BLACKBURN ROVERS

An Illustrated History

BLACKBURN ROVERS
An Illustrated History

MIKE JACKMAN

breedon **books**
PUBLISHING

First published in Great Britain in 2006 by
The Breedon Books Publishing Company Limited
Breedon House, 3 The Parker Centre,
Derby, DE21 4SZ.

ISBN 1 85983 475 2

Printed and bound by Cromwell Press, Trowbridge, Wiltshire.

Dedication

This book is dedicated to my father,
Harry Jackman, who has shared and
encouraged my love of Blackburn
Rovers. Working on this project has
brought back many happy memories of
times shared together at Ewood Park

Acknowledgements

I must begin by thanking Diana Rushton and her staff in the Community History Department at Blackburn Library for their continued help and efficiency throughout this project.

As always with books of this type I am hugely indebted to the various photographers whose work is contained within these pages. In particular I owe a huge debt of gratitude to Howard Talbot, who again guided me through his extensive catalogue of Blackburn Rovers photographs. Howard and his late father, Wally, produced an extensive photographic record of the club which is not only wide-ranging but also of the highest quality. Without Howard this book would not only have been the poorer in terms of photographic content but also would not have been as enjoyable to complete.

Thanks are also given to Anne Barry for her photographs from the club's more recent history and to John Pittard for the loan of photographs from his own collection. Once again thanks are given to Amelia and Harry Jackman for their continued support and help with this project. Finally, I must express my thanks to Steve Caron at Breedon Books for not only providing me with the opportunity to produce this book but for his continued support and guidance during this project. I would also like to express my thanks to Susan Last for her editorial work.

Introduction

THE FIRST edition of this book was published in 1995 to celebrate the winning of the Premiership title. It is, therefore, perhaps fitting that this new edition should coincide with the return of European football to Ewood Park.

The past decade has seen the club continue to defy the odds and remain, with the exception of a two-year spell, a 'small town club' in the elite of English football. That it has been able to do so is down to the benevolence of the late Jack Walker, who, despite his untimely death in August 2000, is still revered by the Ewood faithful.

Founded in 1875, Blackburn Rovers has been at the forefront of English football longer than most clubs. In the 1880s, supported by local businessmen, the Rovers enjoyed unrivalled success in the FA Cup, largely due to the import of Scottish 'professionals'. In the years before World War One the club claimed two championship titles with a team that was littered with big money signings. That it was able to do so was due to the support of Lawrence Cotton, a local businessman who poured his wealth into the club. In 1995 the Rovers again reached the pinnacle of English football thanks to Jack Walker, another 'local boy made good', who, like Cotton before him, provided the funds to rebuild the ground and capture a plethora of expensive signings. While the periods in between these peaks have been filled with moments of elation and despair, the club has continued to remain at the heart of the local community.

While this book tells the history of Blackburn Rovers, it is also a story about the individuals who have been part of the club. As with all stories there are heroes and perceived villains. There are players who won a place in the hearts of the people of the town and brought success and joy to the lives of those who made the regular pilgrimage to Ewood Park. At the other end of the scale there are the stories of players who appeared but fleetingly on the Ewood stage but nonetheless are inextricably linked to the history of the club. Above all this is the story of a club that, despite times of adversity, has continued to play a meaningful part in the lives of many of the townsfolk of Blackburn.

This new version of *The Illustrated History of Blackburn Rovers* differs significantly from its predecessor. In the light of continued research into the history of the club the narrative has been completely rewritten. Furthermore, in a bid to improve the continuity of that narrative the book has been written using a season-by-season framework.

Mike Jackman
Blackburn, May 2006

1875–76

The formation of Blackburn Rovers football club, in November 1875, was greeted by no fanfare or huge enthusiasm by the local populace of the town. At that time Association football was still largely the domain of a clique of 'well-to-do' southern amateur clubs, often populated by public school and university-educated young men. That the early FA Cup finals were monopolised by these metropolitan 'gentlemen's clubs' merely emphasised the fact that football not only had a north–south divide, but that the issue of social class was also prevalent within the fledgling game. Those who occupied William Blake's 'dark satanic mills' of the north had little in common with those who played for clubs like Royal Engineers, Clapham Wanderers, Old Etonians and the university teams of Oxford and Cambridge.

It was, therefore, perhaps not surprising that Blackburn Rovers should have its roots firmly entrenched within the 'upper crust' of Blackburn society. When John Lewis, a native of Market Drayton who had moved to Blackburn in 1868, and Arthur Constantine, a former old boy of Shrewsbury School, met to discuss the possibility of forming an Association club within the town, it was to young men of their own social stratum that they looked for support.

John Lewis, co-founder of Blackburn Rovers, in 1875. (*Copyright: unknown*)

Invitations were issued and, on 5 November 1875, some 17 young men met at the St Leger Hotel on King William Street, Blackburn, to discuss the possibility of forming an Association club bearing the town's name. The men who attended the meeting would have felt perfectly at home within the ranks of those metropolitan clubs that Blackburn Rovers would eventually challenge for supremacy in the English game. The members of the newly formed Rovers came from families that wielded power and influence in late 19th-century Blackburn. They were men who came from a commercial or professional background; factors that were to prove of vital importance in distinguishing Blackburn Rovers from the myriad of local teams that began to spring up at that time.

Walter Duckworth, a former pupil of Clitheroe Grammar School, was elected club secretary, while John Lewis became the club's first treasurer. Thomas Greenwood, another member of a prominent local family, was the captain of the club from its inception until the end of the 1878–79 season. Two of his brothers, Harry and Doctor, were also familiar figures among the playing ranks, with the latter going on to win England international honours. T.J. Syckelmoore BA, another founder member, was a native of Tonbridge and a former student of St John's College, Cambridge, who became a respected master at Queen Elizabeth's Grammar School in Blackburn. Jack Baldwin belonged to a well-known Blackburn family, while Alfred Birtwistle, who became a prominent director of a local firm of cotton spinners and manufacturers, combined playing cricket with Great Harwood and football with Blackburn Rovers. Another member from an eminent cotton family was Richard Birtwistle, whose father, Micah, owned mills in the Daisyfield area of Blackburn.

Others among the 'great and the good' who featured for the club included Sir John Rutherford, who was described as a 'capital half-back', and Tom Dean, who was a regular member of the early forward line. Another front player who was 'noted for his skill as a dribbler' was A.L. Birch, son of the vicar of Blackburn. Two brothers, Jack and Fred Hargreaves, the sons of the Blackburn coroner, both went on to win England international caps; Jack was described as one of the best forwards of his day, while Fred, a half-back, became the first player for Blackburn Rovers to win international honours. Both brothers enjoyed professional careers with local legal firms.

The choice of colours for the new club betrayed the public school background of many of its members. Both of the Hargreaves brothers and Doc Greenwood were Old Malvernians and it was decided to copy their quartered shirt design, but with the traditional green changed to Cambridge blue.

The newly appointed officials opted not to negotiate the use of a field for a home venue, but preferred to play matches on opponents' grounds. Victorian frugality came to the fore as it was decided to test this new venture of Association football before too much expense was incurred.

The first match was played at Church on 11 December 1875 and a very brief report of the game was buried within the columns of the following week's *Blackburn Times*. The Rovers took the lead after approximately 30 minutes' play with Richard Birtwistle – although the paper named him Bertwistle – being credited with the first goal for the club. Church later equalised and the game ended in a draw. Although the team was not named it is generally thought that it consisted of the following players: Thomas Greenwood, Jack Baldwin, Alfred Birtwistle, Arthur Thomas, J.T. Syckelmoore, Walter Duckworth, John Lewis, Tom Dean, Arthur Constantine, Harry Greenwood and Richard Birtwistle.

On 22 January 1876, the *Blackburn Standard* carried a brief report of a match played against Cob Wall and emphasised the potential of the new club. 'Taking it on the whole the Rovers played remarkably well, considering that this is their first season, and they have not got a field of their own. If they can only get a field, and get properly to work, they will have one of the best clubs in the district.' The report on the 0–0 draw also illustrated the *ad hoc* nature of football at this time; the game being played over two 30-minute halves rather than the traditional 90 minutes.

Financially, the first season resulted in the treasurer being able to balance the books – not a common occurrence during the club's history! Members' subscriptions brought in the princely sum of £2 8s, while outgoings included 15s for a football – the only one that the club possessed.

1876-77

Blackburn Rovers secured a ground of their own when officials rented a piece of farmland at Oozehead, near St Silas' on Preston New Road. It was, however, far from ideal for a sporting venue, with a cow pit situated in the middle of the field. While this conveniently collected large quantities of water for livestock, it proved something of a handicap for those trying to play even the most rudimentary form of football. It took an ingenious solution to overcome the problem: it was decided to cover the offending watering hole with boards that were then overlaid with turf. Walter Duckworth's father, a timber merchant, supplied the raw materials that were required so that costs were kept to a minimum.

Little is recorded of the club's second season in terms of matches but, once again, it would appear that local opposition like Darwen and the St George's team of Blackburn featured on the fixture list.

However, there was now sufficient interest in the club for a second XI to be formed, and on 11 November 1876 they visited Mintholme College and achieved a 0–0 draw. Once again, according to the *Blackburn Standard*, the Rovers performed admirably: 'The play of the Rovers under their captain Baguley was good.'

With its own ground, the club was able to collect gate money and the princely sum of 6s 6d was raised, which helped the receipts for the season rise to £8 12s 6d. However, expenditure was also on the increase and on the one occasion when a gate was taken the club had to pay for the services of a policeman to supervise the crowd. The officer concerned received remuneration of fourpence. Other expenses included 2s for tape for the goal, 6s for a leather football case and 3s 8d for four flags.

1877-78

It was soon apparent that a long-term replacement for the field at Oozebooth would have to be found, and it was not long before the Rovers undertook to play matches at Pleasington Cricket Ground. It was at this venue, in December 1877, that a match between Blackburn Rovers and Preston Rovers was brought to an abrupt and tragic end. Henry Smith, one of the Preston players, suddenly collapsed after running over a distance of about 100 yards. He was immediately carried to the nearby Butler's Arms Inn, where attempts were made to revive him. Sadly, before medical aid could arrive, Smith passed away due to a suspected heart attack.

Within weeks of the fatality at Pleasington the club had found a new home at Alexandra Meadows Cricket Ground in Blackburn. On 2 January 1878 the Rovers were able to entertain the famous Scottish club Partick for the opening game on the Meadows.

The *Blackburn Times* noted: 'Considerable interest was excited in the contest, and naturally there was a very large attendance, not only of the residents of the town, but the contingent from the surrounding neighbourhood was numerous.'

An added attraction was that the Rovers included Albert Neilson Hornby in their ranks for the first time. Hornby, whose family owned cotton mills in the Brookhouse area of town, was hugely popular and known to everyone as 'Monkey'. A natural athlete, he excelled at cricket, rugby, soccer and athletics. Hornby made his debut for Lancashire County Cricket Club in 1867 and went on to appear in 292 matches for the Red Rose county. He later went on to captain his country in three Test Matches.

The Rovers match with Partick was a keenly fought affair, but a brace of goals from Richard Birtwistle gave the home side a 2–1 win. Interestingly, the Scottish right-back that afternoon was Fergie Suter, a man who would play a major role in the history of Blackburn Rovers during the next decade.

Although a definitive list of detailed results remains elusive, there is no doubt that this was a disappointing season. Cob Wall, another of the teams in the Blackburn area, enjoyed two 1–0 victories over the Rovers, while local rivals Darwen and Clitheroe both got the better of the fledgling club. The high point of the season was undoubtedly the 2–1 win over Partick but, nonetheless, there was nothing to suggest that, within under a decade, the Rovers would dominate English football.

1878-79

During the summer of 1878 a move was made to improve the structure and organisation of the game within the county of Lancashire. John Lewis was invited to a meeting at The Volunteer Inn, Bromley Cross, to discuss the possibility of forming a Lancashire football association. As a result, in September 1878, representatives of Blackburn Rovers attended a further meeting, held in the Co-operative Hall, Darwen, at which 23 clubs agreed to give birth to the Lancashire Football Association.

While local opposition still provided the bulk of the club's fixtures, the Rovers were also keen to expand the breadth of their itinerary. Matches were now arranged slightly further afield and clubs such as Partick, Sheffield, Manchester Wanderers and Macclesfield Rangers began to feature on the fixture list.

Although results were mixed, defeats being suffered at the hands of Manchester Wanderers, Sheffield and Partick, the club continued to be at the forefront of the development of the game in East Lancashire.

On Monday 4 November 1878 the club hosted an early attempt at floodlit football. A crowd of some 6,000 – with many others taking advantage of the 'free' view from the neighbouring park – gathered at Alexandra Meadows to witness a match played under the most basic of floodlights. The visitors were Accrington and the ground was illuminated by the Gramme light – one being situated at the east end of the Meadows and the other at the west end. Each light was attached to a scaffold that rose some 30 to 40ft from the ground. An 8hp portable engine was required to work the battery and it was said that the system provided the equivalent of some 6,000 candle power. However, it was felt necessary to paint the ball white to aid both players and spectators. The game began at 7.30pm and Fred Hargreaves gave the Rovers an early lead and then scored another before half-time. Although the visitors struck a post in the first half they had little of the play and failed to improve during the second period. The Rovers added a third and also had another goal ruled out as they finished the game as comfortable winners.

However, perhaps the most significant event of the whole season occurred on 15 February 1879 when the Rovers faced Blackburn Olympic at Alexandra Meadows. The Olympic had been formed by the amalgamation of two smaller clubs – Black Star and James Street. Unlike the Rovers, they largely comprised men from a working-class background but, nonetheless, enjoyed the patronage of Sidney Yates of the local iron foundry W. & J. Yates.

The match highlighted a complete contrast in styles between the two teams. While the more robust approach of the physically stronger home side was often more than enough to deflate the keenest of local rivals, the Olympic found the perfect countermeasure. Speed of thought and movement allowed the Olympic to completely overwhelm a Rovers team that looked cumbersome in comparison, by three goals to one. Indeed, the gulf between the teams was such that one local wordsmith was moved to suggest that Blackburn Olympic 'now takes rank as one of the best, if not the best, club in the town.' It came as something of shock for those involved with the Rovers to find that they now had a genuine rival within the town that threatened to undermine their status and ambitions.

Blackburn Rovers, c.1878–79. Thomas Greenwood (10), Doc Greenwood (11), J. Haworth (12), Arthur Thomas (13), Alfred Birtwistle (8), Jack Baldwin (9), H. Ibbotson (umpire, 1), John Duckworth (2), Tom Dean (8), Richard Birtwistle (4), John Lewis (5), Fred Hargreaves (6), Walter Duckworth (7). (Copyright: Blackburn Library)

1879–80

The 1879–80 campaign brought two momentous changes to the ever-expanding itinerary of friendly matches that the Rovers undertook. Firstly, the committee took the decision to enter the FA Cup, and secondly the club supported the inauguration of a Lancashire Football Association Cup. Thus, on Saturday 11 October 1879, Blackburn Rovers embarked on competitive football for the first time, when the team travelled to Enfield for the first round of the Lancashire Cup. It might well have been an all too brief affair if Jimmy Brown had not snatched a goal to allow the Rovers to end the game on equal terms. Indeed, as the match drew to its close the Rovers appeared the stronger of the two sides and Fred Hargreaves, the Blackburn captain, tried unsuccessfully to persuade Enfield officials to play an extra half-hour. The replay was held the following Thursday, at Alexandra Meadows, and the Rovers romped into the next round courtesy of a 5–1 win.

On Saturday 1 November 1879, the Rovers played their first match in the FA Cup when Tyne Association visited Blackburn in the first round of a competition that was still dominated by the clubs in the south. A combination of cold weather and municipal elections restricted attendance and matters were not helped when the game began an hour late due to the tardiness of the some of the home players in assembling at the Meadows. However, two goals from Jimmy Brown and one from John Lewis gave the Rovers a 3–1 lead at the interval and a second-half brace from John Duckworth ensured a comfortable passage into the second round.

By the end of 1879 the club had progressed to the third round of both competitions. Bolton Wanderers had been beaten 4–0 in the Lancashire Cup, while near neighbours Darwen had been defeated 3–1 in the FA Cup. The main point of interest in the game with Darwen was the fact that both teams included men who had played for the Scottish club Partick. Fergie Suter and E. Suter represented Darwen while Hugh McIntyre, who was now with Glasgow Rangers, made his debut for the Rovers. There was already an intense rivalry between the clubs, which meant that the Rovers had to erect a fence around the pitch and arrange for a strong police presence. Fortunately, the police were only called upon on one occasion, when the crowd surged through the fencing and forced the suspension of play until order was restored.

The club's quest to capture the FA Cup came to an unfortunate end at Nottingham on Saturday 31 January 1880. Deprived of the services of Doc Greenwood, Fred Hargreaves and Jack Hargreaves, the Rovers had suggested that the game should be played the following Thursday. However, Forest officials insisted the game be played on the Saturday and so the Rovers travelled to Nottingham with a weakened team. The correspondent of the *Blackburn Times* remarked on the superb hospitality that the Rovers received: 'The Blackburn team were treated in a most gentlemanly and hospitable manner by the Notts club, and, on the arrival of the train at Nottingham Station, they were driven in a coach and four, placed at their disposal, to the Maypole Hotel, where they partook of luncheon and dressed. They were then driven to the field, and, at the termination of the game, back to the hotel.' Sadly, the home team were not quite so hospitable on the pitch and overwhelmed the Rovers 6–0.

With interest in the FA Cup at an end, the Rovers turned their attentions to the Lancashire Cup and a third-round meeting with Turton. In the absence of Fred and Jack Hargreaves the Rovers again turned to Hugh McIntyre and also included Peter Campbell, a playing colleague of McIntyre's at Rangers. Goals from John Lewis and George Avery ensured a 2–1 victory for the Rovers. However, enraged at the inclusion of the Scottish players, the Turtonians immediately launched a formal protest, stating that the two players from Glasgow were not regulars for the Rovers. Fortunately, the Lancashire Football Association turned a deaf ear to these protests and allowed the Rovers to enter the fourth round of their competition. Nonetheless, it was to prove to be a foretaste of things to come as the Rovers pushed the boundaries of the rules to the very limit. The smell of professionalism – highly illegal at that time – was definitely in the air.

A bye in the fourth round was followed by a 3–1 win over Accrington at the semi-final stage. Thus the Rovers progressed to the Final, where they were to meet their old rivals from Darwen. As the Rovers had enjoyed a fairly comfortable victory over Darwen in the FA Cup they were immediately installed as favourites to lift the inaugural trophy. However, before a ball could be kicked, the two clubs became engaged in a vitriolic dispute over team selection. Darwen objected to the inclusion of 'Monkey' Hornby in the Rovers' ranks, while Blackburn officials argued over the eligibility of Kirkham in the Darwen team. The ill feeling became so intense that, on the Wednesday before the Final, the Rovers decided not to play the game. The Lancashire Football Association immediately prepared a long list of charges against the Rovers, which were to be published in the local press should the Rovers fail to appear in the Final. However, common sense prevailed and the Rovers took the field at the Darwen ground, minus Hornby, on Saturday 20 March 1880. Darwen, including Kirkham, enjoyed ample revenge for their defeat in the FA Cup and stormed to a 3–0 win in front of 10,000 spectators.

Away from competitive football, the Rovers continued to build their reputation in a series of friendly encounters. Glasgow Rangers travelled from Scotland in October 1879 and inflicted a 4–1 defeat on the Rovers. The Rangers team that day was captained by the same Hugh McIntyre who would reappear later in the season for the Rovers. His influence on the game was immense and no doubt his power and accuracy of passing caught the eye of Blackburn officials and persuaded them that this was a man around whom a team could be built.

Another heavy defeat occurred on 3 January 1880 when the celebrated Scotch Canadian team visited Alexandra Meadows and romped to an 8–1 win. However, the correspondent of the *Blackburn Times* remarked: 'Although the local club were defeated, they were not in any way disgraced, but sustained their reputation as being one of the principal clubs in the district.' For this game the Rovers had procured the services of C.J. Caborn, a full-back of Nottingham Forest, and McIntyre from Rangers, although the latter, due to the indisposition of one of the visiting team, had to line up with the Scotch Canadians. The visitors were a collection of men from various Scottish clubs, including several from Rangers. The Blackburn goal was scored by Richard Birtwistle after 40 minutes, but by this time the Rovers were already three goals in arrears and the visitors added a fourth just before half-time. Despite the wide margin of defeat, the wordsmith of the *Blackburn Times* was far from disheartened: 'The Blackburn Rovers have obtained some celebrity in the game of football in the country, but they were taught some lessons in the art on Saturday, and will no doubt, profit by them. They, of course, never entertained any hopes of winning against, perhaps, the best players in the kingdom; they were decidedly over matched both in weight and science … but the Rovers deserve great credit for the pluck and determination they exhibited.'

1880–81

Undeterred by the controversies of the previous season the Rovers continued to recruit players from north of the border. Hugh McIntyre transferred his allegiance from Glasgow Rangers to the Rovers and became mine host at The Castle Inn in Blackburn. However, the most controversial arrival came when Fergie Suter, the former Partick player who had been playing with Darwen, opted to join the Rovers. Enraged officials from Darwen immediately accused the Rovers of persuading Suter to join them by offering better terms to the former Scottish stonemason. However, as professionalism was illegal, it was not a line of argument that Darwen could pursue with any degree of conviction without pointing the finger of suspicion at themselves. Darwen had always denied accusations that Suter was in their pay, despite the fact that the player retired from stonemasonry as soon as he arrived in Lancashire. He claimed that the local stone was far too difficult to work and, needless to say, his masonry tools remained untouched during his lengthy stay with the Rovers. In November 1879, another Scottish international, Jimmy Douglas, joined the ranks of the Rovers. This Scottish triumphant would become the backbone of the Blackburn team for several seasons to come and help guide the club to the pinnacle of British football.

Relations between Darwen and the Rovers, and their supporters, reached breaking point on 27 November 1880 when Darwen visited Alexandra Meadows. Before the game, Darwen officials insisted that they would adopt a policy of playing men who were 'Darwen born and bred' – a direct challenge to the path that the Blackburn committee had chosen to follow.

Fergie Suter, whose move from Darwen to the Rovers sparked a heated dispute between the clubs. (*Copyright: Reed Northern Newspapers*)

Thousands thronged around the ground long before the kick-off, with all the seats in the grandstand taken and the perimeter ropes bulging under the strain of those who squeezed into the standing areas. Sensing the hostile atmosphere that existed, Fred Hargreaves, the Blackburn captain, insisted his men 'avoid giving cause of offence, and play throughout a gentlemanly game'.

After 25 minutes the first encroachment occurred when the crowd at the 'sixpenny end' broke through the ropes as Darwen were about to take a corner. As the crowd surged forward the Darwen player, who was taking the corner, moved the ball nearer the goal to take the kick. Uproar followed when his cross was converted to give the visitors the lead. A subsequent piece of dribbling wizardry by Jimmy Brown enabled John Duckworth to equalise matters before half-time. It was during the second half that the match disintegrated into chaos following a clash between Suter and a former Darwen teammate named Marshall. The crowd on the grandstand side, popularly known as the 'shilling side', rushed on to the field as Suter and Marshall were prised apart. During the mêlée that followed, benches were overturned and the gentlemen of the press were forced to stand on the upturned benches to observe the riotous behaviour that was unfolding before their eyes. The game was abandoned and several Blackburn players were immediately hoisted shoulder-high and carried from the ground by a section of the crowd that now covered the entire pitch. After the incident it emerged that the perimeter rope had been cut in several places with shears and that one mirror in the Darwen dressing room had been stolen and another smashed to pieces.

After the embarrassment of the Darwen fracas, the Rovers turned their attention to matters on the field. After an emphatic 6–2 victory over Sheffield Providence at Alexandra Meadows, in the first round of the FA Cup, the Rovers hosted Sheffield Wednesday at the Meadows in the next stage of the competition. Unfortunately, this was to be as far as the club got in its quest to lift the coveted trophy. The correspondent of the *Blackburn Times* succinctly captured the explanation for the defeat at the hands of Wednesday during his opening remarks in his report of the game: 'The condition of the Meadows, owing to the keenness of the frost, was anything but desirable, it being literally coated with one sheet of ice. Notwithstanding this the Wednesday men managed to retain their footing; while the Rovers, in attempting to make runs, came down on all hands.' The explanation for this seemingly paradoxical approach was that the Wednesday team had studded their boots with what were described as 'leather headed nails'. This enabled them to keep their feet, particularly when the wind and sleet blew across the field during the game. Ultimately, the 4–0 win for the visitors owed as much to their footwear as to their undoubted skill.

If external factors could explain the early exit from one Cup competition, failure to progress in the Lancashire Cup was purely due to the obstinacy of the club's own officials. Having disposed of Bradshaw, Clitheroe St Mary's and Turton with ease, scoring a total of 15 goals without reply, the Rovers were drawn against Darwen in the fourth round. Once again, the two clubs became embroiled in a dispute with regard to the date of the fixture. Officials of the Lancashire Football Association listened patiently to the ongoing squabble and then resolved the matter by banning both clubs from further participation in that season's competition.

1881-82

By the end of this season the transition from provincial northern club to the premier football club in England would be complete. Along the way the Rovers would acquire a new ground, reach the FA Cup Final, lift the Lancashire Cup and, perhaps most importantly, become virtually unbeatable.

Alexandra Meadows was no longer deemed to be a suitable venue to stage home games and, as a result, a lease was taken out on a ground on Leamington Street, Blackburn. Some £500 was spent on building a grandstand that could accommodate between 600 and 700 spectators, while substantial boarding was placed along the sides of the pitch in a bid to prevent any further crowd disturbances. In keeping with their ambition, officials also arranged for the erection of a large ornate arch that would bear the name of the club and the ground and would be an imposing entrance to the new arena.

Although early season games had to be played away, while the new ground was prepared, the Rovers began the campaign in fine style. By the time they came to open the Leamington Street ground on 8 October 1881 the team had won all but one of their first six fixtures. A crowd of approximately 6,000 witnessed a 4–1 win over Blackburn Olympic on the day that the Leamington Street ground was officially opened.

The team had undergone something of a transition, with the three Scottish players being at the heart of things. The goalkeeping position passed from Arthur Woolfall to Roger Howorth early in the campaign, while Fergie Suter and Doc Greenwood held down the two full-back positions. The two half-backs were Fred Hargreaves and Hugh McIntyre; at the time the Rovers favoured the 2–2–6 formation. The six forwards, more often than not, were Jimmy Douglas, John Duckworth, Jimmy Brown, Tot Strachan, Jack Hargreaves and George Avery.

It quickly became apparent the Rovers had assembled a team that was capable of beating almost everyone put in front of them. Both Cup competitions brought a glut of goals as the Rovers made spectacular progress on both fronts. The first round of the FA Cup brought a 9–1 victory over the Park Road team of Blackburn and a week later they opened up their Lancashire Cup campaign with a 14–0 win over Kirkham. By the middle of March 1882 the club had reached the finals of both the FA Cup and Lancashire Cup with ultimate ease. Indeed, only Sheffield Wednesday, in the semi-final of the FA Cup, offered serious resistance and took the Rovers to a replay before succumbing 5–1 to a rampant Rovers side.

By the time the team journeyed to London, on 25 March 1882, to face the Old Etonians at the Kennington Oval in the FA Cup Final, they had remained unbeaten all season. Red-hot favourites to capture the trophy, despite the fact that the Old Etonians had appeared in five previous Cup Finals, the Rovers were able to field their strongest team, with the exception that Harry Sharples replaced the injured Doc Greenwood. However, as both clubs had similar colours it was the Rovers who were forced to don an unfamiliar black and white shirt. Luck also deserted them on the day: they lost the toss and had to play against a strong wind in the first half that miraculously disappeared before the start of the second period. However, it was the fast, direct style of the Old Etonians that, coupled with some robust challenges, eventually got the better of the Rovers. Several Blackburn men received nasty blows and George Avery had to leave the field for nearly 10 minutes before half-time due to the severity of his injury. When he returned he was little more than a passenger and could do little to help the Rovers try to equalise the William Anderson goal that had put the Old Etonians ahead after just eight minutes. Sadly, there was to be no fairy-tale ending for the Rovers and thus the first defeat of the season came in the most important match in the club's history up to that point.

Fortunately, the club was more successful in the Lancashire Cup. After the emphatic victory over Kirkham the Rovers easily overcame Accrington Wanderers (7–0) and Church (6–0) to win a place in the semi-final against Blackburn Olympic. The semi-final was played at the Hole-i'-th'-Wall ground, the home of Olympic, on 25 February 1882 amid torrential rain and strong winds. The conditions favoured the physically stronger Rovers as the correspondent of the *Blackburn Standard* suggested in his match report: 'on a fine and very clear day the Olympic had run the Rovers a tight game, [but] it is useless for them to try and master them on a wet day. The Rovers, as usual, went in with the dash that generally characterises their play, and against a powerful wind, blinding rain, and uphill they scored three goals.' They went on to add a further three later in the game, with six different players getting on the score-sheet to complete a 6–1 win.

The Final of the Lancashire Cup was played at Turf Moor on 15 April 1882 when Blackburn Rovers met Accrington in front of some 5,000 spectators. Following the ejection of the Rovers and Darwen the previous season it was Accrington who had who had gone on to capture the trophy in the absence of two of Lancashire's strongest clubs. Before the Final there was an overwhelming feeling that the game would be a mere formality for the men from Leamington Street. As the correspondent of the *Blackburn Standard* wrote: 'A team which had a week or two previously had been held up as the cleverest team in a whole country would have to undergo a phenomenal change ere it descended to the indifferent stage on which Accrington really stands.' Yet the play of the Rovers proved something of a disappointment, as collectively they appeared to still be haunted by their failure at the Kennington Oval. Nonetheless, even an off-key performance was sufficiently powerful to ensure that the club captured the Lancashire trophy for the first time. Goals from Tot Strachan, Fergie Suter and John Duckworth ensured a 3–1 win and a successful end to the campaign.

Blackburn Rovers won the Lancashire Cup for the second time in March 1883. From left to right, back row: D.H. Greenwood, R. Howorth, J. Hargreaves, F. Suter, W. Duckworth (umpire). Middle row: J. Duckworth, H. McIntyre, H. Sharples, F.W. Hargreaves, T. Strachan, G. Avery. Front row: J. Brown, J. Douglas. (*Copyright: Blackburn Library*)

1882-83

Although Blackburn Rovers maintained an excellent record in the endless round of friendly matches, the season as a whole proved to be a disappointment. It began badly with defeat in the previous season's East Lancashire Charity Cup Final. This competition had been founded in May 1882 when the Rovers, Blackburn Olympic, Darwen and Accrington agreed to stage a new competition between the clubs to raise money for various good causes. The two semi-finals had been held towards the end of the previous campaign and after overcoming Darwen 4–1 the Rovers were to face Blackburn Olympic in the Final. It was a major blow to pride when the Rovers slipped to a 5–2 defeat at the hands of their local rivals.

While again looking invincible in their friendly encounters the Rovers found themselves knocked out of the FA Cup before Christmas. The visit of the St John's club from Blackpool, in the first round, provided little trouble for the Rovers and an 11–1 win merely underlined the gulf between the two teams. However, the second round took the Rovers to the Barley Bank Ground in Darwen and a meeting with their fiercest rivals.

The tie was played on Saturday 2 December 1882, on a ground that was hard and slippery with frost, and towards the end of the game snow began to fall. The Rovers were without their captain Fred Hargreaves, owing to injury, which meant that Joe Beverley was moved from full-back to cover for Hargreaves while Doc Greenwood returned at full-back.

The Rovers completely dominated the first half but, thanks to some desperate defending and outstanding goalkeeping by Jamie Richmond, popularly known as 'Long Jamie', the game stood at 0–0 at half-time. The second period continued in the same manner until, with 10 minutes remaining, Mellor put Darwen ahead. The Rovers attacked with even more vigour and, yet again, the match was ended on a note of controversy. The Blackburn players claimed that a shot by Joe Lofthouse had passed inside the Darwen goal, the home team strongly objected and the referee agreed with the Darwen players, so the game ended in favour of the home team by the narrowest of margins. The correspondent of the *Blackburn Times* claimed that Roger Howorth, the Blackburn 'keeper, had enjoyed an embarrassingly easy time: 'The play was so much in the Rovers' favour that Howorth never handled the ball throughout the match.'

Although the Rovers coasted to the Final of the Lancashire Cup, there was little doubt that defeat in the FA Cup had been an immense blow to the club's prestige. It was made even worse when Blackburn Olympic not only reached the FA Cup Final, but also became the first northern club to lift the trophy. The fact that the Olympic had beaten an Old Etonians team that contained 10 of the men who had been victorious over the Rovers 12 months earlier, merely heightened the disappointment felt within the club. In truth the retention of the Lancashire Cup, thanks to a 3–2 win over Darwen in the Final, proved of little consolation to the club. However, some local pride was restored when the Rovers beat Blackburn Olympic 6–3 in the Final of the 1882–83 East Lancashire Charity Cup.

1883-84

Once again the team had begun to undergo something of a transition in terms of personnel. Roger Howorth had handed over the goalkeeping position to Herbie Arthur, while Joe Beverley, the former Blackburn Olympian, had become the permanent replacement for the departed Doc Greenwood at full-back. Jimmy Forrest, who had joined the club from Witton in February 1883, stepped into the half-back spot vacated by Fred Hargreaves. The latter had failed to recover from a serious knee injury, sustained at Aston Villa in November 1882, and had been forced into retirement. Both Joe Sowerbutts and Joseph Lofthouse began to appear with increasing frequency in a forward line that still had Jimmy Douglas, Jimmy Brown, Jack Hargreaves, Tot Strachan and George Avery at its disposal. Indeed, as the season progressed another promising youngster, Herbert Fecitt, began to forge his way into the attack.

The fact that local youngsters like Sowerbutts, Lofthouse and Fecitt were beginning to appear in the senior ranks cut little ice with the national media, which continued to deplore the inclusion of the three Scottish players. The debate over back-door professionalism was now at its height, as questions began to be asked about the status of a number of players with Lancashire clubs. However, far from dousing the flames of the controversy, the Blackburn committee poured more fuel on the fire with the inclusion of John Inglis for the friendly encounter with Darwen on 2 February 1884. Inglis, a Scottish international from Glasgow Rangers, produced a scintillating display as the Rovers crushed their old foes 8–0. The *Blackburn Times* commented: 'The play of Inglis was much admired and he greatly strengthened the forward line of the Rovers.'

The Blackburn committee quickly announced that Inglis would feature in the remainder of the important Cup ties that season; a decision that was not greeted with universal approval. Indeed, the same newspaper that had praised his play against Darwen was quick to condemn the decision taken by the committee. 'There is one point about Blackburn Rovers that does not give entire satisfaction, and this is the introduction of Inglis of the Glasgow Rangers. It is "hard lines" on Sowerbutts or whoever else is supplanted, that after the faithful services of the past he should be pushed out in this manner, and besides that there is a class of people in the town who would rather lose the Cup on their merits than win it with the aid of a specially introduced stranger.'

In fact, the Rovers had managed quite well in the earlier rounds of both the Lancashire Cup and FA Cup without the aid of Inglis. However, when the Scottish player joined the Rovers on the trip to face Upton Park in the fifth round of the FA Cup, he found that he wasn't the only new face on view. The home team had also strengthened their side with several players from southern amateur ranks. Thus J. Pellatt of Oxford University, J.E.S. Moore of Cambridge, Charles King of Oxford University and R.H. Dewing, the Sandhurst College captain, lined up in a team that could well have represented the capital city – yet, curiously, little comment was made about the make-up of the Upton Park team. The match was played at West Ham Park and, because it was a public park, no 'gate' could be collected. To the consternation of the critics it was Inglis who gave the Rovers the lead and set them on their way to a 3–0 victory.

Local objections to the inclusion of Inglis died away as the Rovers beat Notts County at the Lower Aston Ground, Birmingham, in the FA Cup semi-final. Despite the narrowness of the 1–0 scoreline the truth of the matter was that the Rovers, with Inglis in the forward line, completely dominated the game. However, the Nottingham club believed that the inclusion of the former Glasgow Rangers player was against the spirit of the competition and immediately launched an objection with the Football Association. Although Inglis still resided in Glasgow, where he worked as a mechanic and reputedly earned 25s a week, there was no evidence to suggest that the Rovers had offered financial inducements to persuade him to journey down to Lancashire on a regular basis. The objection was quickly dismissed and the Rovers duly faced Queen's Park at the Kennington Oval on 29 March 1884 in the FA Cup Final.

The match was billed as an international affair with the two best teams on either side of the border meeting in the most prestigious game of the year. As one might expect, the match was closely fought, with the Scottish team having two goals disallowed for offside before Sowerbutts gave the Rovers the lead. Forrest added a second and although Christie pulled a goal back for the Scottish outfit it was the Rovers who ended the match triumphant.

The Rovers finally made a lasting impression on those who had previously criticised them in print. The correspondent of *The Sportsman* remarked on the different style that the two teams offered in comparison with their southern counterparts: 'The game witnessed was from start to finish a fast one, and in marked contrast to the style exhibited by the southerners. Of dribbling

there was little, the Glasgowites, if anything doing more than their opponents, who confined their attention almost exclusively to long kicking and head work. For the winners the backs performed capitally, Beverley's defence being grand in the extreme. Forrest, at half-back, cannot be too highly commended, while forward special mention may be made of Lofthouse, Brown and Sowerbutts, the last-named showing wonderful form for a youth.' At the same time *Sporting Life* enthused that: 'The Blackburn team one and all played the game thoroughly, and the combination of the forwards was as good as the defence of the backs was excellent.'

The match not only brought a contrast of styles but it also brought a clash of cultures between north and south. One writer from the *Accrington Times* observed that 'Londoners, who are as a rule devoted to Rugby football, care little for the Association game, and it was evident that a large portion of the crowd had come from Lancashire and Scotland.' The same correspondent also suggested that 'the arrangements for accommodating this huge crowd were ridiculously insufficient, and at each gate there was a dangerous and ugly rush to gain admittance.'

In contrast, in an article that was entitled 'A Northern Horde', it was reported in the *Pall Mall Gazette* that 'London witnessed an incursion of Northern barbarians on Saturday – hot-blooded Lancastrians, sharp of tongue, rough and ready, of uncouth garb and speech. A tribe of Soudanese Arabs let loose in the Strand would not excite more amusement and curiosity. It was a sight not to be forgotten… Strange oaths fell upon Southern ears, and curious words, curious but expressive, filled the air.' It was a sight that Londoners would have to become accustomed to as the Rovers began their domination of the national Cup competition.

The Rovers secured a further trophy when, without the aid of Inglis, they retained the Lancashire Cup. Indeed they might well have had a hat-trick of trophies, but for a narrow 2–1 reverse at the hands of Accrington in the Final of the East Lancashire Charity Cup.

Blackburn Rovers 1883–84. The club won the FA Cup for the first time in its history and went on to capture the Lancashire Cup and the East Lancashire Charity Cup. Back row, left to right: J.M. Lofthouse, H. McIntyre, J. Beverley, W.J.H. Arthur, F. Suter, J. Forrest, R. Birtwistle (umpire). Front row, left to right: J. Douglas, J.E. Sowerbutts, J. Brown, G. Avery, J. Hargreaves. The trophies are: The East Lancashire Charity Cup, the FA Cup and the Lancashire Cup. (*Copyright: unknown*)

1884-85

In terms of achievement, the 1884–85 campaign mirrored that of the previous year. For the second successive season, the club won both the national and county challenge cups but failed to land the East Lancashire Charity Cup. Fortunately, they were able to record these successes without further involvement in the professionalism debate that still raged in English football.

This was also the season that representative honours were showered upon the Blackburn players as both England and Lancashire called upon the services of the men from the Rovers. Unfortunately, this was to prove to be something of a two-edged sword, as a number of friendly matches were lost when players were called away on representative duty. For the first time in two years the team appeared somewhat vulnerable as the aura of invincibility began to fade.

Nonetheless, in the FA Cup the team had little difficulty in reaching the Final in convincing style by beating six clubs: Rossendale 11–0; Blackburn Olympic 3–2; Witton 5–1; Romford 8–0; West Bromwich Albion 2–0 and Old Carthusians 5–1 in the semi-final.

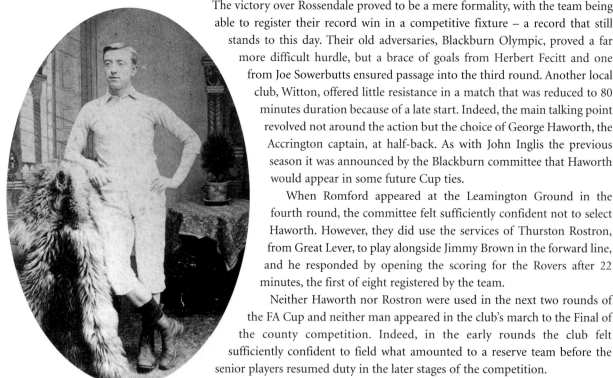

The victory over Rossendale proved to be a mere formality, with the team being able to register their record win in a competitive fixture – a record that still stands to this day. Their old adversaries, Blackburn Olympic, proved a far more difficult hurdle, but a brace of goals from Herbert Fecitt and one from Joe Sowerbutts ensured passage into the third round. Another local club, Witton, offered little resistance in a match that was reduced to 80 minutes duration because of a late start. Indeed, the main talking point revolved not around the action but the choice of George Haworth, the Accrington captain, at half-back. As with John Inglis the previous season it was announced by the Blackburn committee that Haworth would appear in some future Cup ties.

When Romford appeared at the Leamington Ground in the fourth round, the committee felt sufficiently confident not to select Haworth. However, they did use the services of Thurston Rostron, from Great Lever, to play alongside Jimmy Brown in the forward line, and he responded by opening the scoring for the Rovers after 22 minutes, the first of eight registered by the team.

Neither Haworth nor Rostron were used in the next two rounds of the FA Cup and neither man appeared in the club's march to the Final of the county competition. Indeed, in the early rounds the club felt sufficiently confident to field what amounted to a reserve team before the senior players resumed duty in the later stages of the competition.

Joe Sowerbutts.

The FA Cup Final was played on 4 April 1885 when the Rovers again faced the Scottish club Queen's Park at the Kennington Oval. George Haworth reappeared in the Blackburn ranks with Nat Walton stepping down. Goals from Jimmy Forrest and Jimmy Brown ensured that the trophy returned to Lancashire with the Rovers. Two weeks later goals from Herbert Fecitt and Brown retained the Lancashire Cup with a 2–1 win over Blackburn Olympic.

1885-86

Following increasing pressure from clubs in Lancashire, the game finally allowed professionalism in July 1885. Thus, with the payment of players legalised, the Rovers quickly registered themselves as a professional outfit and spent a total of £615 on the payment of wages during 1885–86. However, not everyone at the club welcomed the change. Dr E.S. Morley, a man who had been involved with the club since 1880, abhorred the introduction of a business element into what he regarded as primarily a form of recreation.

Ironically, the advent of professionalism coincided with an extremely disappointing season for the Rovers. Despite continued success in the Cup competitions, no fewer than 24 friendly matches were lost.

Once again the team had begun to evolve and by the end of the season Hugh McIntyre had announced his retirement from the game. Herbie Arthur had spent some time out of the team during the early part of the season to allow Arthur Woolfall to return to duty for a short spell. Dick Turner and Fergie Suter were the regular full-backs, while the half-back positions tended to be shared between McIntyre, Forrest and Joe Heyes, a promising youngster who had switched to the Rovers after making little headway with Blackburn Olympic. Forward talent still abounded at the club with Jimmy Douglas, Jimmy Brown, Joe Lofthouse, Joe Sowerbutts, Nat Walton, Tot Strachan, Herbert Fecitt and Arthur Birtwistle all vying for a place in the team.

Yet, despite this wealth of talent, it was only in the Cup ties that the players really lived up to their reputation. Too many of the friendly games brought indifferent performances and indifferent results, perhaps because team selection for these games became somewhat haphazard. However, in Cup ties the committee always ensured the strongest team was put on the field.

The road to another FA Cup Final produced some surprisingly tough obstacles in the early rounds, with narrow wins being recorded over Clitheroe (2–0) and Oswaldtwistle Wanderers (1–0). However, powerhouse performances against Darwen Old Wanderers (6–0) and Staveley (7–1), coupled with more workmanlike performances against Brentwood (3–1) and Swifts (2–1) enabled the Rovers to reach the Final.

The FA Cup Final, against West Bromwich Albion, was played at the Kennington Oval on 3 April 1886. In truth the game proved something of a drab affair, with both sides being unable to find the breakthrough, although Albion appeared to enjoy the better of the game. The game ended goalless but the Rovers rejected the opportunity to play an extra half-hour, as Turner had injured an ankle, and gladly accepted the opportunity of a replay.

Blackburn Rovers won the FA Cup for a third successive season in 1886. From left to right, top row: Turner, Walton, Strachan, Fecitt. Middle row: Sowerbutts, Suter, Forrest. Bottom row: McIntyre, Brown, Arthur, Douglas. (*Copyright: unknown*)

The replay was held at the County Cricket Ground in Derby on 10 April 1886, the first time the FA Cup Final had been played outside the capital. The Rovers made one change to their line-up, with Nat Walton replacing Joe Heyes. Heyes had endured a difficult afternoon in the first game and his nerves were not helped when he was ordered from the field for having spikes in his boots that were contrary to the rules. After being absent for 10 minutes he returned wearing a pair of ordinary boots and, as a result, struggled throughout the game.

When they arrived at Derby, at dinner time, the Rovers found that their opponents had all been ordered to bed by their trainer to make sure they were properly rested before the kick-off. Fortunately, the Rovers approached the game in a far more energetic mood and totally dominated their hard-working opponents as goals from Sowerbutts and Brown secured the Rovers' third successive FA Cup triumph. By retaining the trophy the Rovers equalled the feat of the Wanderers who captured the FA Cup on three successive occasions between 1875 and 1878. To mark the achievement of the men from Blackburn the Football Association presented Rovers' officials with a specially commissioned silver shield.

1886-87

The signs of a team on the wane had been there for all to see the previous season and 1886–87 merely brought a further acceleration in the decline of the club's fortunes. By the end of the campaign there was no doubt that the Rovers were no longer the dominating force in English football. Certainly the public of Blackburn believed this to be true and attendances at the Leamington Ground began to fall. Not only were 25 friendly matches lost, but the club also made early exits from both the FA Cup and the Lancashire Cup, while the final of the East Lancashire Charity Cup brought a 1–0 defeat at the hands of Accrington.

Once again the team was to undergo a major upheaval, with the retirement of both Hugh McIntyre and Jimmy Brown, although the former made a handful of appearances during the early part of the season. However, the experienced Joe Beverley returned from Blackburn Olympic, while another former Olympic forward, Billy Townley, joined the club. Opportunities were also given to several forwards from the second XI such as William Whitehead, Walter Rushton and Jimmy Costley – another former Olympian.

Undoubtedly the biggest disappointment of the campaign was the manner in which the club relinquished its hold on the national trophy. Having been given a walkover in the first round, when Helliwell scratched from the competition, the Rovers were drawn away to Renton in the next round. The match was played at Hampden Park on 20 November 1886, and the committee sprang something of a surprise when it was decided to play Beverley, an England international full-back and occasional forward, at centre-forward. It was a move that was soon rewarded when Beverley fired in something of a daisy cutter that Lindsay, in the Renton goal, failed to hold and thus gave Nat Walton to opportunity to put the Rovers into the lead. Immediately after the restart Renton snatched an equaliser and the Cup-holders found that they had a real battle on their hands. Another error by Lindsay allowed the Rovers to record a second goal, only for the home side to snatch an equaliser on the verge of full-time. An extra half-hour was played but the Rovers were happy to settle for a replay at the Leamington Ground.

Approximately 7,000 fans gathered for the replay, on 4 December 1886, and witnessed one of the great upsets in Cup football. The Rovers began the game with 10 men as Herbert Fecitt arrived late and when he finally took to the field the Rovers fans hooted their derision at his tardiness. Indeed, the whole team appeared out of sorts, and only the benevolence of the referee, in disallowing two early Renton goals, prevented the Rovers from suffering even greater embarrassment. The first half was a tale of the Rovers resisting increasing pressure from the Scottish side, with only Beverley offering a threat to the Renton goal. Once again the second half found the Rovers relying on the goalkeeping skills of Herbie Arthur and the desperate defence of John Ward and Fergie Suter at full-back. The Rovers crowd tried in vain to lift the team, while a Scottish supporter walked around the ground playing popular Scottish tunes on a concertina. The pressure eventually told when the visitors took the lead and shortly before the end a long-range effort beat Arthur and left the Blackburn 'keeper sprawling forlornly on the frozen ground. It was the club's first defeat in an FA Cup tie since 2 December 1882.

With the club having already gone out of the Lancashire Cup in October 1886 – suffering a crushing 7–1 defeat at Preston North End – there was little to enthuse the public of Blackburn during the remainder of the campaign. The committee constantly chopped and changed the team in a bid to find a winning combination but without much success. However, several younger players were given a chance and one or two promising captures were made from other clubs. The arrival of Jack Southworth from Blackburn Olympic solved the problem of replacing Jimmy Brown, while the veteran Jack Hunter, another Olympian and former England international, shored up the defence over the final weeks of the season.

1887-88

In what proved to be the last season before the formation of the Football League, the Rovers endured yet another indifferent campaign. While results in the endless round of friendly fixtures improved, particularly during the opening months of the campaign, the club suffered mixed fortunes in the Cup competitions.

Familiar faces began to disappear from the Leamington Ground, to be replaced by several up-and-coming youngsters. The forward line was enhanced by Jack Southworth and Edgar Chadwick, while Jack's brother Jimmy began to appear with increasing frequency at full-back. Of the Scottish contingent that formed the backbone of the team during the successive FA Cup triumphs, McIntyre, of course, had long since departed, Suter was restricted to a peripheral role and Jimmy Douglas continued to be a mainstay in the team. Another major loss was that of Herbert Fecitt and Joe Lofthouse, both English internationals who transferred their allegiance to Accrington.

There was a feeling among some of the other clubs within the Blackburn area that the changes to personnel had resulted in a weakening of the Rovers' standing in the game. On the opening day of the season the Rovers faced Blackburn Park Road on the Roadsters ground and suffered an embarrassing 4–2 reverse. Although both Herbie Arthur and Jimmy Forrest were missing from the Rovers line-up, it was still a huge blow to suffer defeat at the hands of a club that was deemed to be of junior rank to the Rovers. A second defeat at the hands of local rivals came on 17 December 1887 when Blackburn Olympic inflicted a 2–1 defeat on a Rovers team that lacked Arthur, Forrest, Joe Beverley and Edgar Chadwick. It merely strengthened the view that without their strongest XI the Rovers had become increasingly vulnerable.

While both Blackburn Park Road and Blackburn Olympic had previously enjoyed a respectable standing within the game, it was the challenge of the rising Witton club that perhaps highlighted the Rovers' fall from grace. Witton, with only one defeat to their name during the season, faced the Rovers at the Leamington Ground on a wet Monday afternoon on 5 January 1888. However, despite the fact that the Rovers were now coming under serious pressure from local rivals, they opted to draft in a number of reserve players for the match. The slippery surface detracted from the quality of the football and the committee might well have begun to doubt the wisdom of their team selection when Horsfield gave the Wittonians the lead in the opening minutes. However, the goal merely galvanised the Rovers into action and for the majority of the game the Witton players spent their time defending as the Rovers coasted to a 4–2 victory.

If local pride had been restored, there was a major shock in store for the Rovers in the sixth round of the FA Cup when they were drawn against the minnows of Derby Junction. Makeshift stands had been erected at the Derby Junction ground to accommodate the sizeable crowd, but the *Blackburn Times* reported that 'the ground is about the worst that can be found the length and breadth of the country, and was altogether unfit to play a Cup tie upon.' The Blackburn committee selected its strongest team for the match and included the veteran Suter at full-back. The bumpy pitch badly affected the Rovers' passing game and the correspondent of the *Blackburn Times* remarked how Jimmy Forrest fell over one of the 'hills' on the pitch as he was about to shoot for goal. After 15 minutes the Rovers snatched the lead when Jack Southworth ran around the full-backs and beat the Derby Junction custodian. However, his superb piece of opportunism was met by a deathly hush from a fiercely partisan home crowd. As half-time approached a scrimmage occurred in the Blackburn goalmouth and Hopkins managed to beat Herbie Arthur from close range, which brought an eruption of noisy celebration from the crowd.

In the second half, it was Hopkins who again beat Arthur to give the home side the lead. Although the Rovers pressed and pressed for an equaliser, their shooting was woeful due to the uneven surface of the Derby Junction ground. As the game drew to a close one of the home full-backs missed his kick and presented Jimmy Douglas with a golden opportunity to snatch an equaliser. With the goal at his mercy he completely fluffed the chance and thus enabled the Junction to register a major upset.

Interest in the Lancashire Cup came to an end at the third-round stage when the Rovers were defeated 4–3 at home. Indeed, the loss to Preston North End occurred just seven days before the defeat by Derby Junction and after these two reversals the season simply drifted to an unsatisfactory conclusion. On 5 March 1888, the Rovers again played Witton at the Leamington Ground but, on this occasion, suffered a 4–3 reverse, while more humiliation was suffered when Blackburn Park Road invited Derby Junction to the town and defeated the Rovers' FA Cup conquerors 3–0.

However, undoubtedly the most important activity with regard to the club's future was taking place away from the Leamington Ground. On 2 March 1888, William McGregor, a Birmingham shopkeeper who was a member of the committee of Aston Villa, sent a letter to five clubs, including Blackburn Rovers, suggesting that a select group of 12 clubs should organise a regular system of home and away matches to replace the *ad hoc* arrangements that surrounded friendly encounters. On 22 March 1888, John Birtwistle represented the Rovers at a meeting at the Anderton Hotel in London that resulted in the formation of the Football League.

1888-89

The inclusion of the Rovers within the newly formed Football League finally ended any debate as to which was the town's premier club. However, officials were also aware that commitment to a 22-match League programme would have a serious impact on the lucrative friendly matches that were normally arranged during the course of a season. Undeterred, the Blackburn committee, under the leadership of club secretary Tom Mitchell, began to arrange a series of midweek away matches that would take the players the length and breadth of the country. Indeed, before a ball had been kicked in the League the Rovers had undertaken away friendlies against Sunderland, Newton Heath and Bootle. Before September was out the Rovers had played League games against Accrington, West Bromwich Albion and Wolverhampton Wanderers, while further trips took them to Boston and Rhyl for friendly engagements.

Determined to maintain the links with Scottish clubs, the committee ensured that the New Year period found Heart of Midlothian and Glasgow Rangers in Blackburn, while Renton and Vale of Leven visited the town in April 1889. During the latter part of that month the Rovers embarked upon one of their regular jaunts north of the border to visit Glasgow Rangers and Vale of Leven.

In view of the hectic schedule that the club had undertaken it was, perhaps, rather surprising that so little squad strengthening took place during the summer of 1887. Indeed, the club suffered a major blow when Edgar Chadwick's father negotiated a move to Everton for his son, who was actually rather reluctant to leave the Leamington club. In his place Tom Mitchell turned to a familiar face when he brought Herbert Fecitt back from Accrington. Another old face to return to the fold was that of Jimmy Brown, who was persuaded to come out of retirement. Unfortunately, his spell out of the game had diminished the speed and trickery for which he was noted and he was restricted to just four League appearances. In defence, Willie Almond, who had joined the Rovers from Witton during the latter stages of the previous campaign, won a regular starting place, while Jimmy Southworth became the automatic choice to partner Joe Beverley at full-back. However, there was some concern that Southworth, a musician by profession, would not always be available for longer away trips. To solve this dilemma, Mitchell journeyed north of the border to sign Johnny Forbes, from Vale of Leven, in November 1888. Forbes, a Scottish international, quickly settled into his new environment and in December 1888 opened a gentleman's outfitters that continued to operate until 1973.

The club's inaugural League match took place at the Leamington Ground on 15 September 1888 – a week after the other clubs had played their first games – when the Rovers and Accrington fought out a 5–5 draw in front of a crowd of around 5,000 spectators. However, it was another of the Rovers' near neighbours that dominated the first season of League football, when Preston North End not only romped away with the first championship title but also captured the FA Cup. The Rovers finished the season in fourth place, some 14 points behind Preston.

Once again the Rovers saved their best form for the FA Cup and proved, yet again, that this was the competition closest to the heart of the club. The Rovers beat Accrington, after a replay, in the first round and four goals from Jack Southworth and a Bob Haresnape hat-trick helped the Rovers to overcome Aston Villa 8–1 in the next round. The semi-final, against Wolverhampton Wanderers, played at the Alexandra Ground, Crewe, was a much tighter affair, with a goal from Haresnape enabling the Rovers to finish the game all square. The replay, also at Crewe, proved a huge disappointment as the Rovers slipped to a 3–1 defeat.

The Lancashire Cup proved an even bigger let down after the Rovers had demolished Witton 7–0 in the opening round. The committee selected a reserve team for the trip to Higher Walton and a creditable 3–3 draw was achieved. However, when the first team faced the same opposition at the Leamington Ground they suffered an embarrassing 5–4 defeat.

1889-90

In terms of achievement the 1889–90 campaign was the most successful that the Rovers had enjoyed for several years. A third place finish in the League, only six points behind championship-winning Preston North End, went hand-in-hand with the capture of the FA Cup for the fourth time in the club's history. Indeed, the only blemish on the season was the fact that the club failed to capture the Lancashire Cup, losing 2–0 to Burnley in the Final.

Yet, in spite of this seemingly successful campaign, the correspondent of the *Blackburn Times,* in writing his summary of the season, commented: 'Although they began the season with a greatly strengthened team their performances have scarcely equalled what was expected of them.' Perhaps this statement reflects the disappointment felt at missing out on a hat-trick of trophies for, until the latter stages of the campaign, it appeared a distinct possibility that the Rovers could win all three competitions.

Once again, under the guidance of club secretary Tom Mitchell, the Rovers had looked to Scotland for new recruits. Tom Brandon, a youngster from St Mirren, was signed to partner fellow Scot Johnny Forbes at full-back. The half-back line was strengthened by the addition of George Dewar, a Scottish international who was signed from Dumbarton. Another Scottish international was added to the squad when Harry Campbell, an inside-forward, was signed from Renton. Joe Lofthouse returned to the fold from Accrington to further strengthen the attacking options. Alas, the one area that had not been strengthened was that of goalkeeper and by the end of the season the committee had used no fewer than six men to try to fill this problem position.

Fortunately, a free-scoring attack helped to cover the deficiencies between the Rovers posts. Jack Southworth led the way with 22 goals in the League while Harry Campbell (15), Nat Walton (14) and Joe Lofthouse (11) all hit double figures in League games. It produced some scintillating football for the crowds at the Leamington Ground, with impressive home wins being recorded against Notts County (9–1), Stoke (8–0), Aston Villa (7–0), Bolton Wanderers (7–1) and Burnley (7–1) in the League. The FA Cup brought a 7–0 win over Bootle, while Irwell Springs were crushed 11–1 in the opening round of the Lancashire Cup.

Nonetheless, while results remained good, the search for a reliable goalkeeper continued unabated. During the opening months of the campaign the role was shared between Billy McOwen and Herbie Arthur. The enthusiasm of McOwen was unable to disguise the errors that often accompany youthful exuberance. Arthur, on the other hand, was reaching the end of his playing career and was but a mere shadow of the great goalkeeper he had once been. In an attempt to remedy the problem, the committee invited a young 'keeper from Scotland, named Ned Doig, to try his luck with the Rovers. He arrived in Blackburn, from Arbroath, on 13 November 1889 and made his debut three days later in the emphatic 9–1 victory over Notts County at the Leamington Ground. Although he had little to do he impressed everyone with his confident handling and appeared set to become the number one custodian at the club.

Ted Doig made his debut in English football with Blackburn Rovers in the 9–1 win over Notts County on 16 November 1889. He later went on to enjoy a long and successful career with Sunderland. (Copyright: unknown, cigarette card)

However, Doig was not happy in Lancashire and made a hasty retreat to Scotland after his solitary appearance in Blackburn colours. The committee were left to rue the loss of a first-class custodian who would later to return to England to enjoy an outstanding career with Sunderland and Liverpool.

Another Scot, named Wilkie, was given an opportunity to make the position his own. He lasted longer than Doig, keeping goal in five League games, before nerves began to eat away at his confidence. His last appearance for the club was in the 4–2 defeat by Everton at the Leamington Ground. Completely overwhelmed by nerves, he struggled to get through the game and, in truth, was fortunate to concede just four goals. After the game he, too, was on his way back to Scotland.

With the FA Cup approaching, the committee gave an opportunity to Arthur Paul, the Lancashire county cricketer who was also a more than useful rugby player. However, he too was deemed to be suspect and, after the first-round win over Sunderland in the FA Cup, he was replaced by McOwen. However, the committee remained unconvinced about their young goalkeeper and sought out Jack Horne, a former Accrington custodian. At 28 years of age, Horne had enjoyed a nomadic career in football, playing for clubs in various parts of the country but, nonetheless, had built up an impressive reputation before leaving the game.

Enticed out of retirement, he made his debut for the Rovers in the 7–0 win at Bootle in the third round of the FA Cup, and then helped the club keep a clean sheet in the narrow 1–0 win over Wolverhampton Wanderers in the FA Cup semi-final.

The FA Cup Final brought the first 'Roses' clash at this stage of the competition with Sheffield Wednesday providing the opposition to the Rovers. The Rovers were overwhelming favourites to lift the trophy as all of their team, bar Jimmy Southworth and Jack Horne, were of international

Blackburn Rovers enjoyed a 6–1 victory over Sheffield Wednesday in the FA Cup Final. From left to right, back row: James Southworth, Jack Southworth, R. Birtwistle (umpire), J.K. Horne, G. Dewar. Middle row: J.M. Lofthouse, H. Campbell, J. Forbes, N. Walton, W. Townley. Front row: J. Barton, J.H. Forrest. (*Copyright: unknown*)

status. Jack Southworth, Jack Barton, Jimmy Forrest, Joe Lofthouse, Billy Townley and Nat Walton were all English internationals, while John Forbes, Geordie Dewar and Harry Campbell had represented Scotland.

The Rovers looked immaculate when they took to the field, being attired in white dress shirts that had been hastily acquired from a London outfitters once it was realised that Sheffield would be turning out in blue jerseys. Prior to the match a representative of the *Blackburn Times* spoke to someone who had been in the dressing room area and he had reported that while the Rovers players were singing and laughing the men from Sheffield were fraught with nerves. He predicted an easy victory for the Rovers and so it turned out. Billy Townley was undoubtedly the star of the show and he became the first man to score a hat-trick in the FA Cup Final as the Rovers romped to a 6–1 win.

Inexplicably, results began to fall away after the FA Cup triumph and, less than a month after lifting the national trophy, the Rovers lost to Burnley in the Lancashire Cup.

1890-91

A season that brought the club's fifth FA Cup success was largely dominated by events off the field. A sharp increase in the amount required to continue the lease on the Leamington ground led to a decision to move to pastures new. Initially, the Blackburn committee secured temporary possession of the old Olympic ground at the Hole-i'-th'-Wall in case the ambition to move to the Ewood racecourse ground failed. Fortunately, club officials were able to negotiate a suitable 10-year lease, with the Rovers paying £60 per annum for the first five years and then £70 per annum for the remaining period. Although, in financial terms, there was little difference between the cost of Ewood and the Leamington ground, there was no doubt that the former offered greater potential with regard to ground development.

Firstly, Ewood was in a more sheltered spot and secondly the area of the ground was far larger than the old Leamington Ground. An initial £1,000 was spent on improvements and a new pitch was prepared for the coming season. Indeed, concerned that the pitch might suffer during the winter months, the committee drew up plans to play reserve games at the Hole-i'-th'-Wall if the need arose.

The efforts of the committee to develop the ground were rewarded in April 1891 when Ewood Park was chosen as the venue for an England v Scotland fixture. However, for some unfathomable reason the England selectors chose to ignore the claims of Jack Barton and Jack Southworth for inclusion in the team. As a result, the public of Blackburn turned its back on the fixture, with the result that an attendance of less than 6,000 produced just £664 in gate money. That the claims of Barton and Southworth had been so easily dismissed by the Selection Committee met with the wrath of the correspondent of the *Athletic News,* who claimed that their exclusion was 'not only an injustice to the men themselves, but an injustice to England'.

The new ground was officially opened when Accrington visited Ewood Park on 13 September 1890 for the second League game of the season. A crowd of around 10,000 witnessed Tom Hay give a faultless display of goalkeeping for Th'Owd Reds and ensure a share of the spoils in a 0–0 draw.

The summer had brought the arrival of two new goalkeepers at the club in the shape of Rowland Pennington and John Lowe. It was Lowe who started the campaign as the first-choice custodian as the new season began with a friendly encounter against West Manchester at Brooks Bar. A Jimmy Southworth hat-trick, in a convincing 6–0 win, suggested that the club might well improve on a third-place finish in the League.

Alas, it was not to be. Nine League games ended in defeat and ensured that the Rovers finished in mid-table – sixth out of 12 clubs. Fortunately, the club did better in both Cup competitions, reaching the finals of both the FA Cup and the Lancashire Senior Cup.

Despite the arrival of two new goalkeepers, the Rovers added a third in October 1890 when John Gow was plucked from the Scottish club Renton. His debut, against Sunderland on 11 October 1890, proved a lively affair, with the Scottish custodian involved in a sharp piece of practice. With the game drifting to a close, and the Rovers holding a lead of 3–2, a Sunderland player stuck a shot at the Blackburn goal. Realising that the ball was out of his reach Gow immediately tugged at the crossbar to ensure that the ball sailed narrowly over. Understandably, the Sunderland players were vociferous in their claims that a goal should be awarded and that the ball had passed under the bar. With no netting to make things easier the referee had a difficult choice to make. However, Mr Duxbury was up with the play and ruled that the ball would have struck the crossbar and therefore ignored the Sunderland claims for a goal, thus enabling the Rovers to hang on for a win.

Further controversy dogged the club when Darwen visited Ewood Park for a friendly match on Christmas Day. With an important League fixture at Wolverhampton the following day, the Blackburn committee chose to field a weakened team for the visit of their neighbours. When the unfamiliar Blackburn players took to the field the Darwen supporters immediately howled their derision at what they perceived as a slight on both themselves and their team. They implored Joe Marsden to take his colleagues back to the changing area – which he promptly did. The cry went up from the Darwen fans that they weren't inclined to pay sixpence to watch a reserve match! Darwen officials then chose to rearrange their team so that a number of their reserve players replaced first-team men. When the new look Darwen team took to the field the crowd poured onto the pitch. The small contingent of police, unable to control the crowd, quickly regrouped outside of the changing area to prevent its invasion by spectators. Unable to get at Blackburn officials to register their displeasure, the Darwen fans smashed goalposts and tore up carpets from the stand before a stone flew through a dressing room window. As darkness fell, police reinforcements were able to disperse the mob and put an end to this not-so-festive occasion.

More controversy followed the club in the first round of the FA Cup. The Rovers had been drawn away to Middlesbrough Ironopolis and, on arrival on Teeside, club officials took one look at the

playing surface and refused to play the match. At the time it was not unusual for games to be replayed if one or other side made a protest about playing conditions. However, after some discussion it was agreed to play the tie and both sides agreed that no protest would be made whatever the result. The Rovers won 2–1; Middlesbrough duly protested and the game was ordered to be replayed the following week, when the men from Ewood enjoyed a rather sweet 3–0 win.

On 14 March 1891 the Rovers faced Notts County at Ewood Park, just seven days before the two sides were due to meet in the FA Cup Final. Without the services of Jack Southworth or Jack Barton, the Rovers succumbed to an embarrassing 7–1 defeat. In the wake of this result the committee elected to replace Gow with Pennington, who had kept goal in the semi-final, for the meeting at the Kennington Oval. The committee was vindicated when goals from Dewar, Southworth and Townley ensured a 3–1 victory that brought the trophy back to Blackburn. Gow, however, remained incensed with the committee and left the club in the summer.

Blackburn Rovers retained the FA Cup with a 3–1 win over Notts County. From left to right, back row: R. Birtwistle (umpire), T. Brandon, R. Pennington, J. Barton, J. Southworth, G. Dewar, J.H. Forrest, E. Murray (trainer). Front row: J.M. Lofthouse, N. Walton, J. Forbes, C. Hall, W. Townley. (*Copyright: unknown*)

1891-92

Undoubtedly, this was one of the poorest seasons that the club had experienced for many years. Not only was it a disastrous season from a football viewpoint, but it was also a disaster in terms of finance. Having had the foresight to move to Ewood Park, with the subsequent investment that that entailed, the committee found scant reward in terms of attendances. Indeed, following the Christmas period of 1891 the gates fell away alarmingly.

Nor was the club blessed with the best of fortune when it came to injuries. Jack Barton was badly hurt on the opening day of the campaign and only appeared once more, against Stoke in November 1891, before being again struck down by an injury that forced him into premature retirement. Both Jack Southworth and Jimmy Forrest broke down at critical times in the season and new signing Mick McKeown was kept out of action for some time after injuring his foot.

The summer of 1891 had seen little in the way of transfer activity at Ewood Park, with the only major departure being that of Tom Brandon who, having fallen out with the Blackburn committee, opted to join Sheffield Wednesday in the Football Alliance. As a replacement the Rovers signed McKeown from Celtic. The club also welcomed Herbie Arthur, who had been playing with Southport, back into the fold.

It was in mid-season that Arthur was involved in one of the more bizarre incidents in the history of Blackburn Rovers. In December 1891 the Rovers travelled to Burnley to fulfil a League engagement on a bitterly cold afternoon. With a snowstorm raging, the referee had great difficulty in getting the Blackburn players to leave the protection of the changing quarters to begin the second half. When the match finally restarted, minus several players, the referee compounded the situation by sending off Joe Lofthouse of the Rovers and Alexander Stewart of Burnley for fighting. The remaining Blackburn players, with the exception of Arthur, retreated to the warmth of the changing area. It was at this point that the goalkeeper entered the annals of Blackburn folklore when he hesitated over the taking of a free-kick. Despite pleas from the referee he refused to be rushed with the result that the hapless official was left with no choice but to abandon the game. The incident resulted in a severe censure for the Rovers and a month's suspension for Lofthouse.

If luck had deserted the Rovers with regard to injury, the same could be said of their fortune in the Cup competitions. In both the FA Cup and the Lancashire Senior Cup they had the misfortune to lose to the eventual winners of the competition. In the FA Cup they were humbled by West Bromwich Albion in a second-round tie at the Hawthorns, while in the county competition they lost to Bury in the Final. The season ended with the Rovers in mid-table, being one of four clubs to finish with 26 points.

1892-93

Once again the close season brought little in the way of transfer activity, with the club merely finding replacements for those who had moved on. Charlie Bowdler, a Shropshire solicitor, joined the Rovers from Wolverhampton Wanderers to replace Billy Townley, who had moved to Stockton, on the left flank. Townley was allegedly offered terms that were far more favourable than those he received at Blackburn and while at Stockton he became an assistant master at Brunswick Street Board School. In defence, Johnny Murray was signed from Sunderland to replace full-back Mick McKeown, who returned to Scotland to join Cowlairs. It was hoped that the signing of Bill Sawers, from Clyde, would add some much needed punch to the attack, while another move brought Matthew Gillespie, a young half-back from Glasgow Thistle, to Ewood Park.

Within weeks of the opening of the campaign it quickly became apparent that the team needed drastic surgery rather than merely tinkering around the edges. After an opening day win, a narrow 4–3 victory over Newton Heath at Ewood Park, the Rovers then began on a sequence that brought five draws and five defeats from their next 10 League games. It was during the latter stages of this sequence that Tom Mitchell was again dispatched to Scotland to find players of genuine quality. Within a matter of a month the club had made several significant signings. George (known as Geordie) Anderson was signed from Leith Athletic to occupy the centre-half position, while Harry Marshall, an outstanding Scottish international half-back, was signed from Hearts. The Edinburgh club also provided the Rovers with William Taylor – an outside-left of some renown. Another Scot with an impressive reputation to sign for Mitchell at this time was George Mann, who arrived from East Stirlingshire.

The influx of the Scottish contingent brought an immediate improvement in results, although Taylor didn't actually make an appearance for the club until January 1893. Nonetheless, despite the importation of so many new players, the club still had the perennial problem of the goalkeeping position to solve. Rowland Pennington survived two games, in which seven goals were conceded, before giving way to the increasingly erratic Herbie Arthur. After Arthur had conceded 10 goals, in

just three games, the committee opted to give the job of custodian to Nat Walton – the same man who had been a regular in the forward line for several seasons and whose attacking skills had won international recognition by England. Walton had played just one game in goal for the reserves before winning instant promotion to the senior XI. The correspondent of the *Blackburn Times* voiced the reservations that many felt in his end of season summary: 'The responsible position of goalkeeper had fallen to Walton, who in this capacity played well, but he was not equal to the majority of League goalkeepers.' After such an indifferent start, the League campaign never really got going and the club ended with 13 draws from their 30 League matches. Fortunately, eight wins produced enough points to keep the Rovers away from the bottom of the table.

Once again, it was the FA Cup that proved to be the highlight of the season as the Rovers reached the semi-final stage with very little resistance. Sadly, particularly for Bowdler, the team was unable to overcome Wolverhampton Wanderers in a closely fought affair at the Town Ground, Nottingham. The 2–1 reversal was a major blow, particularly as the club had already been eliminated by Everton in the first round of the Lancashire Senior Cup. Not even the East Lancashire Charity Cup could provide any solace as the Rovers crashed to a 2–0 defeat at the hands of Burnley.

Blackburn Rovers team group, 1892–93. From left to right, back row: G. Anderson, G. Dewar. Second row: J.W. Murray, J. Forbes, H. Marshall. Third row: E.H. Dodd (linesman), Walton (with cap), J. Hunter (trainer). Front row: G. Mann, W. Sawers, J. Southworth, C. Hall, J.C.H. Bowdler. (*Copyright: unknown*)

1893-94

Only a major end of season collapse, which brought five defeats during the final six League games, prevented the club from chasing Championship honours. As it was, a fourth-place finish was a marked improvement upon the previous two League campaigns. Furthermore, not only did the club improve its League standing, but it also maintained its impressive Cup record, reaching the semi-finals of both the FA Cup and the Lancashire Senior Cup. Sadly, a 1–0 defeat by Notts County, at Bramhall Lane, ended hopes of FA Cup glory while Everton enjoyed a thrilling 4–3 victory in the county competition.

The improved fortunes on the playing field were achieved despite worrying financial problems that were a direct result of the move to Ewood Park. The cost of moving from their Leamington site was estimated in the region of £2,700, but with gates below 10,000 – only the visits of Sunderland in both League and FA Cup had produced estimated six-figure gates the previous season – the Blackburn committee had difficult decisions to make. Before the start of the 1893–94 season it was agreed to transfer Jack Southworth to Everton for the considerable sum of £400. As Southworth's form had begun to slump, his sale appeared good business to the Blackburn committee. The influx of money also enabled the club to address the perennial problem of finding a reliable goalkeeper by signing two new custodians. Although Charlie Watts began the season as the number one choice, by the end of October he had been replaced by Adam Ogilvie. Both the new 'keepers were of Scottish descent and with Johnny Murray, Geordie Dewar, Geordie Anderson, Harry Marshall, Harry Campbell, Coomb Hall and Johnny Forbes also in the squad, there was a distinctive Caledonian flavour around Ewood Park.

These formidable Scots were joined by another in December 1893 when Tom Brandon returned to the club. His original move from the Rovers to Sheffield Wednesday had been embroiled in controversy and his return to Lancashire proved just as complicated. Having become unsettled in Yorkshire Brandon opted to cross the Pennines and join Nelson. However, within a short time the Rovers allowed recently signed Robert MacFarlane, yet another Scottish full-back, to be used by Nelson while Brandon made the move in the opposite direction.

The club continued to raise funds by undertaking its usual series of friendly matches. However, with 30 League games, FA Cup, Lancashire Senior Cup, East Lancashire Charity Cup and Palatine League fixtures to fulfil, these friendly matches put a tremendous burden upon the Ewood first team. Indeed, the demands upon them were so great that the committee began to introduce more and more reserve players to first-team matches. The playing resources became so stretched that for the meeting with Preston North End in the Palatine League in April 1894, the committee had to call upon the services of trainer Jack Hunter, the legendary Blackburn Olympic and England international defender. Due to his lack of fitness and age, Hunter was played in goal while Charlie Watts turned out on the left wing. With the Rovers 2–0 down at half-time, a hasty rearrangement took place to enable Watts and Hunter to swap positions for the second period. Alas the score remained 2–0. It was during this hectic April period that the Rovers fielded a team in a friendly against Southport Central that not only included Hunter, but also his son James. The Palatine League in particular enabled a number of the second XI to rub shoulders with their more illustrious colleagues in competitive action and yet, ironically, the heaviest defeat in this competition, a 6–0 reverse at Preston, came when the team was at full strength. By the end of the season the club had undertaken over 60 matches at first-team level.

1894-95

At the start of the campaign there was a genuine feeling of optimism among those who followed the fortunes of Blackburn Rovers. The long standing goalkeeping problem had finally been solved by Adam Ogilvie, while Tom Brandon and Johnny Murray proved to be one of the finest full-back pairings in the League. The half-back line of Geordie Dewar, Geordie Anderson and Harry Marshall had been tried and tested and not found wanting. In attack the right-wing partnership of Harry Chippendale and Jimmy Whitehead was sufficiently impressive for both players to be capped by England in March 1894. Chippendale was a tall, sturdy individual who had the ability to race down the wing and centre the ball with pin-point accuracy. Whitehead was something of a contrast. Short and stocky, but with no fear of defenders, he not only possessed a thunderous shot, but was also a crafty playmaker. On the opposite flank Jamie Haydock, a Blackburn schoolmaster, was beginning to emerge, although the committee quickly opted to move him on to the right and brought Chippendale to the left flank. With Coomb Hall and Jock Sorley available, there appeared to be a wealth of attacking talent.

However, the one position that had yet to be filled at the start of the campaign was the all-important centre-forward. A replacement for Jack Southworth had never really been found and the committee continued to experiment with several players during the course of the campaign. Ted Killean, James Stuart, Jock Sorley and Josh Hargreaves were all tried in the centre-forward spot with varying degrees of success. Stuart, with his speed and trickery, appeared the most likely to succeed Southworth but, inexplicably, his form fell away after Christmas as first Sorley and then Hargreaves were given extended outings in the team. In truth the constant chopping and changing proved something of a handicap to the team and matters were made worse when the committee signed Paddy Gordon from Liverpool. Gordon was an outside-right of some repute, but his arrival meant that Haydock was axed, much to the chagrin of the Blackburn faithful. Annoyance turned to anger when Gordon failed to live up to his reputation and one contemporary critic wrote: 'Gordon is scarcely worth his place in the team after all. The wiseacres on the Rovers' committee think him a dashing outside-right. But he is not. Haydock is the best they have had for a long time.' Ultimately, the committee was forced to agree and Haydock returned for the final three League games. On 8 May 1895 the committee dismissed Gordon for what was described as 'refractory conduct' during the club's trip to Scotland. Apart from his alleged unruliness, it was also stated that he refused to play for the reserve team against Oswaldtwistle Rovers.

For all the promise of the playing squad, the quality of the football left much to be desired. The form of the team fluctuated wildly during the course of the campaign as the Rovers ended in fifth position in Division One. Nor were they more successful in the Cup competitions. After struggling to overcome Burton Wanderers in the first round of the FA Cup the Rovers went out, albeit unluckily, in a second-round replay against Everton at Ewood Park. Liverpool ended hopes of lifting the County Cup, while Burnley knocked them out of the Charity Cup.

Only the Palatine League provided any solace in terms of success; the Rovers winning four out the six matches. However, these matches were often poorly supported, despite the fact that the Rovers often fielded the first XI. Indeed, the game against Darwen on 25 April 1895 produced gate receipts of just 6s 4d.

As always, the need to boost finances meant that the club undertook no fewer than 17 friendly matches, but of these only five were won. April was again a busy month, with the players involved in 14 matches – three League games, three Palatine League games and eight friendlies.

The financial problems had led to the organisation of a bazaar in the Exchange Hall early in 1895. The appeal was for £1,500 to help liquidate the deficit caused by the move from the Leamington ground to Ewood Park. Thankfully, the bazaar raised net proceeds of £1,200 and the players took it upon themselves to give up a week's wages to support the bazaar fund.

1895-96

When Peter Turnbull was signed from Burnley in April 1895, it was hoped that the club had finally found a suitable replacement for Jack Southworth. Like so many of the recent acquisitions, Turnbull hailed from Scotland and had started his career with Glasgow Rangers before moving to Burnley. During the latter part of 1894–95 he had been loaned to Bolton Wanderers and he came to Ewood Park with an impressive record behind him. A more modest addition to the front line was that of Thomas Tierney, who joined the Rovers from Chorley in June 1895. Another forward to join the club in November 1895 was John Wilkie, who was signed from Partick Thistle.

Unfortunately, despite the addition of new players, the Blackburn attack produced the club's worst scoring record since the formation of the Football League. Only 40 goals were scored in 30 League matches and in the first four League games of April 1896 they failed to register a single goal in 360 minutes of football. Indeed, of the new forwards only Wilkie performed with the consistency that was required. The biggest disappointment was Turnbull who, although joint leading scorer, only managed seven goals from his 25 League outings – a total matched by Jamie Haydock and Harry Chippendale.

It was not surprising that with such a weak attack the team struggled to make much headway in the League. After a reasonable start the Rovers simply faded away and from 28 December 1895 until the end of the campaign the team recorded just four League victories from 16 matches. Indeed, if not for the good start to the season the club might well have struggled to stave off relegation. Nor could solace be found in the FA Cup, as the Rovers fell at the first hurdle, beaten 2–1 at West Bromwich Albion.

Blackburn Rovers 1895–96. From left to right, standing: E.H. Dodds (linesman), J. Hargreaves, J. Whitehead, H. Chippendale, G. Dewar, G. Anderson, P. Turnbull, T. Cleghorn, Jack Hunter (trainer). Seated: J. Haydock, T. Brandon, A. Ogilvie, J.W. Murray. (*Copyright: unknown*)

However, perhaps the greatest disappointment of the campaign was the nature of the departure of Jimmy Forrest – a man who had won five FA Cup-winners' medals while at the club. In October 1895, Forrest claimed that the committee asked him to seek reinstatement as an amateur in order to avoid paying him a wage. The committee, however, vigorously denied this allegation and stated that Forrest left because they could no longer guarantee him a place in the team. Whatever the rights or wrongs of the matter, it was a sad end for a player who had carved his own niche in football history.

Another off-the-field matter that caused serious concern to the club occurred on New Years Day 1896, when a section of the switchback stand at the north end of the ground collapsed and injured five people. It was because of this incident that the club sought the protection of limited liability for its members.

The only gleam of light throughout the whole campaign came in the Lancashire Senior Cup, which the Rovers won. However, even then, a replay was required before Bury were defeated. With no Palatine League or East Lancashire Charity Cup matches, coupled with a reduction in the number of friendly matches undertaken, gate receipts fell compared with previous years.

1896-97

The end-of-season comment by the *Blackburn Times* summed up the frustrations felt by many of the supporters: 'There can be no such thing as standing still in the football world as in many other things, and as the Rovers have not made headway they must have been going backwards. Alas, this is only too plain. The Rovers of today are not the Rovers of yore, when their fame spread far and wide.'

The summer of 1896 brought little in the way of transfer activity to Ewood Park. The biggest capture was John Campbell, a former partner of John Wilkie's at Partick Thistle. Other signings were rather more modest, with Billy Joy, Preston's reserve 'keeper, making the short move from Deepdale. James Stuart returned to Ewood Park from Albion Rovers while Hugh Devlin, another Scottish youngster, joined the club from Cambuslang. Tom Booth, a promising half-back, was signed from Ashton North End and at the end of September 1896, Bob Crompton, an unknown youngster, joined the playing staff from local junior football.

Luck deserted the club from the very outset as the practice matches produced a lengthy injury list that included Thomas Tierney, who twisted his knee, and Josh Hargreaves, who fractured his collarbone. Within weeks of the start of the new campaign, Hugh Devlin, who had made just one senior appearance, was so badly injured in a reserve game that he was forced to return to Scotland with his career in tatters.

The club suffered a major blow in October when Tom Mitchell tendered his resignation. His replacement, Joseph Walmsley, was a local cotton mill manager who had previously played by Blackburn Olympic. Walmsley was a shrewd businessman who reputedly had a good eye for a player. However, he was to suffer a baptism of fire, as by mid-October results were beginning to turn against the Rovers with two consecutive 4–0 reversals at the hands of Liverpool and Preston North End. Both supporters and committee alike became concerned at the sluggish appearance of the players. Further investigation showed that a number of players only appeared spasmodically at training sessions. In November 1896 it was reported in the local press that the players had been ordered to appear before the committee where they were given a dressing down with regard to their attitude towards training under Jack Hunter and Nat Walton. They were told to report for training both morning and afternoon or face the consequences. The first to fall foul of this edict was Geordie Anderson, who was suspended until such time as he could prove his fitness. In truth, many more might well have met a similar fate, but for the fact that the club had insufficient players to replace those who might have been suspended. Indeed, the Rovers were so short of players that they had to entice Herbert Fecitt and Johnny Murray out of retirement to represent the second XI.

The fact that it took the Rovers three games to overcome Chorley, a Lancashire League club, in the Lancashire Senior Cup merely underlined how far the Rovers had fallen in recent times. In the FA Cup the team enjoyed two narrow wins before being eliminated by Everton. By the end of the League campaign only two points kept the club out of the Test Matches. However, nothing could disguise the fact that the team had suffered some embarrassing defeats, including two 6–0 defeats at Derby County and Sheffield Wednesday and a 7–0 drubbing at the hands of Sheffield United.

1897-98

After two seasons of gradual decline the Rovers finally went into complete freefall. A final place of 15th in the League condemned the club to the end of season Test Matches. In the FA Cup they fell at the first hurdle – suffering a 1–0 defeat at Everton – while the only relief was to be found in the Lancashire Senior Cup, where they went down to Newton Heath in the Final.

Before the new campaign began the Rovers found themselves considerably weakened by the loss of a number of senior players. Adam Ogilvie, Geordie Anderson, Geordie Dewar, Josh Hargreaves, Harry Chippendale and Tom Nicol all took their leave of Ewood Park and were replaced by men of lesser experience. The days of expensive raids across the border into Scotland were over and instead the Rovers looked at players from junior clubs. John Bradbury signed from Ashton North End while both William Ball and Ben Hulse came from Rock Ferry. Thomas Briercliffe arrived from Clitheroe and George Hall, an Irish international, came from Belfast Distillery. Albert Knowles, another local youngster, was signed as first-choice custodian, while Jimmy Carter, a more experienced man, was signed from Southern League Millwall Athletic. Another astute signing was that of John Glover, who came from West Bromwich Albion to be the long-term replacement for Johnny Murray at left-back.

The season opened with three straight defeats as the team was chopped and changed to find a winning combination. Bob Crompton played at centre-half on the opening day of the season and was then discarded for the rest of the campaign. A number of the new signings were found to be wanting and both Mills and Bradbury only played two games apiece while Hall made a goalscoring debut on the opening day of the campaign but didn't feature again.

As the season progressed it rapidly became apparent that the newly assembled squad was not equal to the task of competing in the First Division. As the season reached its conclusion the club's officials went to desperate lengths to try to stave off having to appear in the Test Matches. Anderson, Tierney and Hargreaves all returned from New Brighton Tower, the Rovers having retained their League registrations, to make 'guest' appearances in the final games. Another familiar face returned when Harry Marshall came down from Scotland to lend a hand and Peter Turnbull turned out in the penultimate game of the season. Sadly, it was all to no avail.

The Rovers came to the last three matches of the season needing just three points for safety. The first of these games was at Ewood Park, against fellow strugglers Notts County, and it was a major blow when Harry Fletcher grabbed the only goal of the game to give the points to the visitors. Hopes were revived, briefly, when goals from Josh Hargreaves and Tom Booth gave the Rovers a 2–1 win against Bolton Wanderers. As a result survival now rested on obtaining a point from the final match of the season against Bury – a team that was two points behind the Rovers. In another closely fought contest, a single goal settled the destination of the points but, sadly, it was Bury who obtained the goal and the points that took them above the Rovers on goal average. The fight for survival had been so tight that five teams finished on 24 points and goal average settled the final positions, which found Stoke at the bottom and the Rovers, immediately above them, condemned to the Test Matches.

Once again, Anderson, Marshall and Tierney were called upon as the Rovers faced Burnley and Newcastle United in the Test Match series. Unfortunately, the Rovers made a disastrous start by losing both games against Burnley. In the first of these the Rovers had held a 1–0 interval lead before a Toman hat-trick completely turned the game on its head. Even more disastrous was the fact that Tom Booth and Tom Brandon received injuries that kept them out of the return game at Turf Moor, which the Rovers lost 2–0.

For the series of matches against Newcastle United the Blackburn officials made bold changes to the team and axed several of the players who had featured at Turf Moor. Anderson was moved from centre-half to outside-right, while Ben Hulse, John Jackson, Dan Hurst and Fred Blackburn were all brought in and helped the Rovers gain a 4–3 home win. However, two days later the same team travelled to Newcastle and lost 4–0, which meant that the Rovers were condemned to Second Division football. Fortunately, moves were afoot to change the organisation of the divisions that would mean a reprieve for the Rovers. Officials at Burnley had proposed that the top division should be enlarged, which meant that both Newcastle United and Blackburn Rovers would play in the top flight along with Burnley. The proposal was accepted by the Football League despite the opposition of John Lewis, the co-founder of the Rovers.

Bob Crompton made his League debut for the Rovers on the opening day of the 1897–98 season. He went on the make 576 League and Cup appearances for the Rovers and won 41 England caps. (Copyright: Blackburn Library)

1898-99

Having been granted a stay of execution with regard to relegation, the officials of Blackburn Rovers opted for a different strategy with regard to team building. All the Scots, with the exception of the trusted veterans Geordie Anderson and Tom Brandon, left the club. Anderson, who had spent the previous campaign with New Brighton Tower, returned to the fold as the Rovers had retained his Football League registration. In place of those who had taken the club to the brink of relegation came signings of a rather more modest nature. Bill Williams, an orthodox winger who could operate on either flank, had spent four seasons at Everton without ever establishing himself as a first choice. Thomas Wilson had operated on the wing with Swindon Town, while Peter Chambers was a promising half-back with Workington. To these new faces were added a glut of the club's own youngsters, including Bob Crompton, Bob Haworth, John Jackson, Dan Hurst and Fred Blackburn.

In terms of results the 1898–99 campaign was a huge improvement on what had been endured 12 months earlier. The team finished in a highly respectable sixth place as a mixture of youth and experience began to flourish at Ewood Park. Indeed, the only problem, from a playing point of view, surrounded the goalkeeper. Jimmy Carter, who had dislodged Albert Knowles the previous season, began to show faltering form towards the end of the campaign and was replaced by Robert Thompson, another of the many youngsters who were beginning to emerge at Ewood Park.

The Cup competitions brought mixed fortunes for the club. The team suffered defeat in the first round of the FA Cup, 2–0 at Liverpool, and elimination from the East Lancashire Charity Cup at the first hurdle, 3–2 at home to Burnley. However, in the Lancashire Senior Cup the Rovers reached the semi-final before narrowly losing by the odd goal in three to Bolton Wanderers at Ewood Park.

1899-1900

Once again, the emphasis was placed on youth as the Rovers opted to avoid expensive signings. In truth, with the finances in a far from healthy position, there was little choice but to back the blossoming talent at the club. Following the summer departure of Jimmy Carter, the inexperienced Robert Thompson was entrusted with the goalkeeping position, with Albert Knowles, the only other 'keeper on the books, acting as backup. At full-back the youthful Bob Crompton was paired with the veteran Tom Brandon while the club re-signed Art Blackburn, who returned from a stint in the Southern League with Southampton, as cover. The half-back line had a very youthful feel about it with Tom Booth, Bob Haworth and Kelly Houlker forming the first-choice trio. Again, another youth, Sam McClure, who had been signed from Workington as a possible goalkeeper, was to prove a more than useful deputy for any of the half-back positions. In attack the Rovers added Albert Crook, from Stalybridge Rovers, to play at inside-forward and line up alongside Bill Williams, Ben Hulse, Fred Blackburn and Dan Hurst. Another promising young forward, Arnold Whittaker, had been signed from Accrington Stanley, while Tom 'Chip' Briercliffe was still on the books having impressed during the latter part of the previous campaign.

Sadly, the improvements of 1898–99 could not be maintained. The Rovers found themselves embroiled in another relegation battle and little joy was gained from the FA Cup. It took three attempts to overcome Portsmouth in the first round, while Preston North End inflicted a 1–0 defeat on the Rovers at Deepdale in the second round. Indeed, relegation began to have a look of inevitability about it as the team struggled to lift the gloom that had enveloped Ewood Park.

It was at this stage that the directors gambled by bringing Walter Whittaker and Peter Somers to the club. Whittaker was a tall and agile 'keeper who had built up a favourable reputation with clubs such as Newton Heath and Grimsby Town. He was plying his trade in the Southern League, at

Reading, when the Rovers directors snapped him up and installed him as first choice at Ewood Park. As the season drew to a close the Rovers returned to Reading to snap up Joe O'Brien, a full-back who it was felt would challenge Allan Hardy for the left-back position. Somers, who was 21 when the Rovers paid £200 to borrow him from Celtic, was a player who had begun to gain an impressive reputation in Scottish circles. He was an industrious forward who created opportunities for others and was immediately given the inside-right berth at Ewood Park.

Gradually, results began to improve but, even so, the Rovers embarked on their penultimate game of the season, at home to Notts County, knowing that a win was necessary to avoid relegation. Win they did, by 2–0, which was just as well because two days later they lost 2–0 at Deepdale, a result that enabled Preston North End to avoid relegation at the expense of Burnley.

1900–01

The summer of 1900 brought major changes to the structure of the playing staff at Ewood Park. Two old favourites, Geordie Anderson and Tom Brandon, finally called time on long and illustrious careers with the Rovers and moved to Blackpool and St Mirren respectively. While age had caught up with these two fine servants of the club, the departure of Tom Booth was an altogether different affair. Booth, an England international, was approaching the peak of his career but had become disenchanted with life at Blackburn. He was lured to Merseyside by an attractive offer from Everton, after the Ewood directorate decided that there was little to be gained from keeping a disgruntled player in their ranks. Other familiar faces to depart included Tom Briercliffe and Albert Crook, who both moved to Stalybridge Celtic, and Ben Hulse, who joined New Brighton Tower. The club also allowed Percy Slater, a young reserve full-back, to link up with Manchester City.

To fill the gaps the Rovers raided Reading, the club that had provided Walt Whittaker and Joe O'Brien, and snapped up James Hosie and Michael Kelly. Bill Bryant, a speedy and tricky winger was signed from Newton Heath, while Hugh Morgan, a creative inside-forward, moved to Ewood from Liverpool. Another signing brought Wilfred Oldham from Everton to lead the Blackburn attack. However, news that the club had acquired Jimmy Moir, an inexperienced youngster from Celtic, created little enthusiasm among the followers of the club as it was expected that he would merely understudy Hosie.

In view of the considerable changes to personnel, a respectable mid-table finish was deemed a satisfactory outcome to the campaign. This was particularly true in view of the fact that a number of the new men took time to settle and a few proved totally inadequate to the task. Indeed, of the former Reading contingent only Whittaker proved his worth and his consistency between the posts infused confidence throughout the defence. The decision to switch Fred Blackburn to the left wing reduced Kelly to the role of understudy while Hosie was totally overshadowed by Moir. The correspondent of the *Blackburn Times* commented that 'the boyish-faced Moir knew a lot more about half-back play than any of his new comrades. He was as lucky a catch as ever the club had made.' Indeed, he was so successful that the club felt able to release Hosie in January 1901, and allow him to move to Manchester City.

After an indifferent start to the campaign, just three wins from the first 18 games, the team began to take shape and the second half of the season brought a refreshing brand of creative football to Ewood Park. Unfortunately, the club had failed to unearth a consistent goalscorer, with Oldham proving a huge disappointment. On more than one occasion the team dominated a game but ended up with no points because of their inability to turn chances into goals.

The major disappoint of the campaign came with elimination from the FA Cup at the hands of Woolwich Arsenal. The Second Division side snatched a surprise 2–0 victory in a match that had been postponed for a fortnight due to the public mourning for the death of Queen Victoria. Sadly, the postponement came at a time when the team was enjoying a particularly rich vein of form and contemporary observers believed that the delay seriously affected the form of the players. However, some consolation was gained in the more provincial surrounds of the Lancashire Senior Cup with a 4–0 victory over Burnley in the Final at Hyde Road, Manchester.

1901-02

It was during this campaign that Blackburn Rovers finally managed to shed its image of a Cup team and be seen as a power in the race for the championship. After beating Everton on 22 February 1902, the club stood second in the table, ahead of third-placed Everton and tucked in behind the leaders Sunderland, who were due to visit Ewood Park seven days later. Alas, despite continual pressure it was Sunderland who grabbed the only goal of the game and went on to claim the title, while the Rovers had to settle for fourth place.

Blackburn Rovers at the start of 1901–02. From left to right, back row: J. Walmsley (secretary), W. McIver, W. Whittaker, S. McClure, A. Hardy, B. Crompton, N. Walton (trainer), A. Blackburn, W.H. Ball, J. Dewhurst, W. Bryant, R. Haworth, J. Hunter (groundsman), F. Blackburn. Front row: A. Whittaker, P. Somers, A.E. Houlker, H. Morgan, W.H. Gate. (*Copyright: unknown*)

The final position was all the more commendable as the team had gained just five points from the first seven matches of the season. Indeed, but for this slow start the Rovers might well have captured their first Championship crown.

However, there was little joy to be gained in a first-round exit of the FA Cup at the hands of Derby County. On a frozen pitch the Rovers produced an indifferent display and the vastly experienced Jack Darroch, in particular, endured a personal nightmare at left-back. Darroch, who had won a Cup medal with Bury, had joined the Rovers in December 1901 and featured in 17 League games before returning to his native Scotland in the summer of 1902.

The Rovers fared better in the County Cup despite surviving a second-round tie with Bury that took five matches to settle. A comfortable 4–0 victory over Burnley in the Final came just two weeks after the Rovers had been eliminated from the FA Cup.

It was, therefore, rather unfortunate that one of the more successful campaigns in recent years should close on a sour note. When the season ended it was announced that 'Kelly' Houlker would leave the Rovers to sign for Portsmouth in the Southern League. Houlker, an England international, was extremely popular with the Blackburn faithful and he let it be known that he had been prepared to sign for the club at a figure that was under the limit allowed. However, when terms couldn't be agreed, criticism of the directors quickly followed. Local journalists questioned the wisdom of allowing such a talented individual to slip from their grasp.

1902-03

'The directorate have worked in their own peculiar style this season, and are undoubtedly to blame for many things. They have signed plenty of useless men, and few good ones', was the comment of 'Ranger' in an end-of-season summation in the *Blackburn Times*. Having struggled to survive in the top flight, the Rovers became embroiled in a match-fixing controversy that proved sufficiently serious to end the career of Joseph Walmsley, the Rovers secretary.

The summer of 1902 had been a busy one for player movements. The main loss to the club had been Peter Somers, who returned to Celtic, and, of course, 'Kelly' Houlker. Another Scot to return to his homeland was Jack Darroch, who signed for Dundee. To replace Somers the Blackburn directors signed another Scot, Billy Bow from St Bernard's. Neil Logan, a half-back with Swindon Town, came with a favourable reputation made in Southern League circles. Another Southern League player to join the Rovers was goalkeeper John 'Tiny' Joyce, who arrived at Ewood Park via Burton Albion, having spent some time with Millwall.

Unfortunately, the new acquisitions made little impact as the season, once again, began in disastrous fashion for the Rovers. A meagre haul of two points from the first nine games had set the scene for the season, but, unlike 12 months earlier, there was to be no instant revival. During the dreadful early season run the directors continued to strengthen the squad and signed George Robertson, a rather young and inexperienced half-back from Clyde. Another new face to arrive, in October 1902, was that of Lionel Watson, a cultured inside-forward who was signed from Manchester City. The following month another inside-forward, Albert Monks, joined the club from Everton. At the beginning of December, the rather erratic goalkeeping of Joyce was replaced by the steadier hands of Billy McIver, who was promoted from the second XI.

Before the end of February the club had been eliminated from the FA Cup by Derby County and had crashed out of the Lancashire Senior Cup at Everton. First Division survival became the only priority. As the club slipped closer to relegation, Walmsley was again entrusted with the task of finding new blood and February brought the signing of Blackpool's half-back Jack Birchall and a month later Adam Bowman, a goalscoring forward, arrived from Everton.

However, results continued to go against the Rovers and many of the new signings, not just Joyce, proved unequal to the task of turning things around. Bow was reputed to have cost £200 but proved a poor substitute for the guile of Somers. Logan was said to be too lethargic to be successful, while Robertson was unable to retain his place in the first team.

As the club entered the month of April, their plight at the bottom of the table looked desperate. The main relegation rivals for the Rovers were Bolton Wanderers and Grimsby Town. However, when the Rovers beat Bolton 4–2 at Ewood Park, on 4 April 1903, it virtually condemned the Wanderers to Second Division football. With four games remaining the final relegation place was between the Rovers and the 'Mariners'.

On Good Friday 1903, the Rovers visited Gigg Lane to face a Bury team that was looking forward to an FA Cup Final. However, the same 11 players who would thrash Derby County just eight days later and win the FA Cup were inexplicably held to a 1–1 draw by the Rovers. If it was an unlikely point it was nonetheless a welcome one, particularly as the Rovers travelled to Middlesbrough the following day and crashed to a 4–0 defeat.

On Easter Monday the Rovers made the short journey to Liverpool to face an Everton side that was in the lower half of the table. With only a point separating the Rovers and Grimsby Town it was obviously imperative that the men from Ewood Park should take something from the game on

Merseyside. However, not even the most optimistic of Rovers fans could have expected the 3–0 win that a brace of goals from Bowman and another from Fred Blackburn delivered. Five days later lowly Newcastle United visited Ewood Park and lost 3–1, when Bowman again notched two goals. During this same four match period Grimsby had beaten West Bromwich Albion, drawn with Derby County and lost to Sheffield United and Aston Villa to finish the season some four points behind the Rovers.

As the public of Blackburn celebrated their good fortune the Grimsby area was awash with rumours of subterfuge on behalf of the Lancashire clubs. Doubts were cast about the legitimacy of the results the Rovers achieved against Bury and Everton, results that had condemned Grimsby to relegation after just one season of top-flight football. Officials at Grimsby lodged an official protest and an inquiry was held into events that had occurred immediately before the Rovers' fixture at Goodison Park. The result of the inquiry, which was fiercely contested by Walmsley, stated that there was no question of collusion of the part of Everton, but that there was a belief that Walmsley had tried to arrange a win for the Rovers. The Blackburn secretary was immediately suspended *sine die* from any further involvement with football. The result, however, was allowed to stand, as the inquiry could find no evidence of collusion on the part of any other official of Blackburn or Everton. Thus it was the opinion of the inquiry that the final League placings should remain unaltered.

Walmsley continued to plead his innocence and few in Blackburn believed him capable of such deceit. Indeed, the view of those who knew him suggested that he was guilty of little more than making an ill-advised jocular remark that was somehow misconstrued by others. Nonetheless, the services of Walmsley were lost to the Rovers and in November 1903 he took over the licence of the Florence Hotel in Blackburn, an establishment that had previously been occupied by Bob Crompton's father.

1903-04

Following the departure of Walmsley, the directors appointed Robert Middleton as their new secretary in July 1903. Unlike his predecessor, Middleton came from a football background, having been secretary of Blackpool before joining the Rovers. Before his stint with the 'Seasiders' Middleton, originally a schoolmaster by profession, had held similar posts with both Darwen and Rotherham United. He had built up a reputation for being a shrewd operator who hid his calculating business mind behind a genial and courteous disposition.

Middleton inherited a difficult situation, considering the dire season that the club had just endured. However, there was to be no mass influx of new blood but merely a tinkering with various aspects of the playing staff. The major close-season acquisition was Bob Evans, Wrexham's Welsh international goalkeeper, who cost a reputed £150. John McDonald, a full-back from Ayr, and George Smith, an inside-forward from New Brompton, also arrived but with very little fanfare.

In view of the lack of signings it was, perhaps, inevitable that the team should continue the struggles of the previous campaign. New players arrived as the season progressed but failed to make much impact on a struggling team. Moir returned from Celtic but appeared a mere shadow of the energetic youth who had taken the club by storm just three years earlier. Fred Pentland, a recognised goalscorer, managed to notch seven goals in 18 League appearances following his move from Blackpool in November 1903. Nonetheless, the team proved incapable of being able to drag itself from the lower reaches of the division.

The FA Cup brought some relief, with victories over Liverpool and Nottingham Forest at Ewood Park, before a trip to Derby County in the third round brought an abrupt halt to interest in that particular competition.

The Blackburn Rovers team that finished in 15th position in the First Division. From left to right, back row: A. Bowman, B. Evans, N. Walton (trainer), J. McDonald, S. McClure. Middle row: A. Whittaker, G. Smith, B. Crompton, A. Monks, F. Blackburn. Front row: J. Dewhurst, B. Bradshaw. (*Copyright: unknown*)

Only a 2–0 win over Middlesbrough in the penultimate game of the season lifted the Rovers to the relative safety of 15th position in the table. Nonetheless, only two points separated the Rovers from a relegation spot as yet another season came to a disappointing conclusion.

1904–05

'Like its two predecessors, the season of 1904–05 has been one of disgrace to the Rovers', was the opinion of the correspondent of the *Blackburn Times* at the end of a difficult season for all concerned at Ewood Park. Yet it had all started so brightly in the late summer sunshine of 1904. The first three League games had produced three victories with 10 goals scored and not one conceded; talk of winning the Championship reverberated around the terraces of Ewood Park.

Unfortunately, the team merely flattered to deceive and a season of inconsistency, in both performance and results, found the club embroiled in yet another relegation battle. Enough points were gathered to enable the club to scramble to the relative safety of 13th place, but there could be no disguising the ineptitude of what was on display. In the 15 League games between 2 January 1905 and the end of the season the Rovers scored just 11 goals. Of these, two came from Crompton via the penalty spot, while Bowman bagged five of the others. Indeed, without the 12 goals that Bowman scored that season the Rovers would have been well and truly in the mire.

The Rovers were almost relegated, thrown out of the FA Cup in the first round by Sheffield Wednesday at Ewood Park, hammered 5–1 by Liverpool in the second round of the Lancashire Senior Cup and beaten by Second Division rivals Burnley 3–0 in the East Lancashire Charity Cup. It was little wonder that the public of Blackburn felt disenchanted with their performances.

The summer of 1904 had seen little in the way of team-building, with the only major signings being Sam Wolstenholme, Everton's England international half-back, John Bennett, a full-back from Leicester Fosse and Alfred Oliver, a Welsh international winger signed from Bangor. The latter two made little impression, with Bennett making one League appearance and Oliver restricted to just two League matches.

The performances of the reserves did little to lift the gloom as they contrived to get themselves relegated to the Second Division of the Lancashire Combination. In many ways this was the ultimate humiliation for the club although, fortunately, another revamp of the competition resulted in the addition of two clubs to the top tier and meant that the Rovers survived.

However, the event that would have the most far reaching affect on the future of the club occurred not on the field, but in the boardroom. On 28 March 1905, Lawrence Cotton was appointed chairman of Blackburn Rovers. He was no stranger to the club, having been a director between 1891 and 1901 before returning to the boardroom in 1903. Educated at Blackburn Grammar School, he had entered the cotton trade in 1875 and later went into business as a cotton manufacturer in partnership with his brother, Clement. As a successful businessman it was hoped that he could use his business acumen to aid the financial stability of the club.

1905-06

After several seasons of mediocrity, the Rovers finally gave their supporters some cause for cheer by achieving mid-table respectability. Indeed, there were occasions during the campaign when their play suggested that Championship aspirations might well be harboured. Unbeaten at home until the third week in January 1905, the Rovers went on to amass 40 points, their highest total since the inception of the League, although the First Division now contained 20 clubs as opposed to 18. Furthermore, not only were improvements made on the pitch, but in 1905 the Darwen End of the ground, with a capacity of 12,000, was also covered at a cost of £1,680.

The improvement in the team was all the more remarkable because there had been little in the way of transfer activity during the summer of 1905. Indeed, the departures of Jack Dewhurst to Brentford and Fred Blackburn to West Ham United had seen the loss of two regular first-team men – although there were differing views of the importance of their loss. The correspondent of the *Blackburn Times* stated that Dewhurst 'required a benefit as well as the maximum wage. He was not worth both, and we believe, his departure will hardly be felt by the club.' However, the loss of Blackburn was more keenly felt and, although he had not been at his best in recent seasons, there was some concern that his departure came through a conflict with the directors over a promised benefit.

The new acquisitions were of a more modest nature, with Darwen's Miles Chadwick, a winger, and centre-half Joe Wilson both signing professional forms for the Rovers in April 1905. In the same month the Rovers signed Billy 'Tinker' Davies, Wrexham's Welsh international centre-forward who had scored 21 goals in 21 League games when the Welsh club captured the Combination championship of 1904–05. Arthur Cowell joined the Rovers from Nelson in May 1905 and Ellis Crompton was signed from Padiham in the same month. From further afield the Rovers captured Jimmy Robertson, a promising inside-forward, from Vale of Leven.

The success of 1905–06 was achieved on the back of a number of sound defensive displays. Bob Evans produced a season of immaculate goalkeeping, while in front of him Bob Crompton and Cowell formed an excellent understanding at full-back. Indeed, Cowell's development was so rapid

that he had ousted the experienced Jock Cameron after only four League games. The only real concerns that the management had about the defence revolved around the centre-half spot. Sam McClure and Jack Birchall vied for the place until the latter received an injury at Sheffield Wednesday in November 1905 that would keep him out for the season. While McClure was not as creative in his distribution of the ball as Birchall, his defensive play remained second to none.

There were, of course, disappointments. The FA Cup brought little cheer with a first-round exit at Stoke, while interest in the County Cup ended at Bolton in the second round. Nonetheless, after the disappointments of the previous three campaigns, the improved form of 1905–06 was a welcome relief to the Blackburn faithful.

1906-07

After the moderate success of the previous campaign the Rovers returned to their old inconsistent ways. Once again, exasperated supporters were forced to witness another season in which the club courted relegation for most of the campaign. A final League position of 12th rather flattered a team that relied upon three wins and a draw from their final four fixtures to haul them to a position of comparative respectability.

Tragedy struck the club before the campaign began with the sudden death of Sam McClure on 17 July 1906. McClure had suffered ill health for some time and two years previously it was felt that health problems might force him into premature retirement. However, he recovered sufficiently to make 21 League appearances during the 1905–06 campaign. Sadly, he fell ill again but it was still a major shock when an abscess in the ear spread inwards towards the brain and brought a premature end to a life that was lived with boundless energy and a terrific sense of fun.

Under the stewardship of Cotton the club continued to redevelop Ewood Park, and on New

Blackburn Rovers 1905–06. From left to right, back row: B. Holmes (trainer), S. Wolstenholme, J. Birchall, J. Wilson, J. McGill, B. Crompton, J. Cameron, J. Moir, R.B. Middleton (secretary). Middle row: F. Pentland, A. Whittaker, G. Smith, B. Davies, A. Bowman, W. McIver, B. Bradshaw. Front row: T. McAllister, J. Robertson, B. Evans, M. Chadwick, S. McClure. (*Copyright: Blackburn Library*)

Year's Day 1907 the newly constructed Nuttall Street Stand was opened. A crowd of 35,000 gathered at Ewood to watch a 1–1 draw with Preston North End and admire the imposing construction. Designed by the famous football stadium architect Archibald Leitch, the stand could accommodate 4,112 supporters seated in the upper tier, with room for a further 9,320 standing in front. Like the cotton mills that Cotton owned, there was little of the ornate on the outside of this building. A combination of plain red brick and windows, with a cobbled street in front, merely reinforced the image of austere Edwardian working-class functionality. Yet, inside, there was a boardroom of panelled oak with a resplendent fireplace that reflected the riches that the cotton industry had provided for its entrepreneurs.

Ellis Crompton made his debut for Blackburn Rovers in November 1906. He went on to score 20 goals in 35 League appearances before joining Tottenham Hotspur in December 1910. (*Copyright: Blackburn Library*)

While the construction of the stadium would occupy much of Cotton's wealth for the next few years, he was also aware of the need to strengthen the playing squad. The summer brought a return to Ewood Park for old favourite 'Kelly' Houlker, while Jack Martin, who was signed from Lincoln City, scored 17 League goals during his debut season at Blackburn. However, perhaps the two most significant signings during the season were Eddie Latheron and Wattie Aitkenhead. Latheron, a youthful and gifted inside-forward, arrived from Grangetown in the Lancashire Combination, while the versatile Aitkenhead, of Partick Thistle, trod the well-worn route from Scotland to Blackburn.

Fortunately, the Rovers displayed their best performances at Ewood Park, winning no fewer than 10 of their League games on home soil. The Rovers played five FA Cup games during the season, but still couldn't get further than the second round. They overcame Manchester City after two games, but lost in the third meeting with Tottenham Hotspur, played at Villa Park, by the narrow margin of 2–1. Fortunately, the team had already delivered one trophy for the supporters by capturing the Lancashire Senior Cup, at Ewood Park, thanks to a 3–0 win over Liverpool. The only other game in this competition to be played at Ewood Park brought a convincing 8–1 victory over Southport Central. It was little wonder that the Rovers took the County Cup competition seriously, as it provided the only chink of light in an otherwise gloomy season.

1907-08

Supporters of Blackburn Rovers had to tolerate yet another season that was just as lamentable as many of those that had gone before. Indeed, it was not until mid-April that safety was assured as the Rovers scrambled to 14th place in the table. Nor was there any comfort to be found in the Cup competitions. In truth, the fact that famous Cup fighters like the Rovers should be humbled in the first round by Leicester Fosse of the Second Division merely followed the pattern that had been established in recent years. The Lancashire Senior Cup brought a first-round exit at the hands of Bolton Wanderers, while Burnley enjoyed a 4–2 win over the Rovers in the Final of the East Lancashire Charity Cup.

In a bid to secure their status as a top-flight club, Cotton and his fellow directors launched a desperate bid to strengthen the squad in February 1908. Three players were signed from Brighton and Hove Albion during that month, with wingers Dick Wombwell and Walter Anthony immediately being installed in the first team while Joe Lumley, a utility forward, had to settle for reserve-team football. As the season drew to a close, the club captured Archie Kyle, a talented inside-forward, from Glasgow Rangers.

The club's dealings in the transfer market were the main topic of debate among supporters. There was no doubt that the Rovers had a sizable squad, but many of the players at their disposal were simply not good enough for the First Division. A couple of the signings made during the summer of 1907 helped to prove the point. Jim Ferguson, who arrived from Airdrieonians, and John Manning, a signing from Raith Rovers, were bought to strengthen the half-back line. However, Ferguson played in only nine League games, while Manning was selected on just four occasions before being allowed to join Northampton Town during the summer of 1908.

'Ranger', writing in the *Blackburn Times*, believed there was a need to adopt a different policy to transfers. 'The second-rate players might advantageously be reduced and the money thus saved be utilised in paying the maximum wage to first-class men.'

1908–09

The greatest enigma of 1908–09 was the inability of the team to reproduce its impressive away performances at Ewood Park. Despite winning just six matches at home, the team still finished in a creditable fourth place. Indeed, the 41 points that the club accumulated was the highest total that the Rovers had gained up to that point and with more consistency at home, a challenge for the championship might have been a real possibility.

The summer of 1908 had brought three major acquisitions to Ewood Park, with Jimmy Ashcroft, Arsenal's England international goalkeeper, being the one that caught the headlines. Billy Garbutt, Arsenal's veteran outside-right, also made the move to Lancashire from Plumstead. The third major signing, although at the time he was a virtual unknown, was George Chapman, a young, raw but highly talented centre-half who joined the club from Raith Rovers. Another two unknown players who joined in the summer of 1908 were Bob Ellis and John Laurie, who both arrived from Workington.

The money that was being spent on the team was beginning to pay dividends for Cotton and his fellow directors and by the end of the campaign the team was beginning to become more settled. Ashcroft established himself as first-choice custodian, while Bob Crompton and Arthur Cowell continued to be a formidable full-back pairing, with Tommy Suttie proving an excellent understudy. Albert Walmsley, a half-back who rarely caught the eye but whose performances were steady and reliable, had begun to make the right-half slot his own. Chapman, whose passing had been a little inconsistent, had proved to be one of the strongest centre-halves in the country. On the left of the trio Billy Bradshaw continued to perform at the highest level.

Bob Ellis scored on his debut on the opening day of the season. It proved to be his only senior appearance for the club. (*Copyright: Blackburn Library*)

Unfortunately, the front line continued to perform erratically, although Billy Davies notched 19 goals in 27 League appearances, which included two four-goal hauls against Everton and Bristol City, both away from home. The experienced Garbutt gave a number of virtuoso performances on the right wing to justify fully the reputation he had gained during his long career. Although Eddie Latheron had made sufficient progress to gain Inter-League honours, others who had occupied forward positions proved rather inconsistent. Kyle was a major disappointment and before the start of the next campaign he had returned to Scotland to join Bo'ness. Anthony continued to occupy the outside-left berth but lacked the necessary aggression to make the same impact as Garbutt. Aitkenhead had a disappointing campaign despite notching five goals in nine outings. However, the emergence of Ellis Crompton, who scored nine goals in 11 outings as understudy to Davies, proved to be an unexpected bonus.

While the Rovers finished in their highest League place since 1901–02, the FA Cup produced a shattering blow when the Rovers crashed to a 6–1 defeat at Clayton against Manchester United. However, both the Lancashire Senior Cup and East Lancashire Charity Cup were won as the Rovers ended the season on a note of real optimism.

1909-10

This was undoubtedly the most successful season that the club had enjoyed for many years. With no new additions to the squad, the club was able to mount a serious challenge for the First Division Championship. Indeed, from the latter part of October 1909 until the first week of January 1910, with the exception of a few days, the club sat proudly on top of the table. Sadly, the slump in form that followed left the team with too much leeway to make up over the final stages of the season. A third-place finish, coupled with the highest points total that the club had ever accumulated, continued to underline the progress that was being made on the field as well as off it.

Once again the success was built on the continued excellence of the defensive unit. Ashcroft, Crompton, Cowell, Walmsley, Chapman and Bradshaw again proved to be not only talented individually but, more importantly, able to work well together as a team. Garbutt continued to belie his years with his vintage performances on the right flank, while Anthony found a greater degree of consistency on the opposite wing. Latheron and Aitkenhead both performed creditably at inside-forward, but the centre-forward position began to cause concern. Davies was beginning to labour under the numerous injuries he had suffered and Ellis Crompton, while always a danger in front of goal, lacked too many of the attributes required of a top-class centre-forward. A makeshift solution was found when Walter Cameron, a Scottish utility player who had joined the Rovers from Bolton Wanderers in April 1908, was given an extended run in the position. However, it was the failure to find a permanent solution to this problem that undermined the team's performances at critical times of the season.

The FA Cup again brought success in the early rounds before the team crashed to a 3–1 defeat at Newcastle in front of a crowd of 54,772. Similarly, the Rovers fought their way to the Final of the Lancashire Senior Cup, only to be thrashed 4–0 by Everton at Goodison Park. However, the team managed to retain its hold on the East Lancashire Charity Cup with a convincing 4–0 win over Accrington Stanley.

1910-11

After the promise of the previous two seasons, the events of 1910–11 came as a major blow to all concerned at Ewood Park. A poor start – five defeats and three draws in the opening eight fixtures – blighted the whole of the League campaign. However, even when performances improved results continued to elude the Rovers on their travels. Twelve home wins made Ewood Park something of a fortress, but the team had to wait until the last game of the season before they were able to record an away victory in the League.

With no hope of the title, but free from the worries of relegation, the main focus of the campaign revolved around the FA Cup. Drawn away to Southend United in the first round, the Rovers agreed to pay their opponents a sum of £400 to switch the tie to Ewood Park. It proved a good investment in terms of the result, as they romped to a 5–1 win. However, financially it was not a success as the visitors only attracted 10,278 spectators to Ewood. The second round brought a goalless draw with Tottenham Hotspur at Ewood Park before goals from Bradshaw and Davies in the replay at White Hart Lane ensured their passage into the next round. Middlesbrough were beaten 3–0 on their own soil in the third round, while the fourth round brought yet another away victory with a 3–2 win at West Ham United. Curiously, while the team had yet to register an away win in the League, three successive wins away from Ewood Park had taken the club to its first FA Cup semi-final since 1893–94.

In view of their impressive record in reaching the semi-final, the Rovers were red-hot favourites to beat Bradford City at Bramall Lane. However, inexplicably, the team suffered an off day and goals from Frank O'Rourke, Archie Devine and Frank Thompson helped the Yorkshire club to a 3–0 win. The club enjoyed better luck in local competitions and, once again, the Lancashire Senior Cup and the East Lancashire Charity Cup were captured by the Rovers.

The team had begun to undergo something of a transition during the season. Chapman had departed for Glasgow Rangers in the summer of 1910 while Ellis Crompton, unable to win a regular place, moved to Tottenham Hotspur in December 1910. The major addition to the staff in the summer had been Percy Smith, Preston North End's long-serving centre-forward. However, the club appeared reluctant to utilise the services of Smith and when he did win a regular place in the team it was at centre-half, the position the club had struggled to fill following Chapman's departure.

In the midst of the Cup run the Rovers rocked the football world by signing the great John Simpson from Falkirk for a record fee of £1,800. Simpson, known popularly as Jock, was born in England but had moved north of the border as a youngster and gone on to become an outstanding outside-right with the Scottish club. He was chosen for the Scottish League against the Southern League and was likened, in many quarters, to the great Billy Meredith of Manchester United and Wales fame. Many top clubs in England had tried to sign him and it took several attempts before Lawrence Cotton and Robert Middleton were able to return to Blackburn, in February 1911, with his signature. It was this signing that was to herald one of the greatest periods in the club's history.

Blackburn Rovers signed Jock Simpson from Falkirk in January 1911 for a fee of £1,800.

1911–12

An inauspicious start to the campaign, one win and two defeats, did little to suggest that this would be the season that Lawrence Cotton's investment in the team would reap dividends. The only new face in the starting line-up was that of Alf Robinson, a goalkeeper who had joined the club from Gainsborough Trinity the previous May. Robinson had travelled with the team on its end-of-season tour of Austria and Hungary and made a real impression on the Ewood staff. Defensively, the team went into the season with a tried and trusted formation in front of the new 'keeper, with Bob Crompton and Arthur Cowell at full-back and a half-back trio of Albert Walmsley, Percy Smith and Billy Bradshaw. In attack, Jock Simpson and Eddie Latheron formed the right-wing partnership, while on the opposite flank Joe Clennell and Walter Anthony operated in tandem at the start of the campaign. The only area of concern appeared to surround the centre-forward position.

Despite the unimpressive start, Wattie Aitkenhead had scored three goals from the opening three games while occupying the centre-forward role. However, Aitkenhead's strengths lay in an inside-forward berth and, after the first four games had brought just three points, he was moved to inside-left and Davies returned to lead the attack. Sadly, this was not the Davies of old and he managed just two goals before giving way to Smith. The latter had found his defensive role usurped by the return of George Chapman, from Glasgow Rangers, in October 1911. Ultimately, it was Chapman who made the best show at centre-forward, with Smith restored to the centre-half position. However, despite Chapman's success, nine goals in 23 League outings and another six in seven FA Cup ties, his limitations as the leader of the front line were glaringly obvious. His ball control was not the best and his ability to feed his fellow front players was questionable. However, he did possess pace, a tremendous work ethic and had the build to trouble the strongest of defenders. Gradually, the changes in attack began to bear fruit and the Rovers were able to harvest enough points to stay in contact with the early pace-setters, Newcastle United and Aston Villa.

In mid-season the team went on an unbeaten run that lasted three months, with 17 points out of a possible 22 being won, which took the Rovers to the top of the League. Nor did panic set in when the run came to an end at Burnden Park, with a 2–0 defeat by Bolton, for nine points were taken from the next available 10.

The League campaign came to an exciting conclusion in April 1912. A major stride towards the Championship was taken when the Rovers produced a truly Championship-worthy display in the second half of their meeting with title-chasing Everton at Goodison Park. Despite being a goal behind, the Rovers fought back, with two goals from Clennell and another from Latheron, to claim two vital points. Two days later the team virtually assured themselves of the championship when a

Blackburn Rovers, 1911–12. From left to right, back row: J. Simpson, E. Latheron, G. Chapman, W. Aitkenhead, W. Anthony. Middle row: A. Walmsley, P.J. Smith, B. Bradshaw, R.B. Middleton (secretary). Front row: B. Crompton, A. Robinson, A. Cowell. (*Copyright: Howard Talbot*)

Latheron goal proved sufficient to claim the points against Oldham Athletic at Ewood Park. The hiccup of a 5–1 defeat away to Woolwich Arsenal proved nothing more than an annoying delay in sealing the championship. However, when West Bromwich Albion visited Ewood Park, three days after the débâcle in London, the Rovers cruised to a 4–1 win, thanks to a brace of goals from both Aitkenhead and Clennell.

It was perhaps fitting that the championship should be won against the Albion, for it was the men from The Hawthorns who had prevented the Rovers from capturing a possible League and Cup double. While the club had mounted its assault on the League title, it had also enjoyed success in the FA Cup. The opening rounds brought convincing victories over Norwich City, Derby County and Wolves, while Manchester United were disposed of in the fourth round after a replay. The Rovers met West Bromwich Albion in the semi-final at Anfield and fought out a goalless draw, although the Rovers dominated the game and had the best chances to win. Sadly, the attack also had another 'off' day when the teams met at Hillsborough for the replay. Goalless at full-time, the only goal was scored in injury time of the extra period, when a move between Ben Shearman and Claude Jephcott provided Bob Pailor with the opportunity to smash the ball past Robinson and end the Rovers' hopes of a League and Cup double.

Incredibly, the Rovers were unable to capture either the Lancashire Senior Cup or the East Lancashire Charity Cup. A full-strength Rovers team crashed 3–1 at Ewood Park in the semi-final of the county competition, while the Clarets enjoyed a narrow 1–0 win at Turf Moor in the Final of the Charity Cup.

As champions the Rovers were due to meet Queen's Park Rangers, champions of the Southern League, in the FA Charity Shield at some point during the following season. However, it was agreed that the match should be brought forward so that the proceeds could go to the *Titanic* Relief Fund. The match was played at White Hart Lane on 4 May 1912, in front of a crowd of 7,111. The Rovers beat their Southern League rivals 2–1, thanks to a brace of goals from Aitkenhead, to end a wonderful season with yet another honour.

Danny Shea joined the Rovers from West Ham United in January 1913 for a British record transfer fee of £2,000. (*Copyright: Blackburn Library*)

1912-13

Although the Rovers failed to retain their title, the season still gave great satisfaction to all concerned at Ewood Park. With the exception of an indifferent spell around Christmas, the team played an exciting brand of football that met with an enthusiastic response from the supporters.

After the success of the previous campaign there were no major additions to the playing staff in the summer of 1912. The Rovers began the campaign in the sort of form that they had ended the previous season and it was not until 14 December 1912 that they met with their first defeat. The 3–1 defeat at Maine Road at the hands of Manchester City also knocked the Rovers off the top of the table. There then followed another four successive defeats as the Rovers hit a mid-season slump in form.

The response of Lawrence Cotton was to sanction another two major signings. Firstly, a British record fee of £2,000 was paid to bring Danny Shea, West Ham United's talented goalscoring forward, to Ewood Park. Within less than a fortnight, another £1,000 had been spent to capture Joe Hodkinson from Glossop, an orthodox outside-left who possessed plenty of pace and the ability to deliver the ball with pin point accuracy.

Sadly, too much ground had been lost in the League for a realistic challenge to be maintained during the latter part of the season. However, although Hodkinson was unable to participate in the competition, the club embarked on yet another run in the FA Cup. Even without Hodkinson or Shea, the Rovers thrashed Northampton Town 7–1 in the first round of the competition. Victories over Barnsley and Reading followed and gave the Rovers a fourth-round tie with neighbouring Burnley at Ewood Park. Victory over Burnley would have meant that the Rovers would reach their third successive semi-final. A banner carried by Burnley supporters that proclaimed 'THE PARTING OF THE WAYS – IT'S HARD LUCK BOB BUT WE'VE GOT TO DO IT' was an acknowledgement that the FA Cup was the one honour Bob Crompton had never captured during his long and illustrious career.

Despite the comments on the banner, the Rovers were favourites to beat their Second Division neighbours. Unlike today's meetings between the two clubs, the match was played in a friendly atmosphere, with good-natured banter passing between the supporters of both sides. The Rovers faced a strong wind in the first half and the game was, perhaps, more even than most Blackburn supporters would have wished. The defining moment of the game occurred midway in the first half. Tommy Boyle, Burnley's slightly built centre-half, rose to meet an Eddie Mosscrop corner and was able to guide his header past Alf Robinson to give his team the lead.

The second half produced an onslaught on the Burnley goal but, despite the best efforts of Jock Simpson and Shea, the Burnley defence, superbly marshalled by Boyle, held firm. When the Rovers did get the better of defenders they found Jerry Dawson in superb form between the posts. It was a major blow to the Rovers and their supporters to be tossed out of the Cup at the same time as their grip on the Championship was slipping.

Although the Rovers reached the Final of the Lancashire Senior Cup they lost a thrilling encounter with Manchester United, played at Bloomfield Road, Blackpool, by the odd goal in five. Incredibly, despite the scintillating football that the club produced, the team ended the season without a major honour to its name.

A fee of £1,000 was paid for Joe Hodkinson, Glossop's talented outside-left, in January 1913. (*Copyright: Blackburn Library*)

1913-14

During the summer of 1913 several improvements were carried out on the side of the ground that was backed by the River Darwen. Designed by Archibald Leitch, the man responsible for the Nuttall Street Stand, a new stand was erected which was thought to have cost in the region of £7,000. The stand, which was of a semi-double-decker type, provided covered accommodation for some 12,000 spectators, of which 3,000 were seated. The improvements meant that the Riverside section of the ground was now capable of holding 20,650 spectators. It was the ambition of the directors to reach a maximum capacity of 70,000 at Ewood Park. It also meant that some £17,000 had been spent on improvements to Ewood Park in the decade between 1903 and 1913.

Cotton, despite the expensive signings made in January 1913 and the money spent on the Riverside Stand, was keen to add to the overall strength of the playing squad. Therefore, in July 1913, he paid £700 to bring Manchester United's experienced South African half-back, Alec Bell, to the club. Approaching the veteran stage of his career, Bell, who had won two League championships and the FA Cup with United, was signed despite the cost to act as cover for the half-back trio of Walmsley, Smith and Bradshaw.

However, the lack of a natural goalscoring centre-forward remained an ongoing problem at the club. Over the past two seasons the Rovers had experimented with several players in this key position. George Chapman remained the most successful, but Cotton told shareholders that the right man would be found and that they were prepared to pay a high price to capture him.

Despite the lack of a goalscoring centre-forward the Rovers got off to a flying start, with seven wins coming from the first eight matches. Nor was there a lack of goals, with no fewer than 26 goals being scored in these games. However, as the season settled down it quickly became apparent that there was an over-reliance on Danny Shea in terms of goalscoring. In January 1914, the Rovers accepted a reported fee of £1,500 from Everton for Joe Clennell, a player who had scored one goal in his four League appearances before losing his first-team place.

January brought one win for the Rovers from four League games, and on three occasions they failed to find the back of the opposition net. It merely underlined the need for new blood in attack. On 21 February 1914 the Rovers slipped out of the FA Cup when Manchester City visited Ewood Park and enjoyed a 2–1 win. A few days later Cotton sanctioned the creation of a new transfer record when the club paid £2,500 to Heart of Midlothian for Percy Dawson. Although Dawson took time to settle in English football, the club was able to maintain its title challenge. Ironically, the title was sealed with a goalless draw at Newcastle United on 10 April 1914.

Eleven days after capturing the national headlines with a second League Championship in three years, the Rovers became embroiled in more parochial matters. Once again, it was neighbouring Darwen who attempted to ruffle Blackburn's feathers. Despite the history of antagonism between the clubs it was reported that Cotton had made a personal donation to Darwen after they had fallen on hard times. However, scenes at the semi-final of the East Lancashire Charity Cup on 21 April 1914 brought back memories of the many unsavoury conflicts between the clubs.

Alec Bell, the South African former Manchester United star who joined the Rovers in July 1913. (*Copyright: Blackburn Library*)

A late George Porteous goal gave the reserves a 4–3 win over Darwen in the semi-final of the Charity Cup. When the final whistle blew a number of Darwen youths ran onto the pitch and pelted the Rovers players with stones, one of which struck 'keeper Harry Langtree on the back of the head. Only the intervention of a Darwen player prevented the referee from being assaulted as he left the field. As an angry crowd waited outside the front of the ground, the referee had to be escorted by Darwen officials to the station. A number of Rovers players made their escape by crossing a field at the back of the ground. However, when a group of Rovers players reached the main road they were followed by a crowd of baying youths. Once again, the unlucky Langtree was struck in the back and also hit by a lump of turf. Alec McGhie was also struck on the head by sods of turf before the players could board a tram and return to the safety of Blackburn.

In light of the above it was, perhaps, hardly surprising that the Rovers officials were reluctant to answer another appeal for cash from their neighbours.

1914-15

As the players of Blackburn Rovers basked in the summer sunshine of 1914, events had already begun to conspire to bring an end to the club's domination of English football. When Gavrilo Princip, a Serb nationalist, assassinated Archduke Franz Ferdinand in Sarajevo, he not only killed the heir to the throne of Austria-Hungary but set Europe on a path to war. In its wake, Blackburn Rovers became one of the many casualties, albeit a minor one when compared with the tragic human loss.

Percy Dawson finished 1914–15 as leading goalscorer with 20 League goals to his credit. (*Copyright: unknown*)

By the time the Rovers opened their defence of the Championship, Europe was already at war. Injuries and loss of form also conspired to undermine critical areas of the team. While Albert Walmsley remained as consistent as ever, both Percy Smith and Billy Bradshaw began to show signs of age creeping up on them. With the effectiveness of the half-back line reduced, the Rovers struggled in both attack and defence. Matters in attack were not helped when Percy Dawson was injured against Middlesbrough on 19 December 1914 and ruled out for 10 matches. Then, to make matters worse, Danny Shea suffered a serious knee injury on New Year's Day which kept him out of action for the rest of the season.

In January the club suffered a major setback when they were eliminated from the FA Cup at the hands of Swansea Town. With Shea and Dawson missing, the Rovers had to draft in Johnny Orr and McGhie as replacements and the result merely underlined the lack of cover in critical positions. A number of the reserve-team players enlisted in the armed forces, so the club had to draft in local amateur players to fulfil Central League fixtures.

As the season progressed, the appetite for football among the public of Blackburn appeared to diminish and several four-figure gates were recorded at home matches. The realities of war became increasingly difficult to ignore. Indeed, the fact that the Rovers finished third in the League and suffered a humiliation in the FA Cup seemed to be of little significance when measured against the losses in Europe.

1915-16

Before the official meeting of the Football League in July 1915, the League sent out a circular to all clubs explaining its recommendation to halt its competitions for the duration of the war. It explained: 'Owing to many professional players having enlisted and many more being engaged on munition work, which must not be interfered with, some clubs have been so seriously depleted that a competition providing for promotion and relegation would be grossly unjust, would produce the greatest hardship to those who have made the greatest sacrifice; and would favour the club whose players have failed to realise their higher duty to the nation.'

At its meeting in London on 19 July 1915, it was agreed to suspend the League competition. In its place the management committee organised regional competitions, but it was stressed that clubs would be free to decline to take part. The Football Association also announced the suspension of the FA Cup and all international matches. The FA also announced that existing contracts with players would be suspended and that players would not be paid during wartime.

To the regret of both John McKenna, the President of the Football League, and John Lewis, a co-founder of the club, the directors of Blackburn Rovers decided to suspend activities for 1915–16. It was the belief of the Ewood directorate that football would divert attention from the war effort and that, no matter what the cost to the club, a sense of patriotic duty must take precedence over football. In defending the stance the club took and its likely financial consequences Lawrence Cotton stated that, 'We shall pull through some way or other, and then, after the war is over, we shall try to build up what we have lost. But for the present the one thing, and the only thing, is the war.'

The players found alternative clubs for the season and during the course of the campaign Bob Crompton, George Chapman, Eddie Latheron and Joe Hodkinson represented Blackpool; Arthur Cowell, Albert Walmsley and Johnny Orr played with Burnley; Percy Smith played for both Preston North End and Chorley; Jock Simpson returned to Falkirk while Danny Shea returned to West Ham United; Tommy Suttie represented Accrington Stanley; and Alec McGhie played with Liverpool. Others, like Alec Bell and Billy Bradshaw, transferred their allegiance to Blackburn Trinity.

However, as the season neared its end the players reassembled at Ewood Park to represent the Rovers in three charity matches. On Good Friday the team travelled to Newcastle United and won 4–0. The following day the two clubs met at Ewood Park, and on this occasion it was Newcastle United that triumphed 5–4. On 6 May 1916 the Rovers played Burnley, at Ewood Park, and enjoyed a 9–3 victory. The money raised from the two games at Ewood Park amounted to £443 16s 11d and was shared among various charities, with the largest contribution of £150 going to the Belgian Refugees' Fund.

1916-17

Once it became clear that both players and supporters were fully committed to the war effort the Ewood directorate reversed its decision with regard to the participation in the regional competitions. However, the fact that the majority of the Blackburn players were now in uniform would have a devastating impact on the quality of football at Ewood Park.

In September 1916 the Rovers opened their campaign with the majority of the Championship-winning side of 1914 still available. The result was that the season opened with five straight wins and the Rovers sat proudly at the head of the Lancashire Section of the League until 21 October 1916. Unfortunately, it was at this point that players began to drift away as the needs of the military took precedence over the needs of the football club.

Team selection resembled a revolving door as more and more youngsters from the local junior clubs donned the colours of Blackburn Rovers. Nor was the scramble for players restricted to youth. Willie McIver, who had made his League debut for the Rovers in October 1901, returned to the club to keep goal in 19 of the 36 matches played. Another, if rather older, familiar face to turn out for the club was Edgar Chadwick, who had made his senior bow for the Rovers in 1887! He made an appearance on the left wing at Ewood Park, in the 2–1 defeat by Manchester United, some nine years after last appearing in the Football League.

The competitions were split into two sections. The Principal Tournament ran from September 1916 to March 1917 and consisted of 30 matches. However, as this was regional football the Rovers met the likes of Southport Central, Rochdale, Oldham Athletic and Port Vale. Yet, of these minnows the Rovers only completed the double over Southport Central, and went on to finish in 11th position in this competition.

A Subsidiary Tournament, consisting of six games and incorporating the Lancashire Cup, was played over Christmas and continued after the Principal Tournament had ended. Having lost four of the six matches the Rovers finished in 14th place in this particular competition.

During the course of the campaign the Rovers used no fewer than 50 players and it was, perhaps, understandable that the gates at Ewood Park remained hugely disappointing. The public of Blackburn appeared to have little interest in watching what had become a pale imitation of the team that had won two championship titles not so very long ago.

1917–18

'In the principal competition of the Lancashire Section of the League, the Rovers, represented almost entirely by youngsters, have had to meet elevens so superior in craft and experience that the results have almost been a foregone conclusion.' This analysis by one local wordsmith concisely explained the plight of the club during 1917–18.

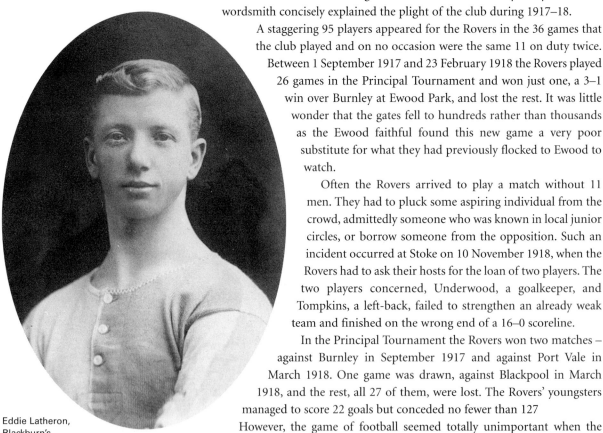

Eddie Latheron, Blackburn's talented England international forward, was killed in action in October 1917. (*Copyright: Blackburn Library*)

A staggering 95 players appeared for the Rovers in the 36 games that the club played and on no occasion were the same 11 on duty twice. Between 1 September 1917 and 23 February 1918 the Rovers played 26 games in the Principal Tournament and won just one, a 3–1 win over Burnley at Ewood Park, and lost the rest. It was little wonder that the gates fell to hundreds rather than thousands as the Ewood faithful found this new game a very poor substitute for what they had previously flocked to Ewood to watch.

Often the Rovers arrived to play a match without 11 men. They had to pluck some aspiring individual from the crowd, admittedly someone who was known in local junior circles, or borrow someone from the opposition. Such an incident occurred at Stoke on 10 November 1918, when the Rovers had to ask their hosts for the loan of two players. The two players concerned, Underwood, a goalkeeper, and Tompkins, a left-back, failed to strengthen an already weak team and finished on the wrong end of a 16–0 scoreline.

In the Principal Tournament the Rovers won two matches – against Burnley in September 1917 and against Port Vale in March 1918. One game was drawn, against Blackpool in March 1918, and the rest, all 27 of them, were lost. The Rovers' youngsters managed to score 22 goals but conceded no fewer than 127

However, the game of football seemed totally unimportant when the weekly newspaper was filled with photographs of young men who had fallen on foreign fields in service of their country. It was particularly poignant for all at Ewood to reflect on the sad tidings that Alec McGhie relayed back from the front. McGhie broke the news that his close friend, Eddie Latheron, had been killed by a German shell on 17 October 1917. At 28, Latheron left a widow and a child and the memory of a wonderfully gifted footballer who had warmed the hearts of thousands who had watched him at Ewood Park.

1918–19

The bare statistics tell the tale of another meaningless season of wartime football at Ewood Park. Some 71 players were called upon to represent the club during the course of the season. The

Principal Tournament ended with Rovers in 16th position, with just five wins and four draws to show from their efforts in 30 games. Of the five victories, three came in the final month of the season, when Percy Dawson was available to lead the forward line. Yet again, the forwards consistently struggled to find the net and only 35 goals were scored while 83 goals were conceded; the heaviest defeat was the 9–0 thrashing at Everton on 4 January 1919.

Nor did the Rovers fare any better in Subsidiary Tournament, coming bottom of their section, with two draws and four defeats.

However, the biggest story of the season was the resignation of Lawrence Cotton, on 19 February 1919, as chairman of Blackburn Rovers. Cotton had become Mayor of Blackburn in 1917 and it was stated that 'the increasing pressure of civic and other duties' led to his decision to step down from his position at the club. However, his fellow directors elected him as the club's first president and then appointed his brother, Clement, as the new chairman.

1919-20

The Championship years were but a distant memory when the players reassembled for pre-season training in the summer of 1919. As with all other communities in Britain, war had taken its toll on Ewood Park. If the loss of Eddie Latheron was immeasurable, there were others too who were unable to return after the guns had finally fallen silent. Wattie Aitkenhead was forced to follow medical advice and hang up his boots while Jock Simpson, who had been injured playing with Falkirk during the war, was unable to resume his career. In May 1920, the Rovers held a benefit match for Simpson, which raised some £1,100 for a player who had been so instrumental in bringing two Championships to Ewood Park. Other old favourites returned but found that age was an enemy that couldn't be defeated and Bob Crompton, Arthur Cowell and Billy Bradshaw made their final appearances for the club during the course of the campaign.

Initially, the Rovers made a bright start, with an opening-day 4–0 win over Preston North End at Ewood Park. However, this proved to be something of a false dawn, as the team didn't win another match until the 1–0 victory over Arsenal at the beginning of October. Ironically, a railway strike had meant that the team had had to travel to the capital by road, but this didn't affect their performance. Sadly, the supporters had to wait until 20 March 1920 before they could celebrate another victory on enemy soil.

With the team in a slump, the directors sanctioned the acquisition of two new defenders in December 1919. David Rollo, an Irish full-back, arrived from Linfield, while Frank Reilly, a Scottish centre-half, was signed from Falkirk. Both players made their debuts in the 2–0 win over Derby County on 6 December 1919 and five days later they played in the 4–1 victory over Bradford City at Ewood Park. However, after the Bradford match the Rovers endured a run of 15 successive League games without a win.

Fortunately, the tide began to turn with a 3–1 win over Chelsea on 11 March 1920 and this was followed by another three victories. The improvement was a direct result of further investment in the playing staff. Both Ronnie Sewell, a goalkeeper, and Levy Thorpe, a half-back, were signed from Burnley, while Norman Rodgers was snapped up from Stockport County.

Norman Rodgers joined Blackburn Rovers from Stockport County in February 1919. His 13 goals helped the Rovers to avoid relegation. (*Copyright: unknown, cigarette card*)

The improvement in results enabled to Rovers to became involved in a frantic race for survival which wasn't resolved until the final day of the season. However, on that day, 1 May 1920, a hat-trick by Rodgers helped the Rovers to a 4–0 win over Sheffield United at Ewood Park, while Notts County suffered a 2–0 home defeat by Manchester United and slipped into the Second Division.

Survival couldn't hide the fact that the Rovers had endured a tortuous campaign in which no fewer than 39 players had been called upon. Ultimately, only substantial expenditure had saved the club from relegation. However, despite the influx of new players, there were still areas of the team that remained a problem. Nine men had tried, unsuccessfully, to fill the vacancy on the right wing that Simpson's departure had caused. Meanwhile, Danny Shea, another hero of the Championship years, had lost form, was placed on the transfer list and was ultimately sold back to West Ham United in May 1920 at a substantial loss.

1920-21

The season proved something of a curate's egg. Mid-table security went hand in hand with embarrassing defeats at the hands of Fulham in the FA Cup and Burnley in the East Lancashire Charity Cup.

Levy Thorpe was the only player to appear in all 42 League games during 1920–21. (*Copyright: unknown, trade card*)

A combination of injury and individual underachievement undermined any attempt to attain consistency in team selection. Arthur Cowell, who still harboured hopes of a comeback, was injured before a ball was kicked. Dick Walmsley, the young full-back who had stepped into Bob Crompton's role just 12 months earlier, was another long-term casualty. Percy Dawson, who had had surgery in the summer, broke a rib in November, yet still finished as the campaign as the club's most prolific marksman. Injury restricted Norman Rodgers to just six League outings, while Peter Holland broke a collarbone and John McDonald suffered a serious knee injury. To add to the club's tale of woe, Fred Duckworth broke an arm during an East Lancashire Charity Cup match and never played for the first team again.

After the expensive signings of the previous campaign, the directors, despite an injury crisis of epic proportions, opted to operate on a more modest budget. As a result they cast their net far and wide to bring in young players at reasonable fees. William McCall and Jimmy McKinnell, a winger and inside-forward respectively, arrived from Queen of the South, as did Tom Wylie, a young full-back, who made his first-team debut after just one Central League outing. Bert Ralphs, an outside-right, was signed from Nuneaton, while another dip into non-League football brought Fleetwood centre-forward, William Sandham, to Ewood Park. From Ireland the club signed Pat Robinson, Distillery's international winger.

Despite the problems with regard to team selection there was general satisfaction at a mid-table finish. Sadly, the team produced one of its worst displays of the campaign in the first-round FA Cup replay at Craven Cottage, when a goal by Billy McDonald proved sufficient to earn Fulham a narrow victory.

The season also marked the end of an era for the club with the death of Lawrence Cotton in May 1921. The loss of the man who had masterminded the most successful period in the club's history was compounded by the resignation of his brother, Clement, from the chairmanship of the club.

1921-22

The Ewood faithful witnessed another season of indifferent football as the Rovers, yet again, struggled to find any degree of consistency. The threat of relegation was once again averted, largely through unexpected away wins at Middlesbrough and Cardiff in the middle of April. A glimmer of light came when the Rovers reached the third round of the FA Cup, but it was quickly extinguished in a 5–0 defeat at Huddersfield.

In a bid to end the problems on the right wing, the directors parted with £2,000 to sign Fergie Aitken, Bury's speedy Scottish winger. However, when the season began it was Bert Ralphs who started on the right and Aitken was selected on the opposite flank. The new man struggled on the left and was quickly dropped in favour of the ageing but reliable Joe Hodkinson. Indeed, Aitken made just two appearances for the club in his favoured position before being discarded altogether. Unfortunately, Ralphs was unable to repeat the form he had shown towards the end of the previous season and, with Aitken out of the picture, the directors were forced into the transfer market once more. The man who was signed was Archie Longmuir, a reserve centre-forward with Celtic, and although he made a creditable job of filling in on the right flank, the season ended with no permanent solution to what had become a serious weakness.

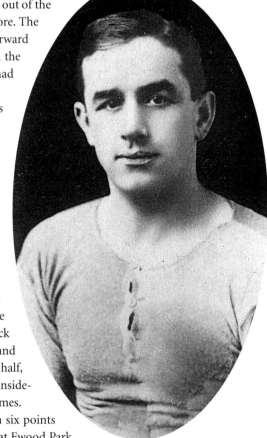

Frank Reilly proved a tower of strength at the heart of the Blackburn defence. (*Copyright: unknown, trade card*)

It was the club's good fortune that the defensive players performed with great consistency, because the forward line became increasingly ineffective. When Percy Dawson and Norman Rodgers failed to find the goalscoring touch of former years, it was all the more unfortunate that both Peter Holland and John McDonald failed to grasp the opportunity presented to them.

It was to improve the performances of the attack that the directors signed Jock McKay from Celtic and Johnny McIntyre from Sheffield Wednesday. McKay, who was signed at the same time as Longmuir, had struggled to win a regular place with his former club. Nonetheless, his 10 League appearances for Celtic had brought six goals and he was a highly regarded deputy for the legendary Patsy Gallagher. McIntyre, another Scot, was a far more experienced player, having begun his professional career with Partick Thistle in 1912. He had joined Fulham during World War One and moved to Sheffield Wednesday in March 1920. Originally a left-half, McIntyre had been transformed by Wednesday into a scheming inside-forward with an eye for goals – he scored 36 goals in 67 League games.

The eight points gained in April 1922 helped the club to finish six points above relegated Bradford City. However, the dearth of excitement at Ewood Park began to result in a gradual decline in attendances. Interest was briefly revived during the FA Cup run and a gate of 45,068 was recorded for the third-round meeting with Huddersfield Town at Ewood Park. It was, therefore, all the more frustrating that the team should crumble in the replay at Leeds Road and suffer a 5–0 defeat.

However, the most significant moment in the season came in February 1922 with the appointment of a full-time manager. Prior to the appointment of Jack Carr, administrative affairs had been run by the club secretary, while a trainer looked after the players from day to day. Carr, an England international full-back, had a wealth of experience both playing and coaching at Newcastle United. The Ewood directors indicated that the necessary funds would be available to restore the club to its former glories.

1922-23

The season ended with the Rovers one place higher in the League than 12 months earlier. Yet, even though the Rovers enjoyed their best results since the war and finished ahead of their neighbours Preston North End and Burnley, there was little cause for satisfaction within the boardroom at Ewood Park. A home defeat in the FA Cup in the second round at the hands of South Shields erased many of the plus points of the campaign.

Jock McKay was a typically tricky Scottish inside-forward who ended the season as the club's leading goalscorer. (*Copyright: unknown, trade card*)

With a new manager at the helm, and the promise of funds to back him, it must have been with some trepidation that Blackburn supporters read of the club's first close-season capture in May 1922. A fee of £300 was spent to bring Dickie Bond, Bradford City's 38-year-old former England winger, to Ewood Park. The fact that he was able to hold down the right-wing spot for over half a season merely highlighted the lack of options available to the new manager.

The highlight of a fairly forgettable campaign was Johnny McIntyre's incredible four goals in five minutes against Everton in September 1922. The Rovers had fallen behind to a George Harrison penalty before a long-range effort from Harry Healless on the stroke of half-time brought the Rovers level. After 10 minutes of the second period McIntyre put the Rovers ahead and then blasted another three goals past a bemused Tom Fern, in the Everton goal.

Sadly, the rest of the campaign was pure anticlimax and the FA Cup brought one of the most humbling experiences in the club's history. Having held South Shields, of the Second Division, to a goalless draw at the Horsley Hill Stadium, passage into the third round ought to have been a formality. Certainly, the Rovers fans that assembled at Ewood Park for the replay expected to see a comfortable victory, particularly as the Rovers had beaten Aston Villa at Villa Park in the first round of the competition. As expected, the Rovers totally dominated the game but, sadly, couldn't find a way past Willis Walker in the visitors' goal. In the 14th minute Jack Smith, the visitors' centre-forward, latched onto a pass from George Keenlyside and drove the ball so hard that Ronnie Sewell let it slip from his grasp and allowed it to pass into the net. It was virtually the only shot that the South Shields team could muster throughout the entire match and yet it proved sufficient to win the match.

Jack Byers arrived from Huddersfield Town in April 1923. However, his career at Ewood Park was not particularly successful and the outside-left departed for West Bromwich Albion in January 1924 after making just 28 senior appearances for the club. (*Copyright: unknown, trade card*)

Following the defeat by South Shields, the directors, who included former players Bob Crompton, Johnny Forbes and Jimmy Forrest, acted quickly to strengthen the team. Aussie Campbell, a young half-back, was signed from Leadgate Park after having failed to make much impression in an earlier spell with Coventry City. In March, Jack Crisp, West Bromwich Albion's outside-right, was signed for £3,175, while Carr returned to his roots to sign Stan Dixon, an inside-forward from Newcastle United. The latter two helped to improve the club's position in the League although Dixon, after four games in attack, was successfully switched to centre-half.

A disappointing season ended on a note of optimism when the Rovers defeated Burnley to capture the East Lancashire Charity Cup.

1923–24

The summer of 1923 brought an end to the careers of veteran wingers Joe Hodkinson and Dickie Bond. Hodkinson returned to his native town to join Lancaster in April 1923, while Bond joined him at the same club a few months later. However, there were to be no major signings by the Rovers, just the acquisition of Ted Harper – a raw, untutored centre-forward who came to Ewood Park from Sheppey United in the Kent League. It was said that he cost only 'a railway fare', but he was nonetheless, in view of his inexperience, something of a gamble. Fortunately, the youngster quickly proved his worth and ended his debut season with 18 goals to his credit.

It proved to be the club's best post-war season as there was no anxiety with regard to relegation. However, the team slumped to new depths in the FA Cup and were unceremoniously knocked out of the competition by the Corinthians at Crystal Palace. In the wake of this embarrassing defeat the Rovers lost a valued player and also suffered the financial consequences that waning support brought.

The loss to the Corinthians, in the first-round tie, was a major blow to Rovers' prestige. The appallingly heavy conditions and long, slippery grass quickly negated the passing game that the Rovers favoured. Even after Doggart had given the Corinthians the lead, the Blackburn attack still had enough chances to win the game. Alas, the chances were spurned and Benjamin Howard Baker, in the Corinthians goal, enjoyed his moment of glory against his former club. Even more galling was the fact that it had been the Rovers that had converted Baker from a centre-half into a goalkeeper during his short spell with the second XI at Ewood Park. To heap further humiliation on the club, a fracas occurred at Blackburn station when the players arrived back from London. Jack Byers and Tom Wylie became involved in an altercation with each other and had to be separated as they brawled in public. Subsequently, Byers was given 14 days' notice for unruly behaviour and was quickly sold to West Bromwich Albion – ironically for a fee that allowed the Rovers to show a profit on a player they had bought from Huddersfield Town in April 1923. Shortly after hearing the news of the defeat by the Corinthians, Clement Cotton, the former chairman of the club, collapsed and died while watching a reserve game at Ewood Park.

With interest in both League and FA Cup at an end, the Rovers found that supporters began to lose interest in affairs at Ewood Park. Indeed, seven days after the Cup debacle a crowd of just 5,000 watched a goalless draw with West Ham United at Ewood Park. With attendances

David Rollo appeared in 40 League games during 1923–24 and also featured in the FA Cup defeat away to Corinthians. (*Copyright: unknown, cigarette card*)

falling and finances stretched the directors, nonetheless, invested a small amount to sign Joe Hulme from York City. Hulme was a promising outside-right and after making his debut in the 3–1 win over Aston Villa at Ewood Park, he remained in the team until the end of the season. The form of Hulme and the progress of Harper were the two main positives that could be taken from a season that had disintegrated so chaotically.

1924-25

A season that promised to end in a blaze of glory merely petered out like a damp squib as the Rovers, once again, finished in the lower reaches of the First Division. Yet, if the team had beaten Cardiff City in the FA Cup semi-final, then the indifferent League form might well have been forgiven by the Ewood faithful.

Unfortunately, many of the problems stemmed from the fact that Harper couldn't reproduce his goalscoring exploits of the previous campaign. His 14 League appearances produced just three goals and yet, when relegated to the reserves, he scored 17 goals in 20 outings. Both Holland and McIntyre tried unsuccessfully to fill the void but, without a recognised centre-forward, the Rovers couldn't achieve any degree of consistency in the League.

In truth, the Rovers had done little to strengthen the playing staff during the close season, preferring instead to place their faith in the acquisition of a number of young players. Bob Roxburgh, a speedy full-back, was another capture from Carr's old club Newcastle United, while Philip Hope was a powerfully built half-back from Norwich City. Queen's Island of Belfast provided William McCleery, a tricky inside-forward, and Fred Morton, an outside-right, both of whom had helped their former club lift the 1923–24 Irish championship. While the new men were welcome additions to the squad not one was in the Rovers team on the first day of the campaign.

It wasn't until February 1925 that the club made a major signing, when Syd Puddefoot arrived from Falkirk for a reported fee of £4,000. Although aged 30, Puddefoot, who had previously played with West Ham United, was the type of gifted playmaker that the club desperately needed, and following his arrival there was an immediate upturn in results.

The Rovers made steady progress in the FA Cup, beating Oldham Athletic, Portsmouth and Tottenham Hotspur, before meeting Blackpool at Ewood Park in the sixth round. A record crowd of 60,011 witnessed Puddefoot score the only goal of the game to send the Rovers into a record-

Blackburn Rovers in 1924–25. (*Copyright: unknown*)

breaking 12th FA Cup semi-final. The Rovers were paired with Cardiff City, in a game to be played at Meadow Lane, Nottingham. Having already inflicted a 3–1 defeat on Cardiff earlier in the season, the Rovers went into the match as favourites. Both Cardiff and Rovers wanted to change the venue but were overruled by the FA, and it was a rather small crowd of 20,100 that gathered to witness what was to prove a major Cup upset.

Cardiff adapted better to the windy conditions and launched a number of high balls into the Blackburn area. Within six minutes the Rovers fell behind when a mix up by David Rollo and Ronnie Sewell gifted the Welsh team a goal. Three minutes later Rollo hesitated again and Joe Nicholson edged the ball to Jimmy Gill, who made no mistake with a simple tap in. After 17 minutes Rollo and Sewell failed to deal with a cross and watched helplessly as the ball sailed between them and was easily converted by Harry Beadles on the far post. McKay's goal, 11 minutes from the end, was scant consolation for the Rovers and their supporters.

As the season drifted to its unsatisfactory conclusion, the Rovers began the process of rebuilding their team. John Crawford, a goalkeeper, was signed from Alloa Athletic, while Arthur Rigby, a dashing winger, was bought from Bradford City for £2,500.

1925-26

The club's jubilee season was dominated by one man – Ted Harper. During the course of the campaign he went from reserve-team player to record breaker and then led the English forward line against Scotland, at Old Trafford, in April 1926.

Sadly, tragedy struck the club three times within the opening months of the season. The death of John Lewis, the club's co-founder, was followed by the deaths of Robert Middleton, the secretary for 22 years, and Jimmy Forrest, director and FA Cup-winner on five occasions with the Rovers.

On paper the Rovers began the season with a very strong squad and yet they made their worst start for many years. Three successive defeats, only three goals scored and 10 conceded, brought an immediate response in terms of team selection. Johnny McIntyre was recalled and installed at left-half, while Harper was also promoted to lead the attack. The result was a stunning 7–1 win at Newcastle United, with Harper claiming five of the goals.

Sadly, the team was unable to maintain the level of consistency required to mount a serious Championship challenge. Nonetheless, in Harper they had a goalscoring machine, whose appetite for goals was such that relegation was never in question. Even when the team endured lean patches in terms of results, Harper still scored goals with a relentless monotony. He fully exploited the change in the offside rule and was aided by the brilliant inside-forward play of Syd Puddefoot. The acquisition of Tom Mitchell from Stockport County in February 1926 enabled Arthur Rigby to move to inside-left and provide even more ammunition for Harper.

Other signings that undoubtedly strengthened the club were Herbert 'Taffy' Jones, Blackpool's talented left-back, who cost £3,850 and Joe Walter, an experienced winger who had played over 50 games for Huddersfield Town before dropping into non-League football. Walter was signed to help cover the departure of young Hulme, who was surprisingly sold to Arsenal in February 1926. The inexperienced winger had frustrated both supporters and officials alike with a mixture of brilliance and indifference during his

Harry Healless continued to give excellent service to the club at centre-half during 1925–26. He made 36 League and Cup appearances during the course of the season. (*Copyright: unknown, trade card*)

time at the club, hence the willingness to cash in on a player who would go on to achieve greatness in the legendary Arsenal teams of the 1930s.

However, the season belonged to Ted Harper and a final tally of 43 goals from 37 League appearances ensured his place in the record books. Sadly, a 12th-place finish and a third-round elimination at the hands of Arsenal in the FA Cup meant that the supporters had little to cheer but Harper's individual success.

1926-27

Yet another unsatisfactory season passed into history without bringing supporters much cheer. Once again, the club flirted with relegation and only a mid-season spurt that brought four wins from five games in February saved the club from being stranded at the foot of the table. Of the club's final 11 League games just one was won, three were drawn and seven ended in defeat. This included a disastrous spell at Easter, when the team failed to produce a single goal in four consecutive games. Nor was the general gloom lifted by the ignominy of a third-round exit from the FA Cup at the hands of Southport, of the Third Division North.

While the team might have been average, Ted Harper, with 35 goals, remained one of the leading marksmen in the First Division. Furthermore, only eight teams bettered the 77 goals that the Rovers scored that season. However, no fewer than 96 goals were conceded – the worst record in the top division and 10 more than West Bromwich Albion, the bottom club, conceded. It was also 16 more than the club had ever conceded since the Football League began in 1888.

The blame clearly lay with the defence, with only 'Taffy' Jones and Harry Healless able to produce the consistency required. Consistency was certainly not helped by the constant changing

Bob Roxburgh made 26 League appearances at full-back. (*Copyright: Howard Talbot*)

of the goalkeeper. Three goalkeepers were used, with Sewell, now at the end of his career, quickly replaced by Jock Crawford, who in turn was replaced by Horace Cope, a 'keeper who was signed from Mexborough Town in October 1926. However, when Cope was injured Crawford returned, in January 1926, and finally made the first-team spot his own with a number of excellent performances.

In October 1926, the Rovers also signed a new full-back in the sturdy form of Jock Hutton. The Scottish international was signed from Aberdeen for £5,000 and it was hoped that his physique and not inconsiderable weight at over 13 stones would bring more solidity to the Blackburn defence. Unfortunately, he was dogged by misfortune and injury and only completed 17 League games during his debut season at Ewood.

Stability at the club was rocked in November 1926 when Jack Carr announced his resignation as manager. Carr, who had also inherited the role of secretary following the death of Robert Middleton, had been an excellent administrator but had been unable to restore the club to the glories of the immediate pre-war period. The directors looked for continuity in the appointment of his successor and promoted Arthur Barritt to the role of secretary, while director Bob Crompton took up the position of honorary manager.

Crompton quickly began to strengthen the squad in the wake of the embarrassing Cup exit at Southport. Tom McLean, a tricky inside-forward, was signed from St Johnstone in February 1927 and a month later John Whyte, a competitive half-back, was signed from the same club. Another Scot to join the Rovers was Bill Rankin, a rugged centre-half, who was signed from Dundee in April 1927 at a cost of £4,000. While a total of more than £13,000 was spent, the club also invested in youth, acquiring the likes of Peter O'Dowd, Sam McCulloch, Malcolm Marson and George Grass.

To offset the cost of team-building, the Rovers allowed Crisp to move to Coventry City, while McKay was sold to Middlesbrough. Nonetheless, at the AGM in March 1927, the club reported a loss of £1,573 over the previous nine months.

1927–28

In the jubilee year of the Lancashire Football Association it was, perhaps, fitting that so many of the major honours should be won by clubs from the Red Rose county. Everton won the First Division championship, with Dixie Dean breaking all records with his 60-goal haul. The Second Division title was won by Manchester City, while Blackburn Rovers captured the FA Cup for a sixth time.

Having spent a considerable amount of money during the previous campaign, the directors chose not to enter the transfer market until December 1927, when George Thornewell, an experienced outside-right, was signed from Derby County. Thornewell was immediately installed on the right-wing after Joe Walter, Peter Holland and Jack Roscamp had all failed to make the position their own. Unfortunately, Thornewell broke his collarbone in the second-round Cup tie at Exeter and didn't return until a week before the FA Cup semi-final.

Once again, FA Cup football dominated the town, as the Rovers opened their Cup campaign with an impressive 4–1 win over Newcastle United. Having held the Rovers at home, Exeter visited Ewood Park and proved a tough nut to crack, taking the match into extra-time before being beaten

Blackburn Rovers, 1927–28. From left to right, back row: Barritt (secretary), Rankin, Roxburgh, Hutton, Crawford, Campbell, Jones, Mitchell, Atherton (trainer). Front row, left to right: Thornewell, Puddefoot, Roscamp, Healless, McLean, Rigby, Holland. (*Copyright: Howard Talbot*)

3–1. Both Port Vale and Manchester United were beaten at home in successive rounds to give the Rovers a semi-final date with Arsenal at Filbert Street, Leicester.

Under the guidance of Bob Crompton and Mo Atherton, the first-team trainer, the Rovers developed a settled side that appeared to raise its game for Cup ties while being plagued with inconsistency in the League. Jock Crawford had become first-choice 'keeper, with Jock Hutton and 'Taffy' Jones being automatic choices at full-back. The half-back line of Harry Healless, Bill Rankin and Aussie Campbell was as strong as any in the top flight. The acquisition of Thornewell had given the front line more balance with Arthur Rigby operating on the left flank. Syd Puddefoot and Tom McLean complemented each other perfectly as inside-forwards. Puddefoot remained one of the most gifted footballers of his era. His vision and passing ability made him the supreme play-maker, the man who made the bullets for others to fire. The pigeon-toed McLean was more unorthodox but no less effective. McLean was a player who liked to run at opponents with the ball seemingly tied to his feet. His wizardry in dribbling past the opposition made him the perfect foil for

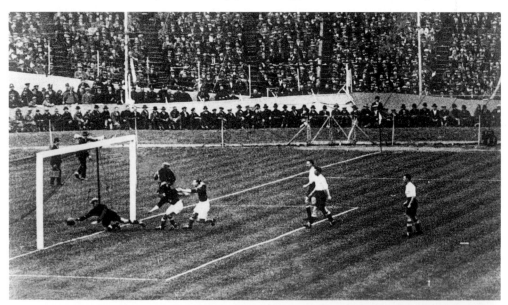

Jack Roscamp puts the Rovers ahead in the 1928 FA Cup Final. (*Copyright: Howard Talbot*)

Tom McLean scores the Rovers' second goal in the 1928 FA Cup Final (*Copyright: Howard Talbot*)

Puddefoot. The man who reaped the benefit from the ingenuity of Puddefoot and McLean was Roscamp. Following the departure of Harper, sold to Sheffield Wednesday for a handsome fee, the club had experimented with Tom Mitchell at centre-forward. However, it was felt that the former Stockport winger didn't have sufficient aggression to make the switch permanent and so the more robust style of Roscamp was used.

The Rovers went into the semi-final meeting with Arsenal as underdogs. The task was made even harder when McLean was ruled out and Holland stepped into the breach. It was, therefore, something of a shock when Roscamp raced clear of the Arsenal defence and gave the Rovers the lead. A magnificent defensive display followed, which enabled the Rovers to hang on to their narrow lead.

Although at full strength, the Rovers went into their seventh FA Cup Final, their first at Wembley, as rank outsiders. While Huddersfield Town were challenging for the Championship, the Rovers were entrenched in the lower reaches of the division. However, within a minute of the kick-off the Rovers completely overturned all those predictions of gloom. Puddefoot and Thornewell worked the ball upfield for Roscamp to chase. With Ned Barkas, Huddersfield's highly rated left-back, between Roscamp and the goal there appeared little danger. It was then that Roscamp revealed an exquisite touch and chipped the ball over a bemused Barkas. It was an unexpected piece of impudence from a player who was noted more for energy than subtlety. However, even then, the ball appeared destined to float into the hands of Billy Mercer in the Huddersfield goal. It was then that Roscamp relied on his more natural assets and simply dipped his shoulder and headed straight for the startled goalkeeper. From the resultant collision the ball slipped from Mercer's grasp and entered the goal with the badly shaken 'keeper following close behind.

The shock of the first goal gave the Rovers the confidence to match Huddersfield for possession during the opening period. Then, after 22 minutes, Rigby found McLean who, in turn, launched a

Blackburn Rovers
parade the FA Cup
around the town
following their 3–1
triumph over
Huddersfield Town.
(*Copyright: Howard
Talbot*)

rocket-like shot past a bemused Mercer, which gave the Rovers a two-goal lead. Half-time gave Huddersfield the opportunity to make a tactical switch, which took Alex Jackson, their Scottish international, from the wing to the centre. The move unsettled the Rovers defence sufficiently for the Scottish player to snatch a goal. Huddersfield poured forward as the Rovers held firm against wave after wave of attacking moves. However, five minutes from time Roscamp hit a low shot past Mercer to restore the two-goal margin. It proved sufficient to bring the Cup back to Blackburn for a sixth time and make Roscamp an unlikely hero.

For the season to end on a high was a welcome relief to all at Ewood Park, for there had been some traumatic times during the course of the season. The death of Bobby Marshall, the regular left-back for the reserves, as a result of an injury sustained at Bloomfield Road, was a tragedy that went beyond the bounds of football. He had been injured during a collision with an opponent in the Central League match that was played on Boxing Day. It was not thought to be serious and after the match he left with his fiancée for a nearby house where they were staying. However, he was taken ill during the night with abdominal pains and underwent surgery at Blackpool Victoria Hospital. After a slight improvement his conditioned worsened and he died on 3 January 1928. Before the month was out the club was in mourning again following the death of Johnny Forbes, a former player, committee member and director at Ewood Park for some 31 years.

1928–29

At the end of the season it was a case of 'what might have been' as, at one point, the Rovers looked well set to retain the FA Cup and capture the League title. Sadly, a combination of injuries and loss of form at the crucial moment robbed them of the chance of twin success. Nor did the FA Charity Shield offer consolation; the Rovers went down 2–1 to Everton at Old Trafford. Nonetheless, a

70

seventh-place finish in the League and a place in the sixth round of the FA Cup reinforced the club's position among the elite of the English game.

In the wake of the FA Cup triumph of the previous season and its subsequent increase in income, the summer of 1928 brought increased activity in the transfer market. Clarrie Bourton and Albert Keating were two forwards signed from Bristol City, while David Raitt, an experienced defender who had seen service with Dundee and Everton, was signed to provide cover at full-back. A more speculative move brought James Melville, a promising young inside-forward cum half-back, from Barrow.

The Rovers began the season in disastrous fashion with successive defeats at Derby and Sunderland. However, maximum points were gained from the next four games and the club went on to establish its credentials as Championship challengers. Unfortunately, even in the early stages of the campaign, the club had been struck with serious injury problems. Jock Hutton was injured in the opening game and was kept out of action for four months. 'Taffy' Jones, his full-back partner, was so seriously injured in the meeting with Arsenal in December 1928 that he didn't reappear for the rest of the season. As Raitt had proved a disappointing understudy, Crompton put his faith in Bob Roxburgh to cover at full-back, and later in the season introduced Tom Baxter, one of the club's promising young-sters, at right-back.

Because of the excellent form that Jack Roscamp showed leading the attack, it was November 1928 before Bourton received his first opportunity at centre-forward. When he finally got his chance he quickly made an impression with six goals in his first four games, including a four-goal haul at Old Trafford in the 4–1 win over Manchester United. With Bourton installed as centre-forward, Crompton was able to make use of Roscamp's versatility, switching him to the outside-right berth and then moving him to right-half during the final weeks of the season. When illness kept Tom McLean out for a lengthy spell it gave Keating the chance to step into his role but, following the exit from the FA Cup, the forwards found it increasingly difficult to find the net on a regular basis. Fortunately, the defence proved more reliable and only three teams conceded fewer goals than the Rovers.

Jack Roscamp was the leading goalscorer with 16 League goals and one in the FA Cup. (*Copyright: Howard Talbot*)

The turning point of the season came with the sixth-round FA Cup meeting with Bolton Wanderers at Ewood Park. A record crowd of 62,522 saw the Rovers held to a 1–1 draw and a few days later 65,295 witnessed the Rovers slump to 2–1 defeat at Burnden Park. Following their defeat at Bolton the Rovers failed to grasp their opportunity to concentrate on a Championship challenge. Just four points were taken from the next eight League games as the Rovers' challenge simply evaporated. Bourton, who had been so prominent earlier in the campaign, went 15 League games without a goal as the Rovers' season spluttered to a disappointing conclusion.

1929–30

Although the Rovers confirmed their place as one of the leading clubs in the country, they were dogged by inconsistency throughout the campaign. Those who paid to watch the Rovers were treated to entertainment on a grand scale. No fewer than 192 goals were scored in League games that involved Blackburn Rovers.

A club that was noted for its strong defence and inconsistent attack finally improved efficiency in goalscoring but, sadly, only at the expense of the defence. Nonetheless, the Blackburn public were treated to some extraordinary results at Ewood Park. Birmingham lost 7–5, Burnley succumbed 8–3 and Middlesbrough were trashed 7–0, while tighter affairs brought a 5–3 win over Sunderland and a 5–4 victory over Manchester United. Away from Ewood Park the Rovers enjoyed a 7–5 victory at Sheffield United.

The first contribution to the improved vitality of the forward play came with the signing of Bill Imrie in September 1929. Imrie, who came to Blackburn from St Johnstone, was a Scottish international half-back, whose attacking style of play added zest to the attack, although sometimes at the cost of his defensive duties. In December 1929, the directors spent £6,500 to bring Jack Bruton, Burnley's England international outside-right, to Ewood Park. The acquisition of Bruton was paid for by the release of Arthur Rigby to Everton, Aussie Campbell to Huddersfield Town and Peter O'Dowd to Burnley. Unfortunately, the loss of the latter two left the club dangerously thin in the half-back department. Of the four recognised half-backs that were left, Harry Healless was restricted to occasional appearances, being regarded as in the veteran stage of his career, while Jack Roscamp was now regarded more of a utility player than a specialist half-back.

With 99 League goals being scored, a new record for the club, there was much to admire with regard to individual contributions. Clarrie Bourton, who had spent half the season in the second team, ended as the club's leading goalscorer with 21 goals. Both Syd Puddefoot and Tom McLean notched double figures, as did Arthur Groves. The fifth player to reach double figures was Arthur Cunliffe, who had been signed from Chorley in August 1927 and groomed in the club's junior ranks.

While this attacking brand of football took the club to sixth position in the First Division, there was little joy in the FA Cup. After two 4–1 home victories over Northampton Town and Everton, the Rovers lost, ironically by the same margin, away to Aston Villa.

Team photograph, 1929–30. From left to right, back row: Les Bruton, Bill Imrie, Tom Baxter, Jock Crawford, Taffy Jones, Peter O'Dowd, Mo Atherton (trainer). Front row: Jack Bruton, Syd Puddefoot, Jack Roscamp, Arthur Groves, Thomas Turner, Bill Rankin. (*Copyright: unknown, trade card*)

1930-31

'Those whom the gods wish to destroy, they first make mad.' Certainly this would have been an apt epitaph for a season that was marred by intrigue, accusation and sheer madness on the part of so many in the corridors of power at Ewood Park. On paper the season was fairly mediocre, with a mid-table spot in the League, as many points as games and as many wins as defeats. There was little in the League to entice the public to flock to Ewood Park, particularly as the industrial depression was beginning to have an impact on the town.

Only the FA Cup offered the chance of salvation, after Walsall and Bristol Rovers had been beaten in earlier rounds. The Rovers were drawn away to Chelsea in the fifth round and, having already beaten the Pensioners at Ewood Park, hopes were high that progress in the competition would continue. However, on the eve of the trip to London the chairman received a letter, purportedly signed by all the players, which expressed concern with regard to the management of Bob Crompton. An ageing squad viewed Crompton's attempts to inject more pace into the Rovers' game with suspicion. Ageing legs and a high tempo game were, perhaps, not deemed compatible by those who would have to deliver the new tactics. As soon as he was told about the letter, Crompton immediately withdrew from his position as honorary manager and Mo Atherton, the first-team trainer, took charge for the trip to Chelsea.

Matters went from bad to worse when it was decided to gamble on the fitness of a couple of players who had been on the injured list. The Rovers then opted for a defensive strategy in the hope of a draw. In the event, the home side sensed an opponent in disarray and showed no mercy in putting the Rovers to the sword. A 3–0 defeat, in front of a crowd of 61,170, ended the Rovers' interest in the competition and, to all intents and purposes, ended their season.

While the club turned in on itself, with accusation and counter-accusation, the public of Blackburn turned away from Ewood Park. As the trade depression tightened its icy grip on the old industrial heartlands of Lancashire, the people of Blackburn chose not to spend their money at a club that was embroiled in internal conflict. Incredibly, those who walked the corridors of Ewood Park were totally consumed with the petty jealousies and internal bickering that was rife throughout the club. The only man not to become involved in this tacky episode was Crompton himself.

Jesse Carver made his League debut in the 3–0 win over Sunderland at Ewood Park on 20 September 1930. Carver went on to make 146 senior appearances for the club before joining Newcastle United. (*Copyright: unknown, trade card*)

Although Crompton had a reputation for an autocratic style of management, he was undoubtedly an astute tactician. He had kept the Rovers at the forefront of English football and had masterminded the FA Cup triumph at Wembley. Crompton had made no secret of the fact that he foresaw the need to adopt a faster tempo to the team's play if their success was to be maintained. Sadly, it was his desire to continue to evolve a successful team that ultimately led to his downfall.

Following the removal of Crompton the directors handed managerial duties to Arthur Barritt, who had joined the club in October 1924 as assistant-secretary, becoming secretary in January 1927. Although a first-class administrator, Barritt had no previous experience in handling the playing side of a football club.

At the end of the season the shareholders committed the ultimate act of folly and voted Crompton off the board of directors. Thus a man who had given 34 years service as a player of international repute and as a director and honorary manager was jettisoned in the cruellest of ways. It was a decision that would came to haunt the club time and again over the next few seasons.

1931-32

The club's financial plight worsened as the full effects of economic depression gripped the area. Gross takings at senior matches showed a drop of £250 per game compared with those of 12 months earlier. However, in truth, the inferior quality of football that was on view at Ewood Park was hardly likely to entice people on limited finances to part with their money. The club suffered another season of disappointment and ended the campaign just six points above the drop zone. Indeed, if not for five wins during the last eight League games, they might well have slipped through the trapdoor to the Second Division.

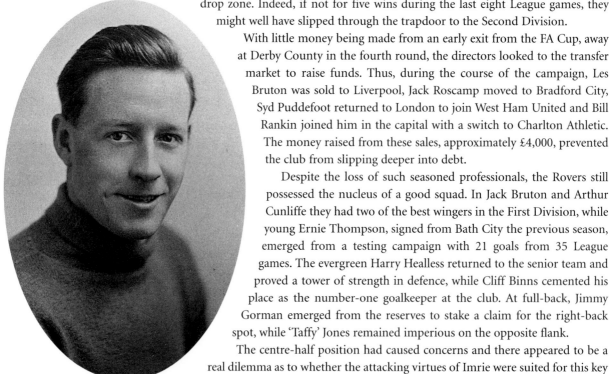

Jock Crawford appeared in seven League games during the course of the season before leaving the club to return to Scotland to join East Stirling. (*Copyright: Howard Talbot*)

With little money being made from an early exit from the FA Cup, away at Derby County in the fourth round, the directors looked to the transfer market to raise funds. Thus, during the course of the campaign, Les Bruton was sold to Liverpool, Jack Roscamp moved to Bradford City, Syd Puddefoot returned to London to join West Ham United and Bill Rankin joined him in the capital with a switch to Charlton Athletic. The money raised from these sales, approximately £4,000, prevented the club from slipping deeper into debt.

Despite the loss of such seasoned professionals, the Rovers still possessed the nucleus of a good squad. In Jack Bruton and Arthur Cunliffe they had two of the best wingers in the First Division, while young Ernie Thompson, signed from Bath City the previous season, emerged from a testing campaign with 21 goals from 35 League games. The evergreen Harry Healless returned to the senior team and proved a tower of strength in defence, while Cliff Binns cemented his place as the number-one goalkeeper at the club. At full-back, Jimmy Gorman emerged from the reserves to stake a claim for the right-back spot, while 'Taffy' Jones remained imperious on the opposite flank.

The centre-half position had caused concerns and there appeared to be a real dilemma as to whether the attacking virtues of Imrie were suited for this key position. Ultimately, the club opted for the defensive skills of Jesse Carver, a youngster who had been groomed in Central League football, rather than Imrie's more cavalier approach. However, by the end of the season it was decided to have the best of both worlds by using Imrie at right-half.

When Puddefoot left the club, in February 1932, he had not featured in the team for some time. Unfortunately, none of the players that the club possessed had similar attributes to Puddefoot in his prime. Tom McLean, Arthur Groves, Les Talbot and Thomas Turner were all tried in the inside-forward positions and yet, while they brought many varied and admiral qualities to the role, none possessed the craft and directness of passing that Puddefoot could display. Ultimately, the club solved the problem with the capture of Ronnie Dix from Bristol Rovers in May 1932. Dix was one of the outstanding young players of his era and had been keenly sought by a number of clubs. It was, therefore, a major coup when the Rovers invested £3,000 to bring him to Ewood Park.

1932-33

The continued industrial depression, coupled with some atrocious performances at Ewood Park led to a further shrinkage in support for the club. The economic problems had begun to weigh heavily on the directors. There was no doubt that the club was in trouble, although there were those, particularly those in the local press, who believed that the ultimate crisis had yet to be faced.

The team struggled all season. Despite the arrival of Ronnie Dix, the Rovers misfired from the very beginning. Five draws and three defeats proved a disappointing start and set the tone for the rest of the season. Fortunately, the Rovers possessed sufficient fire-power in the feet of Dix, Ernie Thompson and Arthur Cunliffe to be able to pull clear of relegation. However, although they finished one place higher than 12 months earlier, they were one point closer to the drop than the previous season. Furthermore, there were some rather ominous defeats that didn't augur well for the future. The worst came at Highbury, on 25 February 1933, when an Arsenal side that would go on and win the first of three successive Championships blasted eight goals past the Rovers without reply. Among the goalscorers that day was Joe Hulme, whom the Rovers had allowed to slip from their grasp several years earlier. Other comprehensive defeats brought a 6–1 hammering at Everton, a 4–0 defeat at Middlesbrough and two heavy defeats at the hands of Aston Villa, 4–0 away and, perhaps more worryingly, 5–0 at home. The Rovers had become a predominantly young and inexperienced outfit that found it difficult to cope with the job they were given to do. The fact that the opposition piled up goals without response merely undermined confidence still further. For the first time in the club's League history 100 goals were conceded in a season. Shamefully, the 102 goals that were conceded confirmed the worst defensive record in the top two divisions.

Two away games in the FA Cup, which brought victory at Lincoln and defeat at Birmingham, meant that the club derived little financial compensation from the competition. As the season progressed the financial burden became ever greater and appeared to anchor the Rovers in a sea of despondency.

Nor was the club immune from further intrigue behind closed doors. In January 1933, Mo Atherton, the long-serving trainer, rocked the town with news of his resignation. Atherton, who had joined the club as a player in 1908 and gone on to train the Championship team of 1914 and the FA Cup-winning side of 1928, was well respected within the game and had been England trainer on five occasions. Within 24 hours of leaving Ewood Park, he was installed as trainer of Grimsby Town. Two months later another member of the FA Cup-winning team departed when Jock Hutton, who had been placed on the transfer list, left the club by mutual consent.

A matter of days before the final League match the Ewood faithful were stunned by the news that the club had agreed to sell Cunliffe and Dix to Aston Villa. Handicapped by financial liabilities, the directors accepted a joint fee of £8,500 for the pair. Dix had been the club's last big acquisition, while Cunliffe was a player whom they had groomed to international status. Many believed the fee to be somewhat philanthropic. Furthermore, the decision to sell Cunliffe and Dix was not unanimous and two schools of thought now operated in the boardroom. However, all were agreed that finance was now the most important issue on the Ewood agenda. To this end the directors negotiated new terms with the players in a desperate bid to trim the wage bill.

1933-34

Following the sale of Dix and Cunliffe, the club's Annual General Meeting turned into an acrimonious affair. The shareholders demonstrated their anger by almost succeeding in preventing Mr J. Walsh, the club's chairman, from being re-elected to the board. The chairman was clearly shaken by the ferocity of the criticism and resigned within a week after more than 21 years' service as a director. Councillor Walter Tempest, who a week earlier had indicated that he would refuse to invest any further money in the club but, on the other hand, would be prepared to sell any player if the price was right, was the man who picked up what many regarded as a poisoned chalice.

Not even the most ardent supporter could have expected the upturn in fortunes that the 1933–34 campaign brought. The Rovers began the season in a perilous state and many predicted that relegation would be their ultimate fate. However, the club was never in any danger and enjoyed a comfortable place in the top half of the table throughout the season.

Despite the improvement in League placing, the team turned out to be something of a Jekyll and Hyde outfit. Invincible at home and totally impotent away was the story of the campaign. Ewood Park was turned into a fortress with the team unbeaten, as 37 points were collected on home soil. Away from home it was a totally different story, with 17 defeats, and just six points were gained from their visits around the country.

The improvement was all the more remarkable as it took place despite the loss of Ernie Thompson to a broken leg in November 1933. Ruled out for the rest of the campaign, the loss of

Bob Pryde made his debut in the 4–2 win over Chelsea at Ewood Park on 21 October 1933. (*Copyright: unknown, Topical Times card*)

Thompson affected the play of the other forwards for a short time. In search of a replacement the directors turned to an old favourite and snapped up Ted Harper from Preston North End. Fortunately, Jack Bruton turned in his best form since joining the club while the arrival of Harper, although in the veteran stages of his career, helped give the attack a timely boost with 15 goals in 22 League appearances. Another veteran who gave good service to the attack was Fred Kennedy, who had been signed from Racing Club Paris in August 1933.

Unfortunately, Thompson wasn't the only major casualty, as Billy Gormlie received an injury against Chelsea in October 1933 that would effectively end his career. Jack Hughes had a brief spell in goal before Cliff Binns was recalled from Workington, where he had gone in the summer, to resume as the number-one custodian.

As the season progressed there was an increased emphasis placed on youth that resulted in Tom Brennan, Les Talbot and Jackie Milne being installed in place of Kennedy, McLean and Turner. Fortunately, the transition was quite successful, with the volatile Milne, in particular, proving a revelation on the wing.

Following the release of 'Taffy' Jones, at the end of the previous campaign, Crawford Whyte, who had joined the club in April 1930, finally took his opportunity to establish himself at left-back. With Gorman in excellent form on the other flank and Carver outstanding at centre-half, the Rovers looked far more impressive defensively than for some time. When Wally Halsall, the automatic choice at left-half, was injured, it enabled two youngsters, Arnold Whiteside and Bob Pryde, to be given a prolonged taste of first-team action.

Sadly, the Rovers had the misfortune to fall at the first hurdle of the FA Cup, albeit to Manchester City, the eventual winners of the competition. Nonetheless, the loss of potential revenue meant that the club needed to take action to ease the financial situation. With some 41 professionals registered, it had become imperative to prune the playing staff. With the emergence of Whiteside and Pryde, the directors took the opportunity to reap some much needed finance by the sale of Imrie to Newcastle United. Sadly, the sale of quality players had become a fact of life at Ewood Park. When the season ended the directors were quick to release a number of the younger professionals who were deemed to be surplus to the needs of the club.

1934-35

A combination of continued economic recession and appalling weather on the day of home matches badly affected attendances at Ewood Park. While these factors were beyond the control of the management of the club, other problems proved to be of their own making. The previous stability in team selection was abandoned in favour of continual tinkering and experimentation. The result was another relegation battle and the loss of public confidence.

By mid-December the club was in turmoil, with only five wins from their first 19 League games. Some of the younger players began to wilt under the strain and, financial crisis or not, the need for experienced players could not go unanswered. During the close season the directors had signed Bobby Crawford, Blackpool's veteran half-back, to play for the reserves and help develop younger players. It was with a view to the continued development of young players that the directors appointed David Taylor, Burnley's former full-back, as coach to the Central League team in November 1934. At the same time the Rovers signed Alex Sharp, a young inside-forward from East Fife but, sadly, he lacked the necessary experience to make a major impact on the club. As Christmas approached the directors dug deep into their limited financial resources to purchase Jack Beattie, an inside-forward, from Wolverhampton Wanderers for £5,000 and Norman Christie, Huddersfield's skilful centre-half.

The acquisition of Beattie and Christie not only helped to gather vital League points, but also enabled the Rovers to enjoy a short Cup run. Although interest in the FA Cup was ended with a dismal home defeat, at the hands of Birmingham, in the fifth round, the competition did bring in around £4,000.

The impact of the new players was a vital factor in the upturn of fortunes during the second half

Blackburn Rovers team group, 1934–35. (*Copyright: unknown*)

of the season. Christie was quickly given the captaincy, such was the impression that he created. Beattie proved the type of forceful inside-forward that was required and Thompson, fully recovered from his broken leg of the previous year, responded with 18 goals, a tally that was equalled by the ever-reliable Bruton.

Although the Rovers climbed to safety in the League, the public remained apathetic to their plight which, of course, meant that the financial crisis continued to deepen.

1935-36

After several flirtations with relegation it was, perhaps, ironic that the club should finally fall in the season that it celebrated its Diamond Jubilee. Curiously, the club was accompanied to the Second Division by Aston Villa who, like the Rovers, were the only other founder member of the Football League never to have tasted life outside the top flight. The fact that such a disaster should befall a club like Villa, with bigger gates and more expensive players, proved small consolation for those on the Ewood terraces. There it was felt that the Rovers, with their tradition, had somehow thought themselves to be immune from such a fate.

For many the writing had been on the wall for some time. The prolonged trade depression had adversely affected revenue at Ewood Park. Yet, the Rovers had contributed to their own downfall and many believed that the decline had begun with the ruthless manner in which Bob Crompton had been driven from the club. This decision, coupled with the continued sale of the club's best talent, led to the plight that the club now found itself in. In a biting assessment of the failure of those at the helm, 'Rover', writing in the *Blackburn Times*, commented: 'There could have been no real recovery without a new and wider vision on the part of those in control.' He went on to note how the club's poor away form over the past three seasons had gone unchecked and that those in charge had relied too heavily on the spirit and enthusiasm of youth.

Ironically, the club had made its best start to a campaign since the war, with eight points being taken from the opening five games. However, inexplicably, a heavy defeat at Sunderland followed and the club then went into freefall. Twice the team conceded eight goals, at West Bromwich Albion and Wolverhampton Wanderers, seven goals were conceded at Sunderland, six at Middlesbrough and five at both Arsenal and Chelsea. No matter how the deck was shuffled the result was always the same. Sadly, the directors no longer had sufficient players of the right calibre to turn things around.

Interest in the FA Cup ended in the fourth round at Bradford City. With League survival the sole ambition, the directors signed Charlie Calladine from Birmingham. Calladine was a seasoned half-

Blackburn Rovers were beaten 8–1 at West Bromwich Albion on 18 January 1936. Back row, left to right: J. Gorman, A. Pinxton, C. Binns, L. Astill, W. Halsall, W. Crook. Front row, left to right: A. Whiteside, J. Bruton, E. Thompson, B. Pryde, F. Talbot, A. Hamill. (*Copyright: unknown, cigarette card*)

back but his contribution was negated when, perhaps out of desperation, he was moved to inside-forward.

Only Ernie Thompson carried a threat in front of the opposition goal and it wasn't until March that the directors entered the transfer market to sign another forward. However, when Tommy Sale arrived from Stoke the battle was all but over.

While matters on the field had reached crisis proportions, the boardroom was again rife with internal conflict. Relations between the directors and Arthur Barritt worsened and, while there were disagreements on several issues, it was thought that team selection was a particularly thorny topic. In March 1936, Barritt announced his intention to resign from the post of secretary-manager and, on 11 April 1936, following a goalless draw with Sheffield Wednesday, he duly left Ewood Park.

Defeat at Liverpool two days after Barritt's departure virtually sealed the club's fate. A home win against Portsmouth and an away win at Aston Villa proved merely academic. By this time the club had lost the services of all three professional goalkeepers due to injury. Against Portsmouth the Rovers fielded an unknown amateur from Merseyside, Kevin Hamill, who helped the Rovers to a 3–1 win despite being at fault for the visitors' goal. At Villa the club turned to another amateur, John Pratt, who performed valiantly as the Rovers left Villa Park with a 4–2 win under their belts. Pratt retained his place for the following week's visit to Stamford Bridge when a 5–1 defeat ended the days of Blackburn Rovers as a First Division club.

1936-37

Following the departure of Barritt, the directors opted on a new course for the management of the club. Reg Taylor, an experienced administrator who had been secretary at Preston North End, was appointed the new secretary at Ewood Park. Arthur Cowell, the trainer-coach, continued to look after the players, while the directors took sole charge of team selection.

If the new arrangements had been intended to galvanise a return to the First Division, they met with little success. Indeed, at one point the club seemed to be in danger of falling straight through to the Third Division North.

The close season had brought little in the way of team strengthening. Sep Rutherford, an experienced outside-left, was signed from Portsmouth and Jock Smeaton, a young inside-forward, arrived from St Johnstone. However, nothing had been done to address the lack of firepower and this problem quickly resurfaced in the Second Division.

As the club continued to slide down the table the correspondent of the *Blackburn Times* continued his assault on those in charge of the club. He blamed the lack of a specialist manager for the club's plight – it was a veiled plea for the restoration of Crompton. However, the plea fell on deaf ears and the directors opted to return to the secretary-manager system, which had patently failed at Ewood Park in recent years. Thus, in October 1936, Taylor was installed as secretary-manager and given the unenviable task of arresting the slide into oblivion.

Since the start of the campaign the Rovers had shed a number of their more experienced players. Alex Hamill and Cliff Binns had left for Barnsley, while Ernie Thompson had joined Manchester United. Before the end of January the club lost Jimmy Gorman to Sunderland and Jack Beattie to Birmingham.

In view of the club's proud traditions in the FA Cup it was, perhaps, fate that decreed that the nadir of the season should be reached in that particular competition. In January 1937 the Rovers faced Accrington Stanley at Ewood Park in a third-round tie. The threadbare nature of the squad meant that Nathan Fraser, a young Scottish import, was given a surprise debut. Although he grabbed the goal that snatched a 2–2 draw, his performance had done little to inspire those watching.

(Left) Ernie Thompson was the leading goalscorer in 1935–36, with 15 goals in 38 League appearances but was sold to Manchester United in November 1936. (Copyright: unknown, Topical Times card)

(Right) Jack Hughes enjoyed his most successful season with the club during 1936–37 and kept goal on 25 occasions. Hughes was transferred to Mansfield Town during the summer of 1937. (Copyright: unknown, trade card)

When the Rovers travelled to Peel Park for the replay Fraser was axed in favour of Jack Lee, a young amateur who was an Oxford Blue. Charlie Calladine gave the Rovers a fourth-minute lead, but Stanley hit back, just before half-time, when Bob Mortimer pounced on Pratt's error to level the score. The game went into extra-time and further goals from Mortimer and Walter Rivers gave Stanley an unexpected victory.

The Rovers had already signed Billy Guest just before the Accrington débâcle, but he was ineligible for Cup ties. Immediately after the FA Cup exit the directors signed Jock Wightman and Len Butt from Huddersfield Town. The three new players transformed 'the rabble of a side into a well-knit and efficient team'.

Suddenly there was a new optimism around the club, and the public of Blackburn responded and began to return to Ewood Park in greater numbers. As the season drifted to a close the Rovers thrashed Nottingham Forest 9–1 at Ewood Park, suggesting that brighter times were just ahead. The upturn in fortunes on the field proved to be rather timely for the directors. In January 1937 a number of the shareholders had demanded an extraordinary general meeting. Held on 24 February 1937, it came in the wake of improved results and the earlier criticisms simply evaporated with the result that the directors received an unlikely vote of confidence.

1937-38

Controversy continued to blight the club during the summer of 1937. At the end of the previous season the directors opted to dismiss the long-serving Arthur Cowell as trainer-coach. It was a move that again resurrected memories of the way that Bob Crompton had been cast aside after long and loyal service.

Another summer had passed without any major activity in the transfer market. Gerry Matier, a young Irish goalkeeper, was signed from Coleraine to replace Jack Hughes, who had moved to Mansfield Town, and Horace Woolley, an orthodox outside-left, was brought from Partick Thistle. However, both men began the season playing Central League football. Then, in September 1937, Percy Dickie, an industrious half-back, was signed from St Johnstone and a few weeks later the club raided Accrington Stanley to sign two forwards in Bob Mortimer and Billy Tyson. Mortimer, the more experienced of the two, enjoyed a two-goal debut in the 4–0 victory over Southampton on 2 October 1937. Sadly, he struggled to make much impression in the higher grade of football and ended the season with just four goals in 16 League appearances.

By November 1937 a decline had set in that resulted in a desperate slide down the table. Furthermore, League failure was accompanied by an early exit from the FA Cup as the club seemed to slump from one crisis to another. Attempts to stem the tide had seen Charles Luke signed from Sheffield Wednesday and Frank Chivers from Huddersfield Town, but the decline continued unabated.

By March it had become clear that the Rovers now faced relegation to the Third Division North unless urgent action was taken. That action arrived with a statement from the directors on 30 March 1938: 'At the meeting last night, Blackburn Rovers directors unanimously endorsed the suggestion of the secretary-manager that in view of the Rovers' position, Mr R. Crompton should be asked to give what assistance he can to the club. Mr Crompton has agreed to do so, and until the end of the season will co-operate with Mr Taylor in the general management of the club. From now onwards Mr Taylor and Mr Crompton will jointly have full control of the team and will suggest its composition for the approval of the Board of Directors.'

It was a dramatic turnaround by a board that had found itself backed into a corner. With the Rovers trapped in a downward spiral they had little option but to bow to public pressure and seek out Bob Crompton. Since his departure from the club, Crompton had managed Bournemouth & Boscombe Athletic for a brief period between June 1935 and February 1936. When he returned from a short, but nonetheless successful, stint on the south coast, he continued to remain silent about the state into which his old club had fallen. When he returned to Ewood he made it clear that he had no magic wand to wave and that patience would be required to turn the club around.

However, his arrival sparked a renewed enthusiasm and vigour among both players and supporters alike. He was able to inspire the team to win four and draw one of their remaining eight games. It proved sufficient to lift the club to 16th place and ensured Second Division football at Ewood Park for the following campaign.

Once the season was at an end, the directors installed Crompton as the club manager and left administrative matters in the capable hands of Reg Taylor. The Annual General Meeting revealed that a loss of £5,256 1s 8d on the season had taken the debts of the club to £26,309 7s 2d. In the wake of such figures Crompton let it be known that the future of the club had to revolve around the introduction of young players. He once again reiterated that there could be no short-term solutions and that patience would be essential if the club was to progress. Ironically, Arthur Cowell, his former full-back partner, who was now trainer of Wrexham, made virtually the same points when he launched a fierce attack on the directors at the AGM. He had slammed the board for the continued sale of the club's best young talent and had

Len Butt finished the 1937–38 season as top goalscorer with 20 League goals. (*Copyright: unknown, trade card*)

argued that too many players who were either inferior, or past their prime, had been brought into the club.

1938-39

In view of the manager's plea for patience, the instant success that he achieved during 1938–39 came as a major surprise to all concerned at Ewood Park. However, after he had taken a club that appeared destined for relegation just 12 months earlier to the Second Division Championship, few could doubt that Crompton really was blessed with the Midas touch. Furthermore, while winning promotion he also helped fill the coffers with a run in the FA Cup that took the Rovers to the sixth round.

Crompton, with the assistance of Len Evans, the trainer, moulded a team that played with spirit, confidence and a basic but simple method. Promotion was not achieved with football of the highest calibre, but it was functional and, above all, successful. Consistency was the cornerstone of success and the Rovers were pacemakers from the very start. One by one the challengers were brushed aside as the team's grip on the title strengthened throughout the campaign. Three wins in the first week of the season set the tone for what was to follow.

Crompton quickly settled on a pattern of play that was ideal for the resources he had available. Jimmy Barron kept goal for all but one match and the full-back pairing of Billy Hough and Walter

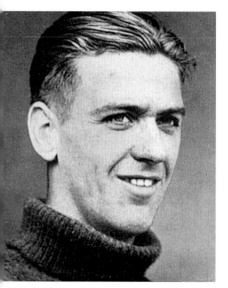

Bill Rogers scored 18 League goals during the Second Division Championship-winning campaign of 1938–39. (*Copyright: unknown, trade card*)

Crook remained unchanged until Hough was injured and Ernest Lanceley successfully stepped in for the final 11 games. Although Crompton had signed George Hardy, Aston Villa's reserve centre-half, and installed him as captain, injury forced him to change his plans. Bob Pryde, who had started the campaign at left-half, was switched to the centre, Arnold Whiteside, who had been deemed surplus to requirements in the summer, returned to make the left-half position his own, and Frank Chivers, who had been signed from Huddersfield in March 1938, became the automatic choice at right-half. Once this trio were installed there was no way back for Hardy. In attack, Billy Rogers replaced Jack Bruton on the right wing, while young Bobby Langton quickly edged Billy Guest out of a spot on the opposite flank. Len Butt and Albert Clarke, a close-season signing from Birmingham, were automatic choices for the inside-forward roles, while Jack Weddle, the veteran Portsmouth centre-forward, was signed to lead the attack.

Only 19 players were used throughout the campaign and of these, seven made only single-figure appearances. The manager adopted a direct approach, which was ideally suited for the players he worked with, and his tactics brought 25 victories and 94 goals. In the FA Cup he took the club to the sixth round before narrowly being edged out, by the odd goal in three, in a replay with Huddersfield Town of the First Division.

Attendances at Ewood Park continued to soar as the team caught the public imagination. While this Blackburn team might not have been a classic side, its unconquerable spirit, amazing courage, stamina and fighting qualities connected with the supporters. Success was due to a collective spirit rather than individual brilliance. But most of all, success was down Bob Crompton, the man who masterminded this approach and assembled a team that would sweep all before them.

1939-40

The shadow of Germany and the possibility of war hung over the country during the summer of 1939. There were to be no major acquisitions at Ewood Park during the close season and the Rovers began the new campaign at Fratton Park with the same XI that had been so successful during the previous campaign. Defeats at Portsmouth and then Arsenal, both by the same 2–1 margin, were followed by a 2–2 draw with Everton at Ewood Park on 2 September 1939. The games had been played in a muted atmosphere with the inevitability of war dominating the minds of most supporters. The day after the Everton game war was declared and the Football League immediately called a halt to proceedings until the end of hostilities.

There then followed a period of limbo during which the Rovers embarked upon a series of friendly matches. However, the authorities, once given the all clear to do so, moved quickly to arrange regional competitions for the duration of the war.

The Rovers began their North West Regional League fixtures in October and played 22 matches in this competition to finish eighth in the table. Fortunately, the standard of play was much higher than that of World War One, as the clubs could call upon guest players from other clubs who happened to be employed or stationed in the vicinity.

Fortunately for the League War Cup competition, the Rovers were able to field the majority of the players who had won the Second Division Championship. Indeed, of the 11 who faced West Ham United in the Final at Wembley on 8 June 1940, only Bobby Langton was unavailable to turn out. During the successful Cup run his place had been filled admirably by Billy Guest. Unfortunately, in front of 43,000 spectators the Rovers failed to capture the trophy; a Sam Small goal was sufficient to clinch a win for the Hammers. After the match the players gathered at the Great Northern Hotel for a celebratory banquet. Sadly, this was to be the last occasion that these sons and adopted sons of Blackburn would assemble together. Once more the ravages of war would take its toll on Blackburn Rovers, as it had done to an earlier generation.

Manchester United's Beaumont Asquith was one of a number of guest players used by the club during the first season of wartime football. (*Copyright: unknown, trade card*)

1940-41

When the season began, the reality of war was quickly brought home to those who visited Ewood Park as a form of escapism. Posters were placed around the ground with instructions to be followed in case of an air raid. Supporters were advised not to leave the ground, but to seek shelter under the Riverside and Nuttall Street stands.

However, like the previous season, wartime attendances remained disappointing. During the course of the campaign the Rovers used no fewer than 53 players in both Regional League and League Cup games. Once again, the Rovers had to rely on guest players to help them out; among those who pulled on the famous blue and white jersey were Tommy Pearson (Newcastle United), Douglas Anderson (Brentford), John Atkinson (Bolton Wanderers) and Jack Fairbrother (Preston North End).

The only senior pre-war Ewood players to feature on a regular basis were Frank Chivers, who only missed one League game, Ernest Lanceley, Bob Pryde, Len Butt and Jock Wightman. Others flitted in and out when wartime duties allowed, but the Rovers were unable to field the same team on two successive occasions.

The club ended the campaign in 24th position in the Regional League, while the first two League War Cup games, against Oldham Athletic, were won. Unfortunately, interest in the Cup competition ended when both games against Manchester City were lost.

However, the events on the field paled into insignificance when news of the death of Bob Crompton was announced. The Blackburn manager had watched the Rovers beat Burnley at Ewood Park on 15 March 1941 but then collapsed shortly afterwards and died that same evening. The loss of Crompton, undoubtedly the greatest servant in the club's history, was a devastating blow to a club that was struggling to come to terms with wartime football.

1941-42

Following the death of Bob Crompton, the Ewood directors chose not to make another appointment but entrusted the managerial duties to Reg Taylor, the club secretary. The Rovers entered both the first and second competitions of the Football League with several matches in the second competition being counted as League War Cup and Lancashire Cup matches.

Sadly, tragedy again struck the club when Frank Chivers was killed in a mining accident in April 1942. Chivers, a member of the Second Division Championship-winning side, had been a mainstay of the Rovers during the early period of wartime football and, prior to his death, had appeared in 27 League games during the season.

The Rovers enjoyed better fortunes on the pitch than in previous wartime seasons. The playing staff had been strengthened with the acquisition of Herman Conway from West Ham United. Conway had kept goal for the Hammers against the Rovers during the 1940 League War Cup Final at Wembley, but his wartime duties took him away from Upton Park. He had become commandant of a supply camp at Accrington and turned out for the Rovers as a guest before joining the club in November 1941.

The Rovers finished the first competition, which ended on Christmas Day, in 26th position in the Football League Northern Section. During the second competition, between December and May, the team enjoyed improved, if slightly erratic, form. A run of six successive victories was followed by four successive defeats but, nonetheless, the club finished the second part of the season in a creditable seventh position. The club also reached the final of the Lancashire Senior Cup, but crashed to a 7–1 defeat at Blackpool.

Once again the Rovers called upon a number of guest players, who included Bobby Ancell and Tommy Pearson (both Newcastle United), Doug Anderson (Brentford), Gordon Bremner (Arsenal) and John Percival (Manchester City).

Despite another season of disappointing attendances, the Rovers announced a profit on the season of £334, which reduced the debit balance to £21,930.

Frank Chivers, a member of the Second Division Championship-winning team of 1938–39, was killed in a mining accident in April 1942. (*Copyright: unknown, trade card*)

1942-43

With the majority of the previous season's players still available, there was cause for some optimism among followers of the Rovers. Keen to continue the encouragement of young players, the Rovers entered an 'A' team in the Blackburn Combination under the guidance of Jack Weddle.

At the Annual General Meeting, held in July 1942, the directors had urged the public of the town to support the club during the season. Yet the size of the task facing the directors was amply demonstrated at the meeting itself. While 12 directors sat on the platform, the body of the YMCA hall held just seven of the 500 shareholders of the club. However, the message was heeded and attendances increased during the season.

Once again the Rovers were able to find a blend of youth and experience that provided the public with some entertaining football. During the first competition the Rovers won half of their 18 League games and finished in 18th place in the table, while the second competition found the Rovers in 15th place at the end of the season.

With Preston North End not participating in the competition, the Rovers were able to make good use of Jimmy Dougal, North End's leading goalscorer during the last season of peacetime football. During the first competition he scored 19 goals in 17 appearances and during the second competition he registered another 10 goals in 15 League outings. Dougal was joined at Ewood Park by two other Preston players, Hugh O'Donnell and Willie Robertson, a youngster just beginning to emerge at Deepdale.

Once again Bobby Ancell, Doug Anderson and Tommy Pearson continued to make guest appearances and the Rovers also introduced several of their promising youngsters to first-team action. Indeed, the policy of encouraging and developing youth was well rewarded when the Rovers 'A' team captured the Blackburn Combination championship and the Birtwistle Cup.

1943-44

There were two familiar faces at Ewood Park at the start of the new campaign, with the return of Ted Harper and Walter Crook. Harper had been discharged from the Army Physical Training Corps because of a knee injury, and had returned to work as first-team trainer at Ewood Park. Crook had also been discharged from the Army because of a knee injury, but had fully recovered and obtained work in Blackburn.

For the first time since the start of the war the Rovers began to find a settled formation with regard to team selection. Conway was the regular 'keeper with Barron acting as an experienced understudy. The right-back position was shared between George Forbes, who had joined the Rovers in 1937, and Walter Taylor, while Crook reclaimed his left-back spot. Arnold Whiteside, Bob Pryde and Willie Robertson, the young North Ender, formed the half-back line on most occasions, with Frank Hindle, a Rovers youngster, and Doug Anderson, guesting from Brentford, used occasionally. It was in attack that the changes tended to be made most frequently. Once again Jimmy Dougal was used successfully, 12 goals in 30 appearances, while another North Ender, Jackie Wharton, made 24 appearances in the Rovers attack. Tommy Pearson played another 16 games while Len Butt returned to feature on 10 occasions.

The Rovers finished the first competition in 12th place, while the second competition ended with the Rovers in 31st place in the Northern Section.

1944-45

The summer of 1944 brought the tragic news of the death of Albert Clarke, the popular goalscoring inside-forward, who had been a key member of the promotion winning team of 1938–39. Clarke had been killed in action while serving with his regiment in Ranville, near Caen, on 16 June 1944.

At the shareholders' meeting in July 1944, thoughts returned to football when the chairman, J. Caton, informed the gathering that the club was actively in search of a big name manager. While the new man was found, Reg Taylor continued to combine secretarial and managerial duties.

The eve of the new season found a different sort of sporting occasion being held at Ewood Park. A crowd of over 2,000 assembled to watch a baseball match between Milton's Yankees and Grigsby's Cubs, two teams made up of American servicemen.

When the football began the Rovers were again able to rely on a number of men that were now

George Mutch, the player who scored the winning goal for Preston North End in the 1938 FA Cup Final, made two guest appearances for the Rovers in 1944–45. (*Copyright: unknown, trade card*)

regarded as recognised first-team players at Ewood Park. Conway, Forbes, Crook, Taylor, Whiteside and Pryde appeared on a regular basis, while a number of the club's younger players began to appear more frequently.

The Rovers finished in 29th position in the first competition while the second competition ended with the club in 12th place in the Northern Section. However, the highlight of the season was the capture of the Lancashire Cup for the first time since 1911. The final two matches of the season, against Accrington Stanley, counted as the two-legged Final. After beating Stanley 2–0 at Ewood Park, the Rovers underlined their superiority with a 4–3 win at Peel Park.

Once again the Rovers were fortunate to call upon the services of a number of guest players who served the club well. Fred Durrant, from Brentford, replaced Dougal in attack and ended the season with 17 appearances and 18 goals. Just behind, in terms of goalscoring, was Frank Coates, a local youngster from Leyland, who scored 17 goals in 32 appearances.

1945-46

Football returned to some degree of normality, with the Rovers involved in a 42-game Football League North competition. Furthermore the FA Cup was re-introduced, although the games were played on a two-legged basis. This interim arrangement was to last for one season, with the Football League earmarked to restart for 1946–47.

Eddie Hapgood, the former Arsenal and England international full-back, took control of Blackburn Rovers on 1 January 1946. (*Copyright: unknown, trade card*)

The search for a manager took the directors to Highbury and Eddie Hapgood, the Arsenal and England full-back. Affectionately known as the 'ambassador of football', Hapgood had appeared in over 400 League and Cup games for the Gunners, and won five League Championship medals, two FA Cup-winners' medals and a host of other medals while at Highbury. He had also represented England on 30 occasions before the war and had featured in 13 wartime international matches. It was agreed that Hapgood would come to Blackburn as soon as he left the RAF.

However, in December 1945 it was reported that he had been demobilised and he was reported to have informed the Rovers that he would continue to play for Arsenal until February 1946. In the meantime he requested that the Blackburn directors should find him a house before he journeyed north to take up his post. The Blackburn chairman, Mr J. Caton, expressed his dismay at the situation and stated, 'It would seem as though his heart is not in the job.' After further discussions, Hapgood arrived in

BLACKBURN ROVERS: AN ILLUSTRATED HISTORY

Blackburn at the turn of the year and explained that his wife's health had been the cause of the delay. Hapgood quickly appointed Horace Cope, a former playing colleague at Highbury, as first-team trainer at Ewood Park.

In a radio broadcast in February 1946, he announced that he had settled in Blackburn and that he appreciated that the board of directors had given him a free hand. He was also taken by the promise of many of the club's younger professionals. However, initial results on the field suggested that the Rovers would have to improve if they were to retain First Division status when the Football League was restored.

The Rovers used no fewer than 46 players during the campaign, with Hapgood making a couple of appearances at left-back. New players included Jackie Campbell from Liverpool, Eric Bell from North Shields and Jack Smith, an experienced centre-forward, who was signed from Manchester United. The Rovers ended the season in 21st place in the Football League North and were eliminated by Bolton Wanderers in the third round of the FA Cup. It all suggested that Hapgood had a major reconstruction job on his hands if the Rovers were to survive for more than one season in the top flight.

1946-47

As expected, the Rovers' first season back in the First Division found them involved in a struggle against relegation. On the field, an undistinguished season was only relieved by two factors; a good away record and a good defensive record. Off the field it appeared that there was always something happening, although two events dominated all else. Firstly, the directors embarked upon an unprecedented bout of spending and secondly, there was a much publicised end to the brief reign of a famous manager.

The Rovers made a good, if rather flattering, start to the campaign with three wins in the opening four games. On the eve of the season, Eddie Hapgood had returned to Highbury to sign George Marks, Arsenal's wartime England international goalkeeper. At full-back the season began with a pairing of Jock Wightman and Walter Crook, while Arnold Whiteside, Bob Pryde and Eric Bell offered a mixture of experience and youth in the intermediate line. The attack was led by the veteran Jack Smith, while Len Butt and George Glaister filled the inside-forward positions. Billy Rogers and Bobby Langton operated on the flanks in a team that mixed vast experience with youthful enthusiasm. Indeed, Langton made such rapid progress that he was rewarded with an England cap in September 1946.

Sadly, the excellent start didn't last and a run of five successive defeats reflected a more realistic view of the nature of the task that Hapgood faced. The manager opted to infuse his team with even more inexperienced youngsters and relations between the manager and some of the more seasoned professionals began to be strained. In January 1947, Crook asked to be put on the transfer list and the captain of the promotion-winning team of 1938–39 made no secret of his conflict with the manager.

As the club's plight worsened, the directors embarked on a radical shift in policy during January 1947. A new club transfer record was established when £10,000 was paid to bring centre-forward Jock Weir from Hibernian. Shortly afterwards a similar amount brought winger Jackie Oakes to Ewood Park from Queen of the South. A further £6,000 was spent to sign Frank McGorrighan, a play-making inside-forward, from Hull City. Unfortunately, the rash of transfer activity merely opened up the rift between manager and directors. Hapgood insisted that none of the new arrivals were players he had identified as possible transfer targets. It was, therefore, no great shock when it was announced that the manager had tendered his resignation on 19 February 1947.

The directors were in no rush to make a new appointment and asked Horace Cope to take

Billy Guest, who joined the club in January 1936, made 22 League appearances during his final season at Ewood Park. (*Copyright: unknown*)

charge until a decision on a new manager was taken. In late February 1947, the directors made the key acquisition of Alec Venters from Third Lanark. Venters, an inventive play-maker, had been a target for the club almost a decade earlier but had gone on to enjoy a splendid career with Rangers. His time with the Glasgow club had brought him three Scottish Championship medals, a Scottish

FA Cup-winners' medal and three Scottish international caps. Although he was at the end of his career when he arrived at Ewood Park, he made the most telling impact of all the new arrivals.

Venters provided the craft and guile that the team, which had relied upon youthful enthusiasm for far too long, had so obviously lacked. In April 1947, the directors announced that Will Scott, the Preston North End secretary and former trainer, would follow Hapgood into the manager's office. A month later the club ended the season with a 1–0 win over Charlton Athletic at Ewood Park and finished in 17th position in the First Division. It was perhaps fitting that the season should end on a high note with victory over the team that had beaten the Rovers in the fifth round of the FA Cup.

While many might have argued that the standard of football was poor, the fact remained that the club's primary target, the retention of First Division status, had been achieved.

1947-48

After two seasons of struggle, the club's relegation to the Second Division in May 1948 proved a bitter pill to swallow. In truth, any one of half a dozen teams could have accompanied Grimsby Town into the Second Division, but sadly it was Blackburn Rovers that failed to show the necessary survival instincts.

There were, perhaps, three main reasons why the club should slip out of the top flight with barely a whimper. Firstly, the continued use of young players before they had been properly groomed for top flight football proved an Achilles' heel. Secondly, the continued managerial changes undermined any chance of continuity at the club. Thirdly, and perhaps most importantly, the Rovers didn't make the most of vital opportunities to beat relegation rivals in March and April 1948.

The club had been thrown into turmoil after just three games, when Will Scott succumbed to illness and had to take a period of leave from Ewood Park. The directors placed the playing affairs in the hands of Jack Bruton, who had been a member of the Ewood administrative staff since his retirement as a player. When Scott returned, Bruton was named as his assistant. Such was the reputation of Bruton that shortly after his appointment as Scott's number two he was approached by Manchester City to become their manager. Fortunately, he opted to stay at Ewood Park.

Scott followed the same policy that had failed Hapgood. Younger players were given their opportunity at the expense of senior staff. Thus, young Verdi Godwin replaced Weir at centre-forward after the Scottish player had failed to justify the fee that had been paid for him. Other youngsters like Bob Tomlinson, George Higgins, Les Cook and Jimmy Baldwin all enjoyed lengthy spells in the team but never threatened to pull the club away from the foot of the table. Higgins, Tomlinson and Cook all featured at full-back but their inexperience proved a major frailty in defensive terms. Unfortunately, of Crompton's successful team of 1938–39 only three players remained and two of those, Bob Pryde and Arnold Whiteside, were in the veteran stages of their career. Apart from Bobby Langton, the Rovers didn't possess influential players who were in or approaching their prime. The team consisted of slowing veterans or inexperienced and raw youngsters. It was to prove a fatal combination.

While the defence was vulnerable, the attack continually stuttered in its attempts to conquer opposition defences. Venters, who had been so vital last season, failed to ignite those around him as age began to take its toll on his magical powers. Without him there was no one to 'make the ball do the work' or use the open spaces. Without him there was no steadying influence in attack. Only Les Graham found the net on a regular basis and without his 15 goals, the attack would have come to a complete standstill in terms of goalscoring.

On 9 December 1947, in the wake of two heavy defeats against Middlesbrough and Sheffield United, Scott tendered his resignation on health grounds. At that point the Rovers had lost 11 of the 19 League games that they had played. The response of the directors was immediate and Bruton was appointed manager.

Although results continued to keep the Rovers anchored in the lower reaches of the table, the fact remained that the fixtures in March and April 1948 gave them the opportunity to meet some of their closest rivals and put some distance between them and the relegation places. Sadly, it was their opponents who took the chance to collect vital points. Bolton Wanderers beat the Rovers at Burnden Park and then Huddersfield Town visited Ewood and left with maximum points. Away

Bill Eckersley made his senior debut on the final day of the season. The Rovers lost 4–1 away to Manchester United. (*Copyright: Howard Talbot*)

draws with Charlton Athletic and Huddersfield Town, coupled with a home draw with Middlesbrough, meant that the Rovers had frittered away any hope of escape. With the Second Division beckoning, the opportunity was taken to give a Southport youngster his first-team debut on the final day of the season. While the 4–1 defeat at Manchester United was of little significance, the debut of Bill Eckersley was to have a major impact on the future of the club, for he would fill the left-back position for the next decade.

1948–49

In the wake of relegation there followed a period of intense activity in the transfer market. Dennis Westcott had joined the club in April 1948 from Wolverhampton Wanderers to add some much-needed punch to a lacklustre attack. In a bid to provide Westcott with the ammunition he required, the club brought in two new wingers, with Jackie Wharton being signed from Manchester City and Don Carter from Bury. The other main close-season acquisition was full-back David Gray, who moved to Blackburn from Preston North End. Unfortunately, at the same time as Gray signed in at Ewood Park, Bobby Langton made the move in the opposite direction. Other departures took Marks to Bristol City while Verdie Godwin and Jackie Oakes switched to Manchester City. It was also hoped that Eddie Crossan, a talented if mercurial Irishman who had joined the club in November 1947, would force his way into the forward line.

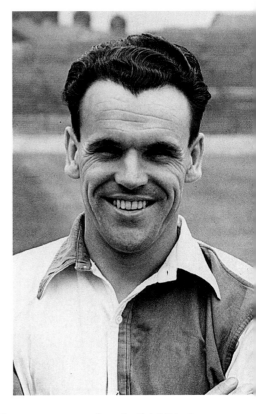

It was a completely new look team that took opened the season against Southampton at the Dell. Stan Hayhurst replaced Marks between the posts, while Gray and young Bill Eckersley formed the full-back pairing. The half-back line was made up of the youthful trio of Jimmy Baldwin, Ken Holliday and Eric Bell. In attack Jackie Campbell and Carter got the nod for the wide positions with Les Graham and Eddie Murphy at inside-forward and Westcott at centre-forward. The new look team lasted for just two games, both of which resulted in defeat, before major changes were made. Out went Holliday, Campbell, Murphy and Carter and in came Bob Pryde, Alf Wheeler, Crossan and Wharton. Results improved and the more optimistic Blackburn supporters talked of a push for promotion.

Alas, the promotion bubble quickly burst. Between Christmas Day and the Saturday before Easter there followed a disastrous sequence of results that brought one win, three draws and nine defeats. The spectre of the Third Division North loomed over the club and the mood was not improved when Hull City knocked them out of the FA Cup. Two crucial wins over Easter and a final-day victory over Brentford helped lift the club to 15th position in the final table. However, the Rovers only finished three points above relegated Nottingham Forest and the directors were left to rue the consequences of a disastrous campaign.

Scottish full-back David Gray joined the Rovers from Preston North End in August 1948. (*Copyright: Howard Talbot*)

Against opposition that looked no better than mediocre, the Rovers had failed to make any headway. Far too often their football lacked imagination and at times the team resembled a rudderless ship. Even during the early part of the campaign, when results were reasonable, the quality of football left much to be desired. Ultimately, Westcott's 21 goals proved to be the key factor in the retention of Second Division status. Indeed, Gray, the right-back, was the joint-second leading goalscorer with five penalties; wingers Wheeler and Wharton also scored five goals apiece. For Graham, the top marksman 12 months earlier, it had been a disappointing campaign with just four goals in 27 League games.

QPR goalkeeper Reg Allen is beaten to the ball by Henry Horton, with Dennis Westcott looking on. This match was played on Christmas Day 1948 and ended in a 2–0 win for the Rovers. (*Copyright: Howard Talbot*)

Fortunately, the Blackburn defence had shown considerable improvement over that of the previous season. Gray and Eckersley had developed into a fine full-back pairing, while the evergreen Pryde continued to defy the years with outstanding performances at centre-half. Bell, despite one or two lapses, made a good impression at left-half, while Baldwin and Cook shared duties on the opposite flank. The club's senior goalkeeper, Hayhurst, was sold to Tottenham Hotspur in October 1948 in a deal that brought Bill Hughes to Ewood Park. Hughes and Jack Patterson vied for the goalkeeping spot until the latter finally made the position his own.

In May 1949 the directors took action to arrest the spiral of decline that had beset the club. Jack Bruton and Horace Cope were both sacked in an acrimonious parting. Bruton claimed that directorial interference in team selection had undermined his position. Nonetheless, the club found no shortage of applicants when it looked for a new man to take the helm.

1949–50

In June 1949, Jackie Bestall, the former Grimsby Town and England international, was appointed manager of Blackburn Rovers. Bestall, who had previously enjoyed a successful spell at the helm of Doncaster Rovers, had a backroom team that included Jack Weddle and Jock Wightman. Although there were no major signings during the summer of 1949, Bestall did sign another experienced defender in September 1949, when Ron Suart was brought from Blackpool. The need for a new defender arose when Bob Pryde decided it was time to bow out of League football and accept the player-manager's job at Wigan Athletic. Pryde also signed Arnold Whiteside, who had been released by the Rovers at the end of the previous season.

Sadly, Bestall's first season at Ewood Park proved to be a disappointment, both in terms of results and the standard of football produced. Relegation, for a time, became a distinct possibility.

Indeed, little comfort was to be found in the fact that ultimately there was a six-point gap between the Rovers and the drop zone.

The highlight of the season was undoubtedly the two meetings with Liverpool in the FA Cup. Although the Rovers narrowly lost a replay at Anfield by the odd goal in three, they won many admirers for their gritty performance against a club that ended the season in eighth place in the First Division. However, this Dunkirk moment could not disguise the continued failure to make any impression on the Second Division.

Like others before him, Bestall was anxious to follow a policy of youth development and this was reflected in some of his team selections. The experienced Suart played only a peripheral role as Bestall favoured the youthful exuberance of Bill Holt at centre-half. It was a decision that reaped dividends as Holt turned in a number of excellent performances at the heart of the defence. Indeed, it was the defence that took the honours during the season. Patterson continued to develop in goal, while Gray and Eckersley formed a full-back partnership that many top-flight clubs would envy. Eckersley's development was sufficiently rapid for him to be included in England's World Cup squad. He made his international debut in July 1950 in the England team that lost to Spain in Rio de Janeiro. Jackie Campbell, who had disappointed in the forward line, proved another of the season's success stories when he was switched to right-half. With Holt and Bell, he made up an impressive half-back trio.

Unfortunately, injuries to a number of key forwards merely underlined the lack of depth in the squad and the departure of Dennis Westcott to Manchester City in February 1950 did little to aid the struggling attack. Indeed, despite his early exit, Westcott remained the top scorer for the season. The hurried transfer of Norman Moore from Hull City failed to add the punch that the forwards so patently lacked. In fact the signing of Moore had been something of a panic measure after moves for Sydney Gerrie of Dundee and Johnny Spuhler of Middlesbrough broke down. The lack of a goalscorer and a playmaker continued to be the crux of the club's problems.

(Above): Bill Holt inherited the centre-half berth after Bob Pryde left to become player-manager of Wigan Athletic. Holt went on to make 80 appearances for the club before leaving to join Weymouth. (*Copyright: Howard Talbot*)

(Left): Eric Bell was the only ever-present during the 1949–50 season. Bell occupied both inside-left and left-half positions during the course of the campaign. (*Copyright: Howard Talbot*)

1950–51

When the season began it was felt that the chief objective would be to keep out of relegation trouble. However, against all expectations the Rovers mounted a serious promotion challenge. The season began with three wins and, on four successive Saturdays in September and early October they were, in turn, second, third, second and first in the table. Indeed, they didn't fall below fourth again until a slump set in during December.

The start had been all the more remarkable because Bestall had made little headway in his search for new players. Paul Todd, a scheming inside-forward, had been signed from Hull City, while Chris Anderson, a young Scottish winger, arrived from Lochore Welfare.

Bestall endured a difficult period as the festive season approached, with the Rovers able to claim just two points from a six-match sequence. The Rovers dropped to eighth in the table and a third-round FA Cup defeat, at the hands of Bristol City, suggested that the revival was at an end. Fortunately, the directors departed from the policy of financial stringency to sign Joe Harris, an Irish centre-forward who cost £2,000.

Harris, who had previously played for Distillery and Larne, immediately added firepower to the attack. As a result the team enjoyed a resurgence that took them back into the heart of the promotion race. The fact that only Preston North End, of the leading teams, showed genuine consistency kept the race for second place wide open. It was a welcome relief for the public of Blackburn to see their team involved in a battle at the top of the table.

Ultimately, the Rovers failed to grasp the chance of promotion because of their financial situation. Glaring weaknesses could not be strengthened. On the right wing Anderson, Bob McCaig, Jackie Wharton and Les Graham had all been tried without success. No matter how the pack was shuffled there was little sustained improvement. Another factor in the decline had been the failure of

Jack Patterson was the only man to play in every match in the 1950–51 campaign. The former Nottingham Forest amateur goalkeeper joined the Rovers in April 1945 and remained until the summer of 1956. However, due to the consistency of Reg Elvy, he only appeared in 127 senior matches for the Rovers. (*Copyright: Howard Talbot*)

Joe Harris arrived from Ireland in January 1951 and scored 10 goals in 17 appearances before the end of the season. (*Copyright: Howard Talbot*)

Opposite page: Ronnie Clayton made his League debut for the Rovers on the final day of the 1950–51 season, when the Rovers defeated QPR 2–1 at Ewood Park. (*Copyright: Howard Talbot*)

Todd to maintain the form he had displayed during the early part of the campaign. His shrewd generalship had been an inspiration but, ultimately, his calm, casual style proved to be his undoing. At a time when 'bite' and battling qualities were required, the Rovers found that those attributes were missing in too many of the players.

However, a sixth-place finish was a vast improvement on previous years and suggested that Bestall had begun to have an impact on the club. As well as improvements at first-team level, where Eckersley again won international honours, Bestall continued the steady development of home-reared players. Frank Chadwick, Ken Clayton, Billy McKee, Derek Leaver, Joe Walsh, Tom Kenny and Geoffrey Jones had all advanced in the Central League side. When the season ended the future at Ewood Park looked considerably brighter than it had done for some time.

1951–52

After the promise of the previous campaign the Ewood faithful were treated to a real Jekyll and Hyde season. On the one hand there was a life-or-death struggle to hold Second Division status, after the most disastrous start that the club had ever experienced. On the other there was an FA Cup

Willie Kelly joined the Rovers from Airdrieonians in September 1951 to add a touch of steel to the defence and went on to appear in 202 senior matches for the club. (*Copyright: Howard Talbot*)

Team photograph taken during the latter part of 1951–52. From left to right, back row: David Gray, Ronnie Clayton, Ron Suart, Reg Elvy, Willie Kelly, Jackie Campbell. Front row: Alec Glover, Eddie Crossan, Eddie Quigley, Bill Eckersley, Albert Nightingale, Chris Anderson. (*Copyright: Howard Talbot*)

run that began with the club anchored at the bottom of the table and ended in a 14th semi-final and two gallant efforts to overcome Newcastle United, the FA Cup holders.

Two points from the opening nine games virtually ended dreams of promotion before September was out. By mid-November the club was in a desperate position with just six points from a possible 32. Once again the directors had to abandon their financial policy in a desperate programme of rebuilding. September brought Alec Glover, Luton Town's speedy winger, and Willie Kelly, Airdrieonians' centre-half, who came with the tag 'Iron Man' attached to his name to the club. Albert Nightingale, from Huddersfield Town, followed in October 1951 to supersede Todd at inside-left. However, apart from Kelly, the two most significant signings arrived in November when Eddie Quigley was signed from Preston North End and Reg Elvy from Bolton Wanderers. Quigley was not only to prove to be an astute playmaker, but he possessed a thunderous shot and an eye for goal. Elvy, a former Halifax Town custodian, had been plucked from the obscurity of keeping goal for the Central League team at Bolton.

The new players cost approximately £53,000 in total but, by the end of the season, they proved that big money spent wisely could turn around even the most dire of situations. However, another factor in improved League form came without a fee attached. Harry Healless, the old, dour, fighting captain of the 1928 FA Cup side, returned to the club in November 1951 as first-team coach.

From December 1951 to February 1952, the Rovers enjoyed seven successive victories and embarked upon a successful FA Cup run. In the third round the Rovers took two attempts to dispose of Nottingham Forest, but Hull City and West Bromwich Albion were beaten at the first time of asking in subsequent rounds. The sixth round brought the visit of Burnley to Ewood Park, on 8 March 1952, when a crowd of 52,920 watched the Rovers conquer their neighbours 3–1. The Rovers faced the Cup holders, Newcastle United, in the semi-final and fought out a goalless draw in the first match, which was played at Hillsborough. The replay was staged at Elland Road and the Rovers faced an uphill task, with both Ron Suart and Bill Holmes missing. The aerial ability of Suart was sorely missed and Newcastle took the lead through a headed goal by George Robledo. However, the Rovers refused to be daunted by the setback and a typically fierce shot by Quigley levelled the score. The Rovers poured forward in an attempt to pull off a major shock but, sadly, the Newcastle defence stood firm and it was the Geordies who won the match with a disputed Bobby Mitchell penalty.

The improved form in the League took the Rovers to 14th position in the Second Division at the end of the season. However, once again the season ended with optimism in the construction of a new side. Elvy proved a steady and reliable custodian, while Eckersley continued to have no peer in terms of cultured full-back play. Kelly had proved to be more than just a dour stopper while the baby of the team, 17-year-old Ronnie Clayton, established himself as one of the game's outstanding prospects. Schoolmaster Bill Holmes, an amateur from Morecambe, had scored seven goals in eight League games and also bagged three Cup goals in four games. Quigley had proved his worth in both generalship of his fellow forwards and his own goalscoring exploits. With Nightingale also proving his worth, the future, once again, appeared to offer promise for the Ewood faithful.

1952-53

Once again, the promise of a previous season failed to materialise at Ewood Park. With financial stringency still of prime concern, the Rovers began the new campaign without any major additions to the squad. The only new face was that of George McLuckie, a Scottish winger who was brought from Lochore Welfare with a view to being groomed in the Central League.

The start to the season was little more than average; the first 10 games brought 10 points, courtesy of four wins and two draws. Holmes and Crossan looked dangerous in attack, while Nightingale and Quigley struggled to find their best form. Nightingale, whose wife was a schoolteacher in Huddersfield, had continued to live in the Yorkshire town and, as a result, found it difficult to settle with the Rovers. In October 1952, he was allowed to move to Leeds United in a £10,000 deal, a transfer which brought a loss of approximately £2,000 for the Rovers.

Although the team had maintained a point a

Bill Holmes, a physical education teacher from Morecambe, scored nine goals from 13 outings but was unable to win a regular first-team place due to the arrival of Tommy Briggs. Holmes moved to Bradford in September 1953. (Copyright: Howard Talbot)

Ken Clayton made his debut for the Rovers in the 2–1 home defeat by Birmingham City on 22 November 1952. Ken went on to make 77 senior appearances for the club before a broken leg curtailed his Ewood Park career. (*Copyright: Howard Talbot*)

game ratio during the opening weeks of the campaign, the quality of the football was desperately poor. From mid-September to the end of November 1952 the Rovers managed just one win and five points from 12 games.

In the last of these matches, Bestall paraded two new signings in Bill Smith and Tommy Briggs. Both had been signed from Birmingham City and both brought different attributes with them. Smith proved to be a more than useful utility player, able to operate at inside-forward or half-back

Tommy Briggs
signs for Blackburn
Rovers in
November 1952.
(*Copyright: Howard
Talbot*)

with equal aplomb. Briggs was an old-fashioned, swashbuckling centre-forward who had won an England 'B' cap in 1950. Sadly for Bestall, both players were to have a limited impact in their first season at Blackburn. Smith was sidelined with injury after only four games, while Briggs managed 17 games before injury brought an early end to his season.

Ironically, the turning point in the Rovers' fortunes came with the injury to Smith. The manager reinstated Quigley to the team after a five-game spell on the sidelines. He returned on Christmas Day and scored both goals in the 2–0 win over Leicester City at Ewood Park. The Quigley who returned to action was not the out-of-form player who managed just two goals from 13 games during the early part of the season. It was the Quigley of old, the astute midfield player who was always a move ahead of the opposition, always on the alert for an opportunity to score or make the telling pass.

Once Quigley was re-called the Rovers lost only four of their remaining 20 League games. Quigley contributed 16 goals of his own, as well as creating numerous chances for his colleagues. Even the jolt of a 6–1 defeat at Luton in the FA Cup didn't prevent the team from gathering a momentum that took them through to the end of the season. Safety was quickly assured and the team climbed to a final position of ninth in the Second Division. They did so with a brand of attacking football, and an abundant supply of goals, that maintained the interest of the Ewood faithful despite the fact that promotion was never a realistic possibility.

1953–54

Blackburn Rovers embarked on a new era with the appointment of Johnny Carey, as manager, in the summer of 1953. The move for Carey came in the wake of the departure of Jackie Bestall in May. Rumours of a rift between Bestall and some of the players had circulated for some time, but in the end the parting proved to be an amicable one. Carey, who had just ended his playing career at Manchester United, arrived at Ewood Park with no management experience behind him.

(Left) Eddie Quigley scored 22 League goals during the 1953–54 season. (*Copyright: Howard Talbot*)

(Right) Bobby Langton returned to Ewood Park in September 1953. (*Copyright: Howard Talbot*)

However, Bestall had left Carey a good foundation on which to build and the former Irish full-back arrived at Ewood with the intention to play 'attractive soccer that wins matches'. However, nobody could have predicted the wonders that he would work with limited resources and virtually no experience.

Carey's first sortie into the transfer market proved an unsuccessful one. During the first week of the season he signed Tommy Bogan, a former teammate at Old Trafford, from Southampton. However, the experienced Scottish winger only made one appearance for the Rovers before being discarded. For the most part, Carey made use of the players that Bestall had left behind. Elvy continued in goal, while Suart and Eckersley held down the full-back places and Kelly remained imperious at centre-half. Indeed, this defensive quartet was so consistent that, between them, they only missed one game during the season and that was when Eckersley was absent on international duty. National service restricted the use of Ronnie Clayton, so the right-half duties were shared between Smith and Campbell, while Bell remained as consistent as ever at left-half. In attack, Crossan and Quigley were automatic choices for the inside-forward positions, as was Briggs at centre-forward. However, the wide positions proved more difficult to fill. Campbell and Glover began the season in these roles with Glover being later switched to the right when Bobby Langton returned to Ewood Park at the end of September 1953. The move for Langton was economically sound and if the former Ewood favourite was older, and considerably slower, his guile and experience, together with his accurate crossing ability, were assets desperately needed by the Rovers. Campbell, McLean, Bogan and Glover all failed to convince Carey that they were the long-term answer to the troublesome right-wing position. In February 1954, the manager returned to Old Trafford to sign Frank Mooney, a lively young winger who had joined United in May 1949.

The atmosphere at the club changed significantly as Carey stressed the importance of teamwork and a collective spirit. He favoured a more intricate style of play that was based on accurate ground passes rather than a long ball for the front men to chase. He inculcated the whole team with this philosophy and expected his defenders to be more constructive in their use of the ball. Even an 8–0 defeat, at Lincoln City, early in his managerial career, failed to shake Carey's belief in the system he adopted.

The new, refined style of play produced a wonderful transformation at Ewood Park. When the final game was played, a 1–0 win over Swansea Town, the Rovers sat in second position in the table. Unfortunately, promotion rivals Everton still had a game to play, against relegated Oldham Athletic. Sadly, there was to be no miracle as the Evertonians romped to a 4–0 win at Boundary Park.

Although promotion hadn't been achieved, there was a genuine feeling that the Rovers' renaissance had begun.

1954-55

Although the ultimate prize of promotion remained tantalisingly out of reach, there could be no complaints about the entertainment value of watching Blackburn Rovers. During the 42 League games that the club played a total of 193 goals were scored, with the Rovers able to claim 114 of them. It was the first time in the club's history – and to date the only time – that the Rovers reached the figure of 100 goals in a League campaign.

All five of the first-choice forwards reached double figures in terms of goalscoring. Briggs led the way with 33 goals, Quigley scored 28, Crossan 18, Mooney 16 and Langton 13. Only three other Blackburn players got on the scoresheet that season – Ronnie Clayton scored two goals, with Eric Bell and Derek Leaver getting one apiece. The 114 tally was made complete with two own-goals.

There were some incredible matches played at Ewood Park with the highest score being recorded on 6 November 1954, when Middlesbrough ended up being thrashed 9–0. Curiously, Briggs failed to get on the scoresheet that day. However, he more than made up for it when he scored seven goals in the 8–3 demolition of Bristol Rovers on 5 February 1955. Seven goals were scored against Doncaster Rovers, while five were hit past West Ham United and Derby County at Ewood Park. West Ham also had the misfortune to concede a further five goals when the Rovers visited Upton Park. Four goals was a common scoreline at Ewood with Swansea Town, Liverpool, Ipswich Town and Hull City all being beaten with varying degrees of ease.

However, while the attack gorged itself on a feast of goals, there was an increasing vulnerability about the defence. The opening day had seen a 5–1 reversal at Craven Cottage and while Liverpool had been beaten at home, the Rovers did concede three goals. In November 1954, there was a 7–3 defeat away at Luton Town, and while Rovers scored four goals in their home match with Notts County they still ended up without a point.

Ultimately, defensive frailties cost the Rovers the chance of promotion and the season ended with the Rovers in sixth place, just four points behind Birmingham City and Luton Town, who were both promoted.

In terms of team selection, Carey was able to achieve a level of consistency that few previous managers at Ewood Park had enjoyed. No fewer than nine players – Elvy (41 games), Eckersley (41), Ronnie Clayton (42), Bell (42), Mooney

Bryan Douglas made his debut for the club against Notts County at Meadow Lane on 4 September 1954. The Rovers lost 1–0 and it was the only appearance Douglas made during that campaign. However, 12 months later he became the automatic choice for the outside-right position. (*Copyright: Howard Talbot*)

(42), Crossan (40), Briggs (41), Quigley (40) and Langton (42) – appeared in 40 or more League games during that thrilling campaign. Of the rest, Kelly played 38 games at centre-half while the right-back position was shared between Suart (25) and Smith (20). The club also gave debuts to three of its youngsters – Alan Bean, Ken Taylor and Bryan Douglas – as concern was again expressed about the advanced years of a number of the senior players at Ewood Park.

1955-56

It was, perhaps, to be expected that 'third time lucky' was the pious platitude that filled the air on the eve of the new campaign. However, apart from the modest signing of Eric Binns, who had spent his career languishing in Central League football at Turf Moor, there were no new faces on view when the season began. Indeed, Binns opened his Ewood career in the reserves, while Kelly took the number-five shirt.

The season opened with two defeats and Kelly, Bell and Mooney were replaced by Binns, Ken Clayton and the veteran Campbell. During the opening phase of the campaign the Rovers never looked more than a middle-of-the-road team. The only ray of light appeared to be the introduction of Douglas, who after three games at inside-left was switched to the right wing for the trip to Bury on 8 October 1955. The Rovers returned from Gigg Lane with a 4–0 win and Douglas remained on the right flank for the rest of the season. Indeed, his progress was such that 'Rover' in the *Blackburn Times* described him as a 'Matthews in miniature'.

However, despite the introduction of Douglas, the Rovers struggled to produce the flowing football of previous seasons. By Christmas the more pessimistic of supporters saw the spectre of relegation looming in the distance. During the first half of the campaign, Quigley, the man who

Tommy Briggs watches the ball flash past Nottingham Forest 'keeper, Harry Nicholson, in a match that ended in a 2–2 draw at Ewood Park on 2 January 1956. (*Copyright: Howard Talbot*)

instigated so many of the attacking moves, had looked a spent force. Indeed, there were several areas where the team appeared to lack genuine quality. Right-back remained a troublesome position, with Bill Smith being dragooned into the role at the start of the campaign, only to be replaced in turn by Tommy Clinton and, more successfully, by Ken Taylor, another of the youngsters that had begun to emerge from the Central League team. Carey, who persevered with Binns at centre-half until Christmas, was forced to recall Kelly as defensive errors began to cost vital points.

An upturn in fortunes began with a 2–1 win against Liverpool at Anfield. From that date, 31 December 1955, until 2 April 1956, the Rovers collected 22 points out of 28 and climbed from 18th position to third in the table. At the same time the club enjoyed a creditable Cup run that ended in a closely fought fifth-round replay against West Ham United at Ewood Park.

The revival was not built on the swashbuckling attack of the previous campaign, but instead a more dour workmanlike approach was adopted. Quigley was reinvigorated and began to oil the wheels of an attack that continued to use Briggs at its cutting edge. Sometimes deadly, sometimes wayward, Briggs nonetheless scored 31 goals to keep the Rovers in touch with their promotion rivals.

Unfortunately, too much ground had been lost earlier in the season and, as a result, minor setbacks proved disastrous. The losses to Swansea and Bristol City in the final month of the season proved decisive in the final outcome and the Rovers had to settle for a fourth-place finish, just four points behind second-placed Leeds United.

Reg Elvy is beaten to the ball by John Ayteo, Bristol City's inside-right, on a day when the Rovers conceded six goals at Ewood Park in a 6–4 defeat. (*Copyright: Howard Talbot*)

Although the Rovers had failed in their prime objective there were, nonetheless, several plusses to be gained from the season. The emergence of youngsters like Douglas, Taylor, Roy Vernon and Ken Clayton was the main source of consolation from the campaign. Ronnie Clayton also progressed from England Under-23 international to full international, although still only 21. However, although veterans like Quigley and Kelly fought back to regain their first-team places, there was clearly a period of transition needed at the club. The best years of Elvy, Kelly, Bell, Quigley and Langton were clearly behind them and with the club no longer 'in the red' the manager would have the necessary funds with which to rebuild his team.

1956-57

The watchword at the start of the season ought to have been patience rather than promotion. After a hat-trick of near misses the manager had to face up to the need to rebuild his ageing squad. The summer of 1956 saw Elvy, Campbell, Mooney, Langton and Quigley pass through the Ewood exit door as the manager looked to rejuvenate his senior team. His biggest signing was Ally MacLeod, who arrived from St Mirren to fill the gap left by Langton. Elvy was replaced by Harry Leyland, who had been released by Everton after 40 senior appearances for the Merseyside club. Leyland had been bound for non-League Tonbridge when Carey stepped in and signed him for the Rovers. Carey returned to Goodison Park to sign a replacement for Willie Kelly and snapped up Matt Woods, in November 1956, for £6,000. Woods had joined Everton in 1947 but had only appeared in eight senior games for the Goodison club before his move to Ewood Park.

Ally MacLeod was signed from St Mirren in June 1956. (*Copyright: Howard Talbot*)

Ken Taylor puts Liverpool's Billy Liddell under pressure, watched by Matt Woods on 16 February 1957. The game ended in a 2–2 draw with Liddell scoring the visitors' second goal. (*Copyright: Howard Talbot*)

In a little over a couple of months, Carey not only reshaped his team, but also found a fairly successful blend. Leyland became the first-choice custodian, while the long-serving Jack Patterson continued in the role of back-up 'keeper. The full-back pairing brought the youthful Taylor in to partner Eckersley. For the bulk of the season the half-back line included the Clayton brothers at wing-half with Woods in the middle. However, when Ken Clayton broke his leg against Middlesbrough on 6 April 1957, Mick McGrath, an Irish youngster who had joined the club in August 1954, stepped in to make the place his own. Douglas and MacLeod were automatic choices for the wide positions, while the inside-forward positions were taken by two youngsters, Roy Vernon and Peter Dobing. Briggs continued to lead the attack successfully with 32 goals, but in spite of his success in front of goal, there was no doubt that his powers were on the wane.

Blessed with an excellent run of results between late October 1956 and early February 1957, the Rovers found themselves involved in another promotion battle. However, whereas the three previous seasons had seen challenges flounder due to the ageing nature of the squad, the opposite was true of the 1956–57 challenge. A lack of maturity in certain areas cost vital points and ultimately the Rovers had to settle for a final position of fourth in the League.

However, the club ended the season in far better shape than it had been for many years. The long-held criticism that the squad was top heavy with ageing players had finally been answered. In truth, the team had used the 1956–57 season to continue its football education and many believed that promotion would have come too soon if the campaign had reached a successful conclusion.

1957-58

The cultured football that Carey had encouraged throughout his tenure at Ewood Park was finally rewarded with the success it deserved. After 10 years in the wilderness of the Second Division, the Rovers finally reclaimed their place among the elite of English football.

During the early part of the season success was built on the firm foundations of a solid defence. Harry Leyland, Ken Taylor, Ronnie Clayton, Matt Woods and Mick McGrath proved a reliable barrier, with young Dave Whelan and Bill Smith being given the opportunity to understudy Eckersley during the latter's increasing bouts of injury. Unfortunately, as expected, Tommy Briggs found it difficult to maintain the standards of previous seasons. Eventually, Carey was forced to move Peter Dobing to centre-forward and introduce Ronnie Cairns, and then Roy Stephenson, to the inside-forward position. Cairns had been with the Rovers since September 1953, but had only made a handful of appearances prior to 1957–58. Stephenson, a former Burnley product, was signed by the Rovers from Rotherham United in November 1957.

While the Rovers led the table during parts of October and November 1957, there was a slight dip in form in mid-season that threatened to undermine the promotion challenge. The problem largely revolved around the use of Dobing in a position for which he was not suited. The lack of a traditional type of centre-forward had become a serious concern for Carey. In a bid to boost the club's promotion prospects, Carey allowed Tommy Briggs to move to Grimsby Town in March 1958 and, just before the transfer deadline, negotiated the £15,000 transfer of Tommy Johnston from Leyton Orient.

Tom Johnston was signed from Leyton Orient to lead the Blackburn attack during the final stages of the successful promotion campaign. Johnston scored eight goals in 11 appearances as the Rovers clinched the runners-up spot in the Second Division. *(Copyright: Howard Talbot)*

Although Johnston had built up a reputation for his strong, bustling type of leadership, Carey envisaged a slightly different role for the much travelled Scot. The manager asked him to play a similar role to that of Quigley: to general the forwards but maintain an eye for goal. Two goals on his debut, ironically against Grimsby Town, helped the team to a 3–0 win and set the Rovers on their path to promotion. The 11 games that Johnston featured in led to nine victories and 40 goals, of which Johnston scored eight.

The Rovers had also embarked on a successful Cup run before Johnston arrived. Away wins over Rotherham United and Everton were followed by victory over Cardiff City after a replay. The sixth round produced one of the most entertaining matches of the season, when Liverpool visited Ewood Park. A titanic struggle ended in victory for the Rovers, thanks to goals from Ronnie Clayton and Ally MacLeod. The semi-final, at Maine Road, found the Rovers in an unfamiliar strip of black and white stripes as Bolton Wanderers reached Wembley thanks to the odd goal in three.

The last week of the season brought a 4–0 win over Leyton Orient at Ewood Park before the Rovers travelled to London for their final two games. On the Wednesday night the Rovers faced a Fulham side at Craven Cottage who needed to win to retain an outside chance of promotion. However, an Ally

MacLeod goal ensured a share of the spoils for the Rovers and ended the London club's bid for top-flight football.

The final match of the season was a promotion battle between second-placed Charlton Athletic and the Rovers, who occupied third spot. A win or a draw for Charlton would ensure that they accompanied West Ham United into the First Division. For the Rovers the task was simple: win at all costs.

A crowd of 56,435 assembled at The Valley to witness one of the most thrilling games in the club's history. Within a matter of four minutes the home side took the lead when a cross from Johnny Summers was headed past Leyland by Fred Lucas. Three minutes later Stuart Leary missed a golden opportunity to put Charlton two ahead. The Rovers

Tommy Briggs (partly hidden by the post) scores his final goal for the club in the 1–1 draw with Charlton Athletic at Ewood Park on 14 December 1957. (*Copyright: Howard Talbot*)

got back in the game after 22 minutes when Dobing headed a Vernon free-kick firmly into the net. On 36 minutes the Rovers took the lead when Eckersley hit a beautifully weighted pass down the left wing for Dobing to run onto and place an oblique right-foot shot past Willie Duff, as the Charlton 'keeper advanced to met him. Three minutes before half-time the Rovers fans were ecstatic when Vernon picked up a loose ball and unleashed a venomous shot from 25 yards that flew past the startled Duff. On 62 minutes the Rovers appeared to have won the game when Johnston was fouled and Douglas converted the resultant penalty. Fourteen minutes from the end Eddie Firmani gave the home supporters hope when he headed past Leyland. The home team continued to attack, but the Rovers' defence, superbly marshalled by Woods, held firm. However, with seven minutes remaining, a clumsy challenge by Woods gave the opportunity for the referee to award the

Bryan Douglas challenges as Fulham's Jimmy Hill clears the ball, watched by goalkeeper Tony Macedo. (*Copyright: unknown*)

Willie Duff gathers the ball as Bryan Douglas just fails to connect with the ball. A crowd of 56,435 watched this promotion decider between Charlton Athletic and the Rovers. (*Copyright: unknown*)

home team with a penalty. Amidst unbearable tension, John Hewie kept his nerve and calmly slotted home the spot kick. Fortunately, the Rovers defence held firm and it was the Blackburn contingent in the crowd who celebrated a welcome return to top-flight football.

1958–59

The primary objectives – security and consolidation – were convincingly achieved despite the early exit of the architect of the club's improved fortunes. Apart from the loss of the manager, there was very little activity in the transfer market as the Rovers tried to adapt to life in the top flight.

The team made a sensational start to the season with three successive wins. A 5–1 win at St James' Park on the opening day of the campaign was followed by convincing home wins over Leicester City (5–0) and Tottenham Hotspur (5–0). Incredibly, the club failed to win any of the next nine games and it was during this lean period that Carey, who had always worked without a contract at Blackburn, accepted an offer to become manager of Everton. Fortunately, Carey agreed to remain with the Rovers until the directors had appointed a successor. The man chosen to follow Carey into the Ewood hot seat was Luton Town's Dally Duncan. A former Scottish international, he had enjoyed a long playing career with Derby County before taking the helm at Luton in September 1947. During his time at Kenilworth Road he had taken Luton into the First Division, in 1954–55, and had been able to keep them there despite the limited resources at his disposal.

Duncan continued the excellent work of Carey and managed to stabilise the club in a comfortable mid-table position. There were, of course, changes to the personnel but, apart from the sale of Johnston and the signing of Derek Dougan, the changes involved those on the existing staff.

Burnley 'keeper, Colin MacDonald, watches a header from Ally MacLeod go wide in a goalless draw played at Turf Moor on 18 October 1958. (*Copyright: Howard Talbot*)

After a bright start it became apparent that Johnston, despite his best efforts, was not the long-term solution to the centre-forward position. In February 1959, he accepted a move back to London to rejoin Leyton Orient, despite the fact that the Rovers had not found a replacement. In the short term, Dally promoted Jackie Swindells, from the Central League team, and the Manchester-born youngster duly scored the winning goal in a 2–1 victory over Portsmouth. Ironically, Derek Dougan, who scored Pompey's goal that day, was the man who would eventually be bought to fill the vacancy left by Johnston. Initially, Duncan had hoped to sign Bill Curry from Newcastle United; however, when terms couldn't be agreed the club turned to Dougan. The young Irishman had been on the Ewood wanted list for some time, with an attempt made to sign him before he joined Portsmouth.

A number of the Rovers players blossomed in the higher division as Ronnie Clayton and Bryan Douglas continued to build upon their international careers with England. Vernon became a regular in the Welsh team as he combined the duties of schemer and sharpshooter as well as any other inside-forward in the country. All three had spent the summer of 1958 in Sweden involved in the World Cup. While the three younger players made their mark at international level, one of the club's former internationals, Bill Eckersley, began to fade from the first-team scene as age and injury took their toll. Whelan, who had lost his place to Taylor, returned to fill the gap left by Eckersley. In May 1959, Peter Dobing was rewarded with his first England Under-23 cap, as the younger players at Ewood began to fulfil their potential.

Youth development had been high on Carey's agenda and the seeds he had sown blossomed in May 1959, when the Rovers' youth team, under the guidance of Jackie Campbell, lifted the FA Youth Cup for the first time in the club's history.

Tommy Johnston challenges Arsenal's Welsh international 'keeper, Jack Kelsey, during the Rovers' 3–2 win over Arsenal at Ewood Park on 25 October 1958. (*Copyright: Howard Talbot*)

1959-60

(Left) Birmingham City's former England 'keeper, Gil Merrick, saves at the feet of Tommy Johnston in the match played at Ewood Park on 8 November 1958. (*Copyright: Howard Talbot*)

(Right) Tommy Johnston fires in a shot against Leyton Orient in the third-round FA Cup tie played at Ewood Park on 10 January 1959. (*Copyright: Howard Talbot*)

(Bottom left) Fulham's Tony Macedo saves at the feet of Bryan Douglas as Jim Lanley keeps a careful eye on the situation. The Rovers enjoyed an opening day 4–0 win at Ewood Park. (*Copyright: Howard Talbot*)

(Bottom right) West Ham United's Ken Brown tries to prevent Ally MacLeod from crossing the ball during the 6–2 win over the Hammers on 12 December 1959. (*Copyright: Howard Talbot*)

Rarely had Blackburn Rovers experienced a season of such sharp contrasts as 1959–60. A season that ought to have ended in relief – at having survived a dismal League campaign – and joy – at having reached another FA Cup Final – ended in rancour, public disillusionment and a catastrophic rift between directors and manager that resulted in the latter's dismissal.

The Rovers ran into difficulty after the first match and for the next five months the club went through one of the worst epidemics of injury and sickness that it had ever experienced. Between August and New Year, the team was never at full strength. However, Duncan's only move into the transfer market was to sign Louis Bimpson, Liverpool's reserve centre-forward, in November 1959.

Fortunately, despite the many setbacks, the team was able to accumulate a respectable number of points during the first half of the campaign. However, the first four months of 1960 produced one of the bleakest periods in the club's history. Rumours of unrest within the camp and lamentable League form coincided with sparkling Cup performances that took the club all the way to Wembley.

The unrest centred upon the relationship between Vernon and Duncan, a relationship that had all but disintegrated. In the end the club had no option but to part company with its star inside-forward. It came as no surprise that Johnny Carey, his former mentor, should return to Ewood to snap up the mercurial Welshman. For a time the departure of Vernon lifted morale, but the fact remained that the team won just three League games between Boxing Day and the end of the season. During that run, a miserable tally of eight points was accumulated out of a possible 38. Without their successes earlier in the season, the club would have been stranded at the bottom of the table. The manager had tried, unsuccessfully, to pep up the attack with the signing of Chris Crowe from Leeds United and Everton's Eddie Thomas.

It was all the more remarkable then that, against the background of such dire performances in the bread and butter of League football, the club should enjoy such a successful Cup campaign. Although two games were needed to overcome Sunderland, in the third round the replay ended in a convincing 4–1 win. In the fourth round a late goal from Mick McGrath prevented the club from losing to Blackpool at Ewood Park. The Rovers travelled to Bloomfield Road, where they had already lost in the League, and surprised even the most devout supporters with the ease of the 3–0 win that they enjoyed.

Once again, the fifth round pitted the Rovers against opponents who had already enjoyed comfortable victories over them. Indeed, the Rovers had been thrashed 4–1 at home by Tottenham Hotspur just seven days before they journeyed to White Hart Lane for the fifth-round tie. Against all expectations the Rovers cruised to a 3–1 win and a meeting with Burnley in the sixth round.

Interest in the FA Cup ought to have come to an end at Turf Moor with the Rovers 3–0 down and with just 17 minutes left to play. However, it was then that fate intervened: a harmless looking-shot by Dobing struck the boot of Alex Elder and flew up and hit his hand. The referee gave what was, to even the most ardent Blackburn supporter, a highly debatable penalty. Douglas duly accepted the gift and three minutes later a speculative drive by Dobing found the back of the Burnley net. In an action-packed finale the Rovers drew level due to another piece of good fortune.

With just four minutes left, Ronnie Clayton hit another speculative shot toward the Burnley goal. The ball fell at the feet of McGrath, who swung his foot at the ball, only to mishit it, and then watched as his sliced shot trickled over the line with 'keeper Adam Blacklaw completely stranded. A crowd of 53,839 packed into Ewood Park to witness a virtuoso performance from Bryan Douglas as the match went into extra-time before goals from Dobing and MacLeod gave the Rovers a 2–0 victory.

The semi-final, against Sheffield Wednesday, was played at Maine Road, and a brace of goals from Derek Dougan ensured a place in the FA Cup Final against Wolverhampton Wanderers. Unfortunately, the luck that had taken the Rovers to Wembley deserted them as the club was to suffer a number of own goals both on and off the pitch. Problems over ticket distribution led to a number of die-hard supporters being overlooked. The result was that a sizeable proportion of the club's following felt alienated. Indeed, for some it was to be a permanent alienation and a number of life-long supporters were lost forever. The team journeyed to Wembley with a major injury doubt over Dougan. To make matters worse, the Irish striker chose the trip down to London as the moment to hand in a transfer request.

After Dougan had given an assurance he was fit to play he was selected by Duncan to lead the Blackburn attack. Within minutes of the kick-off it became clear that Dougan was not as fully mobile as one might have hoped. Things went from bad to worse when McGrath turned a cross into his own goal to give Wolves the lead. Within a minute Dave Whelan and Norman Deeley collided, with the result that Whelan was carried off with a broken leg. Ironically, it was a brace of goals from Deeley that secured a comfortable win in what had been an undistinguished game.

Fortunately, the finances from the Cup run offered some consolation in that the Rovers were able to use the money to erect a cantilever roof at the Blackburn End of the ground. Following an end-of-season tour of Germany, the town was awash with rumours of a rift between the directors

(Left) Derek Dougan scored 16 goals during the season but the FA Cup Final proved a personal nightmare for the Northern Ireland international centre-forward. (*Copyright: Howard Talbot*)

(Right) Dave Whelan broke his leg in the 1960 FA Cup Final but went on to become a successful businessman and, as chairman, took Wigan Athletic to the Premiership in 2005. (*Copyright: Blackburn Library*)

and Dally Duncan. Stories of poor discipline within the club were rife and clearly the team's performance in the League was of major concern to the directors. Duncan was asked to resign but, with a long-term contract in his hand, he declined to accede to the directors' request. When the manager refused to fall on his sword, the directors had no option but to sack him and begin the search for a replacement.

1960–61

After the disastrous public relations exercise that the FA Cup Final had disintegrated into, the 1960–61 season was all about redemption. However, the disenchantment that had pervaded the Ewood faithful was not easily lifted and the average attendance fell from 27,299 (for 1959–60) to an alarming 19,344. In truth, the Rovers weren't the only club who suffered at the turnstile as the bitter struggle between the players and the football authorities began to dominate the back pages.

The Professional Footballers' Association had become committed to the abolition of the maximum wage – £20 a week during the season, and £17 in the summer. Reg Taylor, the Blackburn secretary, expressed his concern that if the limit was lifted it would be detrimental to clubs like the Rovers whom, he believed, would find it difficult to maintain their current numbers in terms of playing staff. However, Harry Leyland, a member of the PFA executive, believed that there was a principle at stake that was worthy of the fight. Thus, with the threat of industrial action in the air, a steep decline in attendance, a loss of public confidence and without a manager at the helm, the Rovers embarked on the 1960–61 season.

The vacant managerial position was filled when the directors chose to offer the job to Rochdale's Jack Marshall. However, the Fourth Division club's directors were not prepared to release their manager until they had found a suitable replacement. As a result the Rovers had already played six League games before the new man was able to take charge of the club.

When Marshall arrived at Ewood Park, he found that his options with regard to team selection had been severely curtailed by injury. Leyland, who had undergone a cartilage operation in the summer, had joined Whelan on the long-term injured list. The ageing legs of Eckersley had shown an increased vulnerability to injury, while a third full-back, John Bray, was also out injured when Marshall arrived. Matters were further complicated with increased speculation with regard to the future of both Dobing and Dougan at the club. The directors had placed Dougan on the transfer list but, as ever, the unpredictable Irishman had opted to stay put and then scored a hat-trick, at Old Trafford, on the opening day of the season.

In January 1961, the maximum wage was abolished and within the month the players celebrated a victory over their contracts. It was a decision that made the long-term prognosis for the Rovers somewhat bleaker.

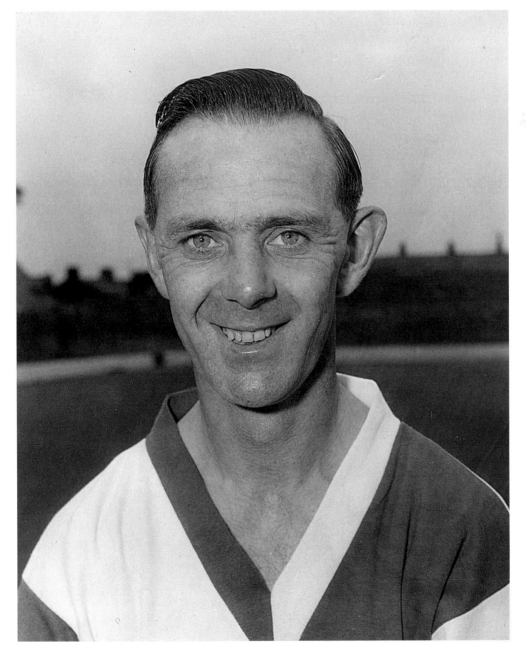

Bill Eckersley brought his long and illustrious career to a close at the end of the 1960–61 season. Eckersley appeared in 432 senior matches for the Rovers and scored 21 goals. The classy left-back was also capped on 17 occasions by England. (*Copyright: Howard Talbot*)

During the course of the campaign the new manager proved adept at utilising the limited resources at his disposal. Fred Pickering, who had replaced the injured Eckersley, had looked a solid, if unspectacular, left-back. However, when Marshall switched him to centre-forward for the final 10 games, he proved a revelation and scored seven goals. Marshall's greatest discovery of the season proved to be Andy McEvoy, an Irishman who had languished in the Central League team as a workmanlike inside-forward. When Marshall switched him to right-half he was rewarded with a player who made such progress that he was capped by the Republic of Ireland. However, no amount of tinkering could solve one persistent problem. With Harry Leyland coming to the end of his time at Ewood, there would clearly be a vacancy between the posts. However, neither of his understudies, Bob Jones or Brian Reeves, did enough to persuade Marshall of their suitability to inherit the number one spot.

Keith Newton (No.3) guards the line as 'keeper Bob Jones battles with Sheffield Wednesday's Bobby Craig during the 1–1 draw at Ewood Park on 1 April 1961. (Copyright: Howard Talbot)

Brian Reeves vied with Bob Jones for the right to inherit the mantle of Harry Leyland during 1960–61. (Copyright: Howard Talbot)

While working with the younger players at the club, the manager looked to strengthen the club's finances with the sale of Peter Dobing and Chris Crowe. A £40,000 deal with Newcastle United was struck for Dobing but he was reluctant to move and the deal collapsed. Marshall arranged for Crowe, who had never really lived up to his reputation, to join Preston North End. However, a last-minute change of heart by the Deepdale club ended the proposed £27,500 transfer.

An eighth-place finish in the League, the highest for 27 years, proved cause for satisfaction for the new manager. The club had also enjoyed a moderately successful FA Cup run that ended at Sheffield United in the fifth round. Although the newly formed Football League Cup was treated with caution by the public, the Rovers enjoyed a brief run before they suffered the embarrassment of an exit at the hands of lowly opposition. After away wins at York City and Swansea Town, two home matches with Rochdale and Wrexham brought pitiful gates of 6,316 and 8,061 respectively. However, when the Rovers lost a replay at Wrexham, there was much criticism with regard to their abysmal performance.

1961-62

The summer of 1961 enabled Jack Marshall to finally unload two of the players whose departures had been long expected. Peter Dobing was sold to Manchester City for £37,500, while Aston Villa paid £15,000 for Derek Dougan. Bill Eckersley, who had enjoyed a well-supported testimonial match in May 1961, hung up his boots, while Ally MacLeod returned to Scotland to join Hibernian. The summer also brought the end of Harry Leyland's tenure at Ewood Park as Marshall set his sights on a new 'keeper.

Marshall's first move into the transfer market brought Ian Lawther to Ewood Park from Sunderland for a fee of £18,000. Lawther, a Northern Ireland international, was a hard-working inside-forward who had scored 41 goals in 75 League games for the Roker Park club. A few days later Marshall added Arsenal's diminutive Irish winger, Joe Haverty, to his squad. Haverty, a regular in the Republic of Ireland squad, cost the Rovers £25,000 and came with a glowing reputation from Highbury.

There was also a major change in the backroom staff with Jack Weddle, the long-serving trainer, being replaced as senior coach by Jimmy Gordon, who held a coaching post at Middlesbrough.

As the pre-season games got under way, the Rovers still hadn't addressed the goalkeeping problem and the opening friendly brought a 4–2 defeat at Deepdale. Three days later the Rovers were due to host a return fixture with North End. On the morning of the match the Rovers successfully negotiated the transfer of Fred Else, Preston's England 'B' international 'keeper. In the evening Else, one of the most highly rated goalkeepers in the country, made his Rovers debut against his former club in a game that ended in a 1–1 draw.

Ian Lawther had a difficult start to his Blackburn career before ending the campaign as leading goalscorer with 20 League and Cup goals. In this picture he incurs the wrath of the local constabulary for the benefit of the photographer. (*Copyright: Howard Talbot*)

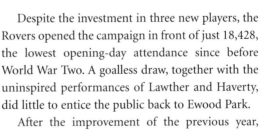

Despite the investment in three new players, the Rovers opened the campaign in front of just 18,428, the lowest opening-day attendance since before World War Two. A goalless draw, together with the uninspired performances of Lawther and Haverty, did little to entice the public back to Ewood Park.

After the improvement of the previous year, 1961–62 proved a major disappointment. Sixteenth place in the First Division reflected the lack of consistency that plagued the team. Lawther, after an indifferent start, finished the season as top goalscorer, with 14 League goals, but not one of the other front players reached double figures. Haverty, in particular, failed to live up to expectations and at the end of the season was placed on the transfer list at his own request.

When Accrington Stanley folded in March 1962, the registration of their players reverted to the

Jack Marshall supervises the signing of Joe Haverty, Arsenal's Republic of Ireland international winger. (*Copyright: Howard Talbot*)

Fred Else joined the Rovers from Preston North End on the morning of a friendly encounter between the two clubs. In the evening he kept goal for the Rovers in the 1–1 draw at Ewood Park on 11 August 1961. (*Copyright: Howard Talbot*)

The opening day of the season produced a goalless draw with Cardiff City at Ewood Park. Fred Else watches a Cardiff shot fly wide of his post. (*Copyright: Howard Talbot*)

Football League. A number had been keenly sought by League clubs, including the Rovers, and to the dismay of Stanley followers these players were bought for a fraction of their true value. The player in whom Jack Marshall was interested was Mike Ferguson, a talented inside-forward who had taken the eye of a number of clubs. Two days after Stanley's demise, both Marshall and Jimmy Milne, the manager of Preston North End, arrived in Accrington in search of Ferguson. Fortunately, it was Marshall who learned that the player was training with the Burnley reserve squad at Gawthorpe. Marshall quickly hurried over to Burnley and agreed terms with Ferguson. The next day the Stanley directors agreed to sign the documents that made Ferguson a Blackburn player for the relatively modest fee of £2,000. Nonetheless, it was to prove to be the most significant signing of the season.

The manager was also able to finally capture Bobby Craig, a long-time target of Marshall's, only after the transfer deadline had passed. As a result, special permission from the Football League was required before Craig could appear in the final two games of the season.

The biggest disappointments for the club came in the two Cup competitions. Having reached the sixth round of the FA Cup, the Rovers drew at Fulham only to lose the replay at Ewood Park. In the Football League Cup the club were again humbled by lowly opposition. However, on this occasion it was an even greater embarrassment, as the club had reached the semi-final stage. Drawn against Rochdale in a two-legged semi-final, the Rovers crashed to a 3–1 defeat at Spotland. Alas, a 2–1 win at Ewood Park was insufficient to prevent another Cup upset in front of the Ewood faithful.

1962-63

The Rovers rounded off their season with a feast of goals and five successive victories. Nineteen goals were scored during this period and only three conceded as this final flourish took the Rovers to a mid-table position. Yet for three-quarters of the campaign the football produced by the Rovers was drab and uninspiring. The public remained unenthused by it and the 20,000 mark was topped on only five occasions at Ewood Park – against the two Merseyside clubs, Manchester United, Burnley and Tottenham Hotspur.

With attendances low, the manager had little room for manoeuvre in the transfer market and the only acquisition he made during the whole campaign was Mike Harrison, Chelsea's England Under-23 international outside-left, who arrived in September 1962 to replace Joe Haverty.

Bobby Craig opened the season with a hat-trick at Portman Road, but the 3–3 draw at Ipswich was followed by an alarming 5–2 home reverse to Nottingham Forest. Two wins and two draws from the opening 10 games left the Rovers in bottom place on 22 September 1962.

Fortunately, the club gradually clawed its way up the table, due largely to the footballing artistry of Bryan Douglas. While arguments raged as to whether Douglas was more suited to the wing or inside-forward, the England international proved he could be devastating in both roles. However, despite the presence of Douglas the Ewood faithful only celebrated four home wins up to the final few days in March 1963. Indeed, between 24 November 1962 and 28 March 1963 the Rovers failed to win any of their 11 League games and the threat of Second Division football began to loom on the horizon.

Consistency was not helped when the icy blast of winter prevented all but one game being played between 22 December 1962 and 2 March 1963. The Rovers' third-round tie with Middlesbrough was postponed on no fewer than 11 occasions before the Second Division side held the Rovers to a 1–1 draw at Ewood Park. The replay ended in a disappointing 3–1 defeat. The club had already been eliminated from the League Cup by Sunderland, another second-tier club.

The greatest paradox of the season was the performance of the forward line. Craig, after his initial impact, quickly departed for Scotland after his wife failed to settle in the town. Fortunately, Celtic offered him an escape route from his brief nightmare at Ewood Park. Lawther endured a difficult season and was axed for the second half of the campaign as Marshall asked McEvoy to revert to his original inside-forward role. Fred Pickering continued to bear the brunt of the goalscoring, with 28 League and Cup goals, but his game was not without flaws. Another youngster,

Bryan Douglas beats Gordon Banks from the penalty spot to put the Rovers ahead in their clash with Leicester City on 20 October 1962. (*Copyright: Howard Talbot*)

Fred Pickering finished as the club's top goalscorer during 1962–63 with 28 League and Cup goals. (*Copyright: Howard Talbot*)

Fred Pickering beats Birmingham City goalkeeper Colin Withers to score the third goal for the Rovers in a 6–1 win on 27 April 1963. (*Copyright: Howard Talbot*)

John Byrom, a former England youth international, forced his way into the team at inside-forward but, like Pickering, suffered through his lack of experience. Ferguson proved his ability to operate on the wing or at inside-forward and grew into top-flight football as the season progressed, but Harrison, despite his blistering pace, failed to live up to his reputation or fee.

Although the Rovers scored 79 League goals, more than most teams in the top flight, there were many occasions when the forward line appeared quite incapable of turning pressure into goals. On one of the few occasions, before Christmas, when the forwards did sparkle, against Arsenal at Ewood Park on 3 November 1962, defensive frailties prevented a win being recorded. Nonetheless, those who witnessed the epic 5–5 thriller were treated to a superb display of attacking football from both teams.

118

The final match of the season, a 3–0 win over Tottenham Hotspur, marked the end of the Blackburn career of Matt Woods. The veteran centre-half had amassed 307 League and Cup appearances with the Rovers and had been a colossus in the heart of the Ewood defence. Woods, with Mike England snapping at his heels, opted to bow out while still at the top and left Blackburn to join an Australian club.

1963–64

Rarely can the Ewood faithful have witnessed such a season of mixed emotions as that of 1963–64. The birth of 'Marshall's Misfits', a potential League Championship, defeat in the FA Cup by lower League opposition and, finally, the sale of the club's leading goalscorer to a Championship rival and with it the evaporation of their own title challenge both delighted and exasperated the long suffering supporters.

The opening months of the season brought some of the most entertaining football that the Blackburn public had seen for many a year. With a limited budget at his disposal, Marshall had been astute in the use of the playing resources available to him. Else, who had been supremely consistent since his move from Deepdale, remained first-choice goalkeeper, with Bob Jones as his understudy. At full-back, John Bray and Keith Newton were automatic choices, with Chris Sims able to cover either man. Newton, who had originally started life as a centre-half, had been successfully converted into a full-back by Marshall and, in February 1964, joined Fred Pickering in the England Under–23 team. Ronnie Clayton and Mick McGrath continued to hold down the half-back positions, while Mike England was entrusted with the centre-half role that Woods had vacated. In attack Ferguson and Harrison operated on the flanks, Douglas pulled the strings at inside-left and the goalscoring was largely left to Pickering and McEvoy. England, Pickering and McEvoy, like Newton, had been switched around by Marshall until he found positions in which they blossomed. As a result the media termed the team 'Marshall's Misfits'. Nonetheless, nobody could argue with the effectiveness of Marshall's changes.

The season opened on a low note when Liverpool enjoyed a 2–1 win at Ewood Park. However, from that moment on the Rovers played some exquisite attacking football that not only kept the fans entertained, but also won matches. On 7 September 1963, the Rovers served notice of their intentions with the 7–2 demolition of Tottenham Hotspur at Ewood Park. The Tottenham team included a host of star names: Danny Blanchflower, Dave Mackay, John White, Bobby Smith and Jimmy Greaves. However, the Rovers, with Douglas at the heart of everything, simply swept them aside. McEvoy hit four goals as he gave an irresistible display of goal-poaching.

Like Carey a decade earlier, Marshall had found a group of forwards who complemented each other to perfection. Although not as prolific as Carey's men, the Marshall forward line was no less effective. Pickering and McEvoy were the spearhead, with Douglas the playmaker in chief. On the wings, Ferguson was a bundle of extravagant tricks, while Harrison was a traditional speed

(Left) Andy McEvoy (on the ground on the left) scores the first of his four-goal haul against Tottenham Hotspur on 7 September 1963, despite the presence of defenders Maurice Norman and Ron Henry. Goalkeeper Bill Brown lies prostrate on the ground after felling Fred Pickering. (*Copyright: Howard Talbot*)

(Right) Andy McEvoy beats Bill Brown to score Blackburn's sixth goal in the 7–2 rout of Tottenham Hotspur on 7 September 1963. (*Copyright: Howard Talbot*)

(Left) Mike Harrison gets in his shot despite the attentions of George Cohen, Fulham's England international full-back. (*Copyright: Howard Talbot*)

(Right) Fred Else saves at the feet of former teammate Fred Pickering as John Bray covers on the line. Pickering had joined Everton just a couple of weeks before this game was played in March 1964. (*Copyright: Howard Talbot*)

merchant with a thunderous shot. From 9 November 1963 to 26 December 1963 the Rovers dropped only one point in a sequence of eight games. This run reached its peak on Boxing Day, when the Rovers romped to an 8–2 win over West Ham United at Upton Park, with both Pickering and McEvoy able to register hat-tricks. Two days later West Ham journeyed north and enjoyed a surprise 3–1 win at Ewood Park. Inexplicably, the result began a slump in form that would seriously undermine the club's title pretensions.

After the Boxing Day victory there followed a sequence of seven League games in which only one was won. Furthermore, the team was humbled in the FA Cup with a 3–1 defeat at Oxford United. Ironically, the Rovers had also been eliminated from the League Cup at the hands of Notts County, another lower League club. Immediately before the Oxford defeat, Marshall had entered the transfer market to sign Walter Joyce, an experienced utility player who had spent his entire career at Burnley, for a fee of £10,000. However, despite the FA Cup débâcle, Marshall continued to keep faith with his team and was rewarded when the poor sequence of results ended with a 5–0 win at Burnden Park, against Bolton Wanderers, and a 5–2 victory over Leicester City at Ewood Park.

Unfortunately, hopes that a rejuvenated team might maintain their Championship challenge evaporated when Fred Pickering expressed a wish to leave the club. Pickering, on the fringe of the England team, naturally wished to maximise his earning potential while at the height of his career. However, the Ewood directors were reluctant to meet his wage demands and placed him on the transfer list. Everton, one of the title challengers, wasted no time in agreeing an £80,000 deal to take him to Goodison Park.

With the transfer deadline on the horizon, the Rovers moved quickly to snap up George Jones, Bury's 18-year-old England youth international. He was signed in the afternoon of 13 March 1964 and was rushed down to Birmingham to make his debut for the club that night at St Andrews. Although he only arrived seven minutes before the kick-off he enjoyed a dream debut and scored one of the goals that gave the Rovers a precious 2–2 draw.

Following the departure of Pickering, the club's title challenge simply evaporated. A week after the Birmingham game the Rovers hosted Everton at Ewood Park. Without the suspended Roy Vernon, another former Ewood favourite, the Rovers were able to subdue the Everton front line with little difficulty. Pickering was kept quiet by England and it was the Rovers, prompted by Douglas, who looked the more likely to score. Twice the Rovers hit the woodwork before Douglas put them ahead. Against the run of play the visitors equalised, but five minutes from the end the Rovers appeared to have snatched the points when Harrison scored. However, at that moment fate intervened and the goal was wrongly ruled out because of offside. In the last minute the Rovers suffered the cruellest of luck when Derek Temple scored to give the visitors an unlikely victory.

In the eight games that the Rovers played after the departure of Pickering only one was won. Four points from a possible 16 resulted in a final position of seventh in the First Division, respectable by the standards of previous years, but a major disappointment in light of what could have been achieved.

1964-65

After the traumas of the previous campaign the Rovers enjoyed another season that was a mixture of highs and lows. Tenth in the First Division, eliminated from the FA Cup in a thriller of a Cup tie at Ewood Park and humiliated at home in the League Cup – these experiences were accompanied by a continued fall in attendances.

The most worrying aspect for the directors was that the average attendance at Ewood Park dropped from 21,543 to 16,110. Yet Marshall continued to adopt a style of football that was

Burnley's Willie Irvine challenges Fred Else, watched by Mick McGrath, during the 1–1 draw at Turf Moor on 10 October 1964. (*Copyright: Howard Talbot*)

Bryan Douglas beats Adam Blacklaw from the penalty spot to score for the Rovers in the 1–1 draw at Turf Moor on 10 October 1964. (*Copyright: Howard Talbot*)

Manchester
United's Pat Dunne
grabs the ball as
John Byrom closes
in, watched by Bill
Foulkes. The Rovers
slumped to a 5–0
home defeat on 3
April 1965.
(*Copyright: Howard
Talbot*)

designed to entertain. In Douglas and Ferguson he possessed two players who were able to beguile the crowds and bewilder opponents by their outstanding craft and skill. However, the appetite of the public for football in Blackburn had simply evaporated. There was also a fickleness about public support that brought an attendance of 29,363 for the visit of Manchester United, in April 1965, while a few weeks earlier only 8,990 turned up for the visit of West Ham United.

After both the opening matches were lost, the Rovers proceeded to win four of the next five and, once again, thoughts turned toward a Championship challenge. However, although Marshall tried to play the game constructively, with a proper balance between attack and defence, consistency continued to be elusive.

Sandwiched between victories against Sheffield United and Everton in the League was a 5–1 drubbing at home by Workington in the League Cup. The fact that only 6,282 fans bothered to witness the débâcle merely underlined the fragile nature of the club's support. The manner of the defeat against Workington was in sharp contrast to the unfortunate exit from the FA Cup. After a 2–2 draw at Filbert Street, the Rovers and Leicester City produced a thriller of a third-round replay at Ewood Park, which the Rovers were desperately unfortunate to lose by the odd goal in three.

In a bid to find a greater level of consistency, Marshall toyed with the newly adopted 4–2–4 system. For a brief period it produced the defensive solidity that Marshall required but, long before the end of the season, the tactic had been abandoned in favour of the more traditional formation.

With limited income through the turnstiles, the club had little option but to concentrate on the development of young players. A nucleus of youngsters from the north-east made up the reserve team that won the Central League championship for the first time in the club's history. In March 1965, Marshall added a little more experience to his squad when he signed George Sharples from Everton. Sharples, a half-back, had joined Everton as an apprentice in April 1959 and had made his

Mike Harrison
scores from the
penalty spot in
the 3–1 win over
Tottenham
Hotspur on 19
April 1965.
(*Copyright:
Howard Talbot*)

League debut as a 17-year-old in November 1960. However, by the time of his move to Blackburn he had only made 10 senior appearances for the Goodison Park club but had a wealth of Central League experience.

The first half of the campaign had brought 11 wins and 26 points, while the second half produced just five wins and 16 points. As the season drew to a disappointing close, the manager took the opportunity to introduce youngsters Ben Anderson, Billy Wilson, Dick Mulvaney and Rowland Horrey to the first team.

1965-66

This was undoubtedly the worst season in the club's long and illustrious history. The Rovers had endured two previous relegation campaigns, in 1935–36 and 1947–48, and on both occasions there had been sympathy for a famous old club fallen on hard times. However, when a 1–0 home defeat by West Bromwich Albion, on 16 April 1966, condemned the Rovers to the Second Division there

Mike England, the Welsh international centre-half, was successfully switched to centre-forward in a bid to add more punch to the Blackburn attack during 1965–66. (*Copyright: Howard Talbot*)

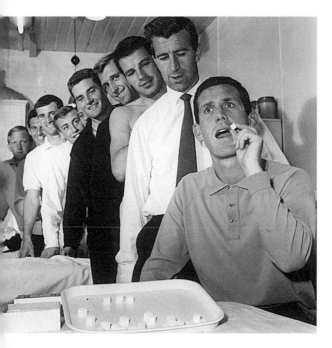

The Blackburn players line up for their sugar lump vaccines during the polio scare. (*Copyright: Howard Talbot*)

was little sympathy among the fans, who jeered the team from the pitch. The fact that there were only 7,637 of them, and the fact that the club still had six games to play, four of which were at home, suggested that the time for sympathy had long since passed.

The season had been an unmitigated disaster from start to finish, and while the team produced a number of deplorable performances, the fact remained that luck had abandoned ship before the voyage began. Having enjoyed a short, but successful, pre-season jaunt to Holland, when Blauw-Wit FC and GVAV Groningen proved useful whipping boys to build up confidence, the Rovers returned to find Blackburn in the grip of a polio epidemic. As a result, opening fixtures had to be postponed and the Rovers found themselves in a catch-up situation from the beginning.

When the season did begin, with an inauspicious 5–2 defeat at Fulham, the Rovers looked a disjointed outfit and lost seven of the opening eight games. To add to their troubles, Bryan Douglas had to sit out the opening games through injury and when he did return, he lasted only five games before he had to undergo the surgeon's knife.

The team's second win of the season, a 4–1 victory at Turf Moor on 9 October 1965, found Mike England switched to centre-forward in a desperate ploy to add some punch to a lacklustre attack. In the short term it proved successful and England, who scored against Burnley, notched seven goals during his 13-game sortie at centre-forward. While his goals were welcome his absence from the defence proved difficult to cover. Dick Mulvaney was asked to fill the vacancy and his inexperience was quickly exploited by the opposition.

The greatest enigma centred round McEvoy and Byrom. The pair had scored 54 League goals between them during 1964–65, but at the end of this relegation campaign the pair could muster a total of only 13 League goals. Yet in six FA Cup ties they managed to equal their League tally. Little wonder that the Ewood faithful found it difficult to accept the slide into the Second Division.

Having been switched to centre-forward, Mike England beats Burnley 'keeper Harry Thompson at Turf Moor on 9 October 1965. (*Copyright: Howard Talbot*)

The fact that the players enjoyed a successful run in the FA Cup made their League form all the more unfathomable. Fans were left to wonder how a team that could beat Arsenal and West Ham United in the FA Cup should struggle to overcome teams of lesser ability in the League. By the time that the Rovers lost their sixth-round tie, at home to Sheffield Wednesday, the question had become largely academic.

Jack Marshall scoured the country for replacements for this battered team but was met with rejection wherever he turned. An ambitious move to sign Terry Hennessey, Birmingham City's Welsh international midfield star, failed and attempts to strengthen the forwards were also doomed to failure. Moves for Allan Gilliver from Huddersfield Town, Colin Bell from Bury and Wyn Davies from Bolton Wanderers all ended in disappointment for the manager. With the transfer deadline on the horizon he managed to sign Martin Britt, West Ham United's former England youth international centre-forward. However, Britt, who had made his debut for West Ham against the Rovers in May 1963, had limited League experience and his acquisition proved little more than a last, ultimately futile attempt, at survival. In truth, Britt was no better than those that the club already possessed, and the reluctance to speculate on a major signing in the end proved fatal.

The Rovers bade farewell to top-flight football with five successive defeats, and three of the final four home games were played before crowds of less than 8,000. The public of Blackburn clearly opted not to witness the last rites of a disastrous and disgraceful campaign. The *Blackburn Times* had carried a headline 'Relegation… or abdication?' – for many the latter seemed a more appropriate epitaph for what they had witnessed.

(Left) Bob Jones collects the ball at the feet of Everton's Fred Pickering as Walter Joyce shadows the former Blackburn centre-forward. Everton won the match 2–1. (*Copyright: Howard Talbot*)

(Right) Martin Britt jumps with Leicester 'keeper Gordon Banks as Bobby Roberts (No.4) covers his goalkeeper. Leicester City won the match 2–0. (*Copyright: Howard Talbot*)

1966-67

Relegation brought several changes to the personnel at Ewood Park. Although the directors continued to keep faith with Jack Marshall, they refused to offer him a new contract. Marshall accepted the decision and continued to work without any long-term security. The summer had brought the departures of Fred Else, John Byrom and Rowland Horrey, while Mike England left on the eve of the season to join Tottenham Hotspur for £95,000. The summer enabled Marshall to capture his long-term target Allan Gilliver from Huddersfield Town. John Barton, Preston's long-serving reserve goalkeeper, arrived to inherit the mantle of Else for £6,000, while £36,000 was spent on Barrie Hole, Cardiff City's Welsh international midfield player. Towards the end of September

John Connelly signs autographs prior to his debut against Ipswich Town on 24 September 1966. He is watched by Barrie Hole, John Barton and Allan Gilliver (behind Connelly). (*Copyright: Howard Talbot*)

John Connelly gets over his cross despite the attentions of Ipswich Town's Bill Baxter. (*Copyright: Howard Talbot*)

the manager spent a further £40,000 on John Connelly, Manchester United's England international winger.

'Back in one season' was the prime objective but, after the club had made the best start to a season since World War Two, a disastrous spell, between mid-September and mid-November 1966, seriously undermined the club's challenge. In the wake of England's World Cup triumph in the summer of 1966, the game had undergone a tactical change. In a bid to strengthen their backroom team the directors opted to appoint Eddie Quigley, the former Ewood favourite, as first-team coach. However, Quigley, who was manager of Stockport County, insisted on the title of assistant manager

with sole responsibility for coaching throughout the club. The directors readily agreed and on the 31 October 1966 he took up his duties at Ewood Park.

By the time Quigley arrived the Rovers had lost the services of Gilliver to a long-standing back problem. He had arrived at Ewood Park with a slipped disc and, following a dispute between the Rovers and Huddersfield, a Football League commission ruled that the Yorkshire club should repay £18,000 to the Rovers. The case also had far-reaching implications for the rest of football as stringent medical examinations became part of transfer procedures.

Eddie Quigley talks to a group of players after his appointment as assistant manager in charge of coaching. From left to right: Mike Ferguson, Ben Anderson (behind Ferguson), Keith Newton, Quigley, Billy Wilson and John Barton. (*Copyright: Howard Talbot*)

Quigley quickly assessed the needs of the team and immediately began to reshape the formation that Marshall had favoured. His first decision was to use the rugged defensive skills of Walter Joyce in midfield rather than at left-back. With Douglas and Hole both operating as attacking midfield players, Quigley added Joyce to the equation to stifle the main playmaker of the opposition. In the centre of a four-man defence, the Rovers used the vastly experienced Ronnie Clayton with the more youthful Mulvaney. However, when an ear infection ruled Mulvaney out, both Dave Holt and Ben Anderson had been tried as Clayton's partner without much success. Finally, George Sharples, who had lost his place to Hole, was drafted in to play alongside Clayton. Despite a lack of aerial presence, the partnership worked well and combined with Keith Newton and Billy Wilson at full-back, the two formed a solid back line.

However, without Gilliver, the attack remained depressingly impotent. In a bid to solve the problem the Rovers paid £10,000 to Stockport County to sign Frank Lord, a veteran centre-forward in the style of Briggs and Johnston. In a lower division, Quigley had been able to rely on Lord's physical and aerial strength; however, in the Second Division he appeared slow and cumbersome and after one goal, in 10 games, he was axed in favour of the more mobile Malcolm Darling.

While Quigley took control of the coaching, it was Marshall who bore the brunt of the dissatisfaction of the supporters. Disenchanted with the situation in which he found himself he tendered his resignation and left Ewood Park on 10 February 1967. The directors immediately installed Quigley as caretaker manager.

Quigley's tactical changes took the club into the thick of the promotion race. On Easter Saturday the Rovers faced a crucial clash with Coventry City at Ewood Park. Unfortunately, Mike Ferguson became embroiled in a clash with City's Dietmar Bruck and was sent off before half-time. Then, five minutes into the second half, Barton failed to gather a cross and Bobby Gould gratefully accepted the chance to score what proved to be the winning goal. It was the first League goal that the Rovers had conceded at Ewood Park since 5 November 1966, but it was sufficient to end the club's hopes of promotion. However, the truth of the matter was that too many points had been squandered earlier in the season, which meant that any slip-up in the final stages would prove fatal.

Impressed with the way in which Quigley had galvanised his limited resources, the directors appointed him as the club's manager on 19 April 1967.

1967-68

Long before the season ended the quest for promotion had stalled and a sense of bitter disappointment filled the air at Ewood Park. Until mid-January 1968, there had appeared to be a genuine belief that promotion was not beyond the Rovers. However, when their promotion

(Left) John Connelly opened the scoring in the 2–0 win over Bristol City at Ewood Park on 9 September 1967. City 'keeper Mike Gibson is grounded as the defenders, Jacobs (No.2) and Tainton, are unable prevent the ball entering the net. (*Copyright: Howard Talbot*)

(Right) Mike Ferguson sends Bristol City 'keeper Mike Gibson the wrong way to clinch a 2–0 win over City at Ewood Park on 9 September 1967. (*Copyright: Howard Talbot*)

credentials were seriously tested, during January and February, the team was found wanting. Both the quality of their football and team spirit disintegrated at the most crucial point of the season. In a division where mediocrity reigned supreme, the failure was all the more painful.

The summer of 1967 had solved two problems that Quigley believed had blighted the previous campaign. Adam Blacklaw, Burnley's vastly experienced Scottish international goalkeeper, was signed to replace Barton, while John Coddington, Huddersfield's long-serving captain, was signed to partner Clayton in the centre of defence. However, the troublesome need for a goalscorer remained unanswered. Quigley had moved for two players in the summer but failed to land either. Huddersfield's Tony Leighton rejected a move to Ewood Park because he was reluctant to move house to be closer to Blackburn. Throughout the summer speculation grew that Fred Pickering would return to Ewood Park. The Rovers engaged in negotiations to sign their former protégé before a dramatic change of heart resulted in their bid being withdrawn and the player joining Birmingham City.

The season began with Ben Anderson, a reserve defender, in the number nine shirt. It was a solution that brought three goals in as many games for the Scottish youngster before the experiment withered and Allan Gilliver returned from his long-term injury. Ultimately, the lack of a genuine goalscorer proved too much of a handicap. Goals became a rarity and of the 16 League wins that the team enjoyed, no fewer than nine were won by a single-goal margin. Indeed, the only time the team sparked in front of goal was at Deepdale in November 1967, when five goals were put past Preston North End.

Jim Herriott, Birmingham City's 'keeper, catches the ball under pressure from Allan Gilliver. (*Copyright: Howard Talbot*)

In view of the lack of entertainment, the decision of Quigley to dispense with the services of Bryan Douglas at first-team level proved highly contentious. While the former England international had struggled with injury, and was coming to the end of his career, the fact remained that the club possessed no obvious replacement.

As the season drew to a close, too many of the senior players struggled to find their form. Even the acquisition of Don Martin, a talented forward from Northampton Town, failed to produce little more than the briefest of rivals. Indeed, signed as a centre-forward, Martin looked happier as a maker of chances rather than a prolific goalscorer.

1968-69

(Left) John Connelly stabs the ball narrowly wide during the opening day encounter with Derby County at Ewood Park. (*Copyright: Howard Talbot*)

(Right) Barrie Hole, the Rovers' Welsh international midfielder, was sold to Aston Villa for £60,000 in September 1968. (*Copyright: Howard Talbot*)

A reported loss of £84,723 hung over the club like the sword of Damocles. The directors hurriedly refuted suggestions that Keith Newton would be sold to recoup some of the losses. However, before the season began, Mike Ferguson was sold to Aston Villa for £50,000 and Ben Anderson joined Bury for £10,000. In September 1968, the club reaped another £60,000 when Barrie Hole joined Ferguson at Villa Park. The only incoming player was Les Chappell, a journeyman inside-forward, who arrived from Rotherham United in a straight swap for Allan Gilliver.

The season followed a familiar pattern; a good start, top of the League by October, only to be followed by the annual post-Christmas slump. Once again the main failing revolved around a lacklustre attack. Quigley had tried to boost his shot-shy forward line with the acquisition of Jim

Keith Newton beats Kevin Keelan from the penalty spot to score Blackburn's second goal in the 3–0 win over Norwich City at Ewood Park on 26 October 1968. (*Copyright: Howard Talbot*)

Don Martin (No.10) helps out in defence against Cardiff City at Ewood Park on 11 January 1969. Other Blackburn players in the photograph are Ronnie Clayton (No.6), 'keeper Adam Blacklaw and John Coddington. (*Copyright: Howard Talbot*)

Two of the club's greatest servants, Ronnie Clayton (below) and Bryan Douglas (opposite page) bowed out of Ewood Park at the end of the 1968–69 season. (*Copyright: Howard Talbot*)

Fryatt from Stockport County. Fryatt, who cost £25,000, was a popular character in the lower leagues with his balding pate, mutton-chopped whiskers and Mexican-style moustache. He was also a more than useful goalscorer at that level and was renowned for his powerful heading ability. However, against Second Division defences he struggled to make much impact and the Rovers failed to make the most of his aerial power. Ultimately, a return of three goals from 24 League appearances merely conformed that Fryatt looked more impressive as a provider of chances rather than as a sharpshooter.

In January 1969 the directors introduced a two-tier system of management, with Quigley in charge of coaching and team selection while Johnny Carey returned to the club as administrative manager. However, the arrival of Carey did little to improve the club's fortunes on the pitch and just one win from the last 16 League games suggested that, far from being promotion candidates, the Rovers were more likely to be embroiled in a relegation battle the following season. The final six League games were all lost and just 4,777 turned up to watch the last home game.

It was particularly sad that two of the club's legends, Ronnie Clayton and Bryan Douglas, consummate professionals both, should finally bow out of Ewood Park on such a low note.

1969–70

Against the background of a stormy Annual General Meeting, the directors sanctioned a major spending spree. Allan Hunter, Oldham's impressive young centre-back, was joined at Ewood Park by Brian Hill, an orthodox outside-

(Left) Don Martin fires the ball past 'keeper Jim Platt to score the third goal in a 4–0 win over Middlesbrough at Ewood Park on 6 September 1969. (*Copyright: Howard Talbot*)

(Right) Eamonn Rogers is on the spot to score the second goal in the 3–3 draw with Bolton Wanderers at Ewood Park on 22 November 1969. (*Copyright: Howard Talbot*)

left, from Huddersfield Town, and Ken Knighton, Preston's midfield dynamo. The total cost of this trio was approximately £100,000 and the money was spent at a time when the directors faced accusations of running a closed shop. The unsuccessful attempts of a local businessman, Derek Barnes, to win a seat on the board had led to a vitriolic AGM at which the directors had been accused of failing to halt the dramatic decline in the club's fortunes.

The sale of Keith Newton, the England international full-back, to Everton came as a major blow to Blackburn supporters. (*Copyright: Howard Talbot*)

The summer also brought changes to the backroom personnel, when Jimmy Gordon, the first-team trainer, left to join Derby County. Brian Birch, the youth team coach, was promoted to chief coach and worked in tandem with Quigley during a testing pre-season programme. The manager also altered the tactics and chose to operate a 4–3–3 system. Blacklaw, who had not enjoyed the best of seasons the previous year, remained in goal with Newton and Wilson at full-back. Hunter was drafted into the centre of defence to partner Mulvaney. Stuart Metcalfe and the mercurial Eamonn Rogers played either side of Knighton in midfield while Connelly, Martin and Hill formed the front line.

The directors quickly reaped the rewards of their investment when the team climbed to the top of the table in October. However, a 4–0 defeat by Sheffield United at Bramall Lane on 1 November 1969 suggested that the team was still not quite promotion material. Nonetheless, the team responded to the defeat with three successive wins and Christmas found the Rovers in the thick of the promotion battle.

It was at that point that the wheels fell off the promotion bandwagon. On 15 December 1969 the club finally parted company with Keith Newton. The England full-back was keen to protect his international place for the forthcoming World Cup in Mexico, and was already on the transfer list when Everton stepped in and signed him for £80,000. Following the sale of Newton the Rovers lost four successive games, including a third-round FA Cup tie at home to Swindon Town. Nor were the defeats marginal – Hull and Portsmouth beat the Rovers 3–0, Middlesbrough 4–1 and Swindon romped to a 4–0 win at Ewood Park. There were mitigating factors for the Swindon defeat as the manager axed Mulvaney and Darling for disciplinary reasons after the pair missed training over the New Year period.

Faced with another fade-out, the directors let it be known that money was available to strengthen the squad. However, moves for Alec Lindsay of Bury and former favourite Barrie Hole came to nothing. Having failed to sign an attacking midfielder, the Rovers ultimately spent £30,000 to sign Roger Jones, Bournemouth & Boscombe Athletic's England Under–23 goalkeeper. The

Jim Fryatt climbs above a Pompey defender to head the ball narrowly wide during the 3–0 home defeat by Portsmouth on 27 December 1969. John Coddington (No.4) is the other Blackburn player involved in the action. (*Copyright: Howard Talbot*)

signing raised eyebrows on the Ewood terraces, as few believed a goalkeeper was the number one priority. Sadly, in the short term, the move backfired on the Rovers when Jones received a serious groin injury and was ruled out until the last day of the season after just four appearances.

The decline after Christmas was truly alarming, with just 14 points taken from 18 League games. Fortunately, the early season form meant that the Rovers ended the campaign in eighth position. Ultimately, the lack of a goalscorer proved the club's undoing, with too much being expected of Martin.

The former Northampton man was easily the top scorer with 13 goals, but all too often he was left to fight for scraps around the opposition area. However, Quigley had little room for manoeuvre, particularly after he had allowed Jim Fryatt to join Oldham Athletic in February 1970. The following month John Coddington left Ewood to join Stockport County, where he had spent a spell on loan, and Quigley signed their utility player Freddie Goodwin to operate in midfield for the Rovers.

As the season drew to a close Quigley blooded several young players – Terry Eccles, Mick Wood, Jeff Whalley and Ray Charter – but it merely underlined the limited number of experienced back-up players the manager had at his disposal. Indeed, once Coddington and Fryatt had left he had no option but to throw untried youngsters into the team as another season quietly faded away.

Jimmy Kerr was said to be the club's record signing when he was transferred from Bury in May 1970. However, after just 11 appearances for the club his career was ended by injury. (*Copyright: Howard Talbot*)

1970-71

The omens for the Rovers appeared bad from the very outset of what was to prove to be an ill-fated campaign. The summer had produced a somewhat puzzling transfer strategy. A record fee of £60,000 was reputedly spent on Bury's talented midfielder Jimmy Kerr. Although Bury sources placed the sum at nearer £40,000, the fact remained that it was a sizeable sum in view of the club's financial difficulties. However, having placed 'all his eggs in one basket', Quigley was then forced to wheel and deal to bring in other new faces. Bryan Conlon, a tall, craggy centre-forward, arrived from Norwich City in exchange for Malcolm Darling. Another exchange deal took Laurie Calloway to Southport in exchange for Alex Russell, a workmanlike midfielder who been at Haig Avenue since 1963.

The club received another blow on the eve of the season when Brian Birch, the first-team coach, accepted an offer to be head coach at Galatasaray in Turkey. This led to the hurried promotion of Ken Waterhouse to the post of senior trainer-coach while, Arthur Proudler, who had been released from Everton's coaching staff, took control of the Central League team.

As the Rovers prepared for the new campaign they had Eamonn Rogers on the transfer list while Dick Mulvaney, having had a transfer request refused, had taken his plight to the Football League. Thus, it was amid a background of unrest that the season got underway. However, things went from bad to worse when Don Martin suffered a broken ankle at Hillsborough in only the third match of the campaign.

The first win of the season didn't come until the fifth game, a 1–0 victory over Swindon Town. The goal was scored by Conlon, his first for the club, and, in the absence of Martin, Quigley gave a debut to another young striker – Tony Parkes ,who had been signed from Buxton in May 1970.

Unfortunately, it was to be the last victory that the team enjoyed until Norwich City were beaten at Ewood Park on 24 October 1970. By this time the club was in dire straits. An independent Football League tribunal had ordered the Rovers to sell Dick Mulvaney and the defender, despite being the first choice centre-half, was placed on the transfer list with a £50,000 fee on his head. In view of the difficult financial situation the directors readily accepted an £80,000 bid from

Tony Parkes, making his first-team debut, congratulates Bryan Conlon (No.10) on scoring against Swindon Town on 5 September 1970. This was Conlon's first goal for the club following his transfer from Norwich City in the summer. (*Copyright: Howard Talbot*)

Birmingham City for Ken Knighton. However, the deal collapsed when the player rejected the opportunity to move to St Andrew's.

Two days before the Norwich game the directors decided to make a change at managerial level. Johnny Carey was asked to take charge of team affairs, while Quigley was put in charge of scouting and the club's young players. While Carey and the directors talked about a mutually beneficial

arrangement, the former manager kept his own counsel and declined to comment. Quigley had come under fierce criticism from the supporters for his defensive approach to the game. Although he favoured 4–2–4 at Ewood Park, he usually adopted a 4–3–3 or 4–4–2 system away from home with the intention of gaining a point.

The Norwich win was followed by five successive defeats and by Christmas the situation had become critical. Jimmy Kerr had been stricken by a serious knee injury after just 11 appearances, an injury that was sufficiently serious to end his career. The Football League tribunal had intervened and reduced the fee for Mulvaney to £30,000, while Ken Waterhouse resigned as trainer-coach to return to management at Morecambe. Carey promoted Proudler to first-team coach but consistency and, more importantly, victories continued to be elusive.

Bill Dunning, a former youth team player at Ewood Park, is watched by other apprentices David Bradford, Chris Rossindale and Dennis Sneath, as he packs his boots for a first-team game. (*Copyright: Howard Talbot*)

In January 1971, William Bancroft, at 39, became the youngest chairman in the club's history. He inherited an appalling situation with the financial plight every bit as serious as the one the team faced on the pitch. In March 1971, he had no choice but to sanction the sale of Knighton to Hull City for £60,000. Of this, only £10,000 was made available to Carey to strengthen his squad. Sadly, the money that remained was earmarked

Fred Pickering fires a shot towards the Cardiff City goal during a 1–1 draw at Ewood Park on 13 March 1971. This was Pickering's first game following his return to the club but a return of two goals in 11 appearances proved insufficient to avoid relegation. (*Copyright: Howard Talbot*)

for the club's survival through the summer. A further blow came when the Football League reduced the fee for Dick Mulvaney to £10,000.

In a last throw of the dice the Rovers finally signed former favourite Fred Pickering. While the return of the prodigal son had long been championed by supporters, the player who arrived from Blackpool bore little resemblance to the buccaneering, free-scoring centre-forward of old. Plagued by injury and weight problems, Pickering could do little to alter the club's destiny.

On 27 April 1971, the Rovers suffered a 2–1 defeat at Queen's Park Rangers and, as a result, lost their Second Division status. On 1 May 1971, a crowd of 3,971 gathered at Ewood Park to witness the last rites as the Rovers played out a 2–2 draw with Bristol City.

1971-72

In the wake of relegation the club's balance deficit stood at an alarming £81,604. In a bid to cut the wage bill, the Rovers released a number of players, including Alex Russell, Brian Hill, Ray Charter and George Sharples. Furthermore, the Mulvaney saga finally came to an end when the player, whom the Rovers had rated at £50,000, joined Oldham Athletic on a free transfer after the intervention of a Football League tribunal. The directors also took the decision to dispense with the services of both Johnny Carey and Eddie Quigley. William Bancroft indicated that the club would revert to a single manager and that that man would be 'a younger man with a more forthright approach and more modern ideas'.

In mid-July 1971, after much speculation, the Rovers appointed Watford's Ken Furphy as the new manager at Ewood Park. An FA coach, Furphy axed Arthur Proudler within a week of his appointment and announced his intention to take control of coaching while Richard Dinnis was put in charge of the reserve team and Jimmy Kerr was given the juniors to look after. However, the latter soon left the club in a bid to resurrect his playing career in South Africa.

The manager sprung a surprise, on the opening day of the season, with the inclusion of Gerry McDonald and David Bradford, two of the club's juniors, in the first team. A 2–1 win over Rotherham United, with McDonald getting on the scoresheet, was followed by victory over Workington in the Football League Cup. However, these victories merely glossed over the deficiencies in the team that were all too apparent.

By early September 1971, the team had lost three of their opening five League games and Lincoln City knocked the club out of the Football League Cup. As result, Furphy decided on drastic action and within the space of two months he virtually rebuilt his team. It began with the departure of Allan Hunter, who was sold to Ipswich Town for £60,000 plus Bobby Bell, who was valued at £20,000, in part exchange. Two weeks later Furphy increased his transfer fund by selling Bell, who had made two appearances for the club, to Crystal Palace for £50,000. A further £20,000 was raised when Furphy allowed Graham Moseley, the youth-team goalkeeper, to join Derby County on his 18th birthday for £20,000.

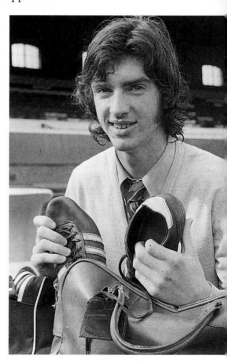

Liverpool's Chris Lawler heads the ball clear under challenge from Terry Eccles in this pre-season friendly. (*Copyright: Howard Talbot*)

New players then arrived in quick succession as the manager rebuilt his team. Terry Garbutt, a powerful midfielder, was signed from Watford for £16,000 while Terry Shanahan, a quick-running forward, was taken on a month's loan from Ipswich Town. A fee of £3,000 secured Johnny Price, a right-winger from Stockport County. Furphy had to pay £15,000 to sign Ben Arentoft, Newcastle United's Danish international midfielder. The manager brought in two new full-backs in Mick Heaton, a £7,000 signing from Sheffield United, and Gerry Farrell, who had been freed by Wolverhampton Wanderers. Furphy had to part with £17,500 and Freddie Goodwin to capture Tony Field, Southport's free-scoring forward. The manager also traded Eamonn Rogers to Charlton Athletic for a small fee and the more robust talents of Barry Endean.

The constant chopping and changing failed to halt the slide in terms of results and the club slipped out the FA Cup, against Port Vale, in the first round. With the Rovers anchored uncomfortably in the lower reaches of the Third Division, Furphy made his key acquisition when he signed John McNamee from Newcastle United. In truth, the former Celtic and Hibernian centre-half was playing on borrowed time. He appeared an unlikely saviour, for a combination of injuries and age had clearly taken their toil on this rugged Scot. However, his steely presence was undeniable and he immediately brought an authority and organisation to the defence. McNamee was a

Graham Moseley was sold to Brian Clough's Derby County for £20,000. Moseley, who had just celebrated his 18th birthday, had yet to appear in the first team at Ewood Park. (*Copyright: Howard Talbot*)

defender of the old school who relished physical battles with opposition forwards. He provided protection for Roger Jones and tutored Derek Fazackerley in the art of defending. In return the young defender used his willing legs to cover the immobility of his more experienced colleague.

With Field in prolific form in attack and the new-found confidence of the defence, the Rovers slowly began to climb the table. At the same time the manager was able to

John McNamee arrives from Newcastle United in November 1971 to shore up the Blackburn defence and lift the club from the bottom of the Third Division. (*Copyright: Howard Talbot*)

Bryan Conlon is unable to get to the ball as Oldham Athletic goalkeeper Harry Dowd watches anxiously. The meeting with Oldham Athletic at Ewood Park ended in a 1–0 defeat for the Rovers. (*Copyright: Howard Talbot*)

reduce the wage bill by allowing the likes of Bryan Conlon, Dewi Atherton, Billy Wilson, Frank Kopel and Fred Pickering to move on. Ultimately, in view of the dreadful start, a 10th-place finish was a highly satisfactory conclusion to the season. Furthermore, the club had also produced a profit of £34,959, the first profit that the Rovers had recorded for several years.

1972-73

A tour of Czechoslovakia in May 1972 enabled Furphy to continue to experiment with the players at his disposal. Ben Arentoft, who had struggled to make much impression in the battleground that was Third Division midfield football, was successfully converted into a left-back. In attack, Barry Endean, who had endured a difficult time at the Rovers due to illness and injury, rediscovered his goalscoring touch.

During the close season Charlie Woods, a former Watford player, was appointed coach to the revived 'A' team. However, Furphy also registered him as a player, in case of emergencies. The only new face on the playing staff was Don Hutchins, an orthodox outside-left, who was signed from Plymouth Argyle.

An abysmal run of injuries disrupted the start to the season and forced Furphy to enter the transfer market. Kit Napier, an experienced forward, was signed from Brighton and Hove Albion while Dave Turner, a veteran

(Left) Danish international Ben Arentoft was successfully switched from midfield to left-back and only missed one game during the season. (*Copyright: Howard Talbot*)

(Right) The much-travelled Kit Napier was signed from Brighton and Hove Albion to add a little more guile to the Blackburn attack. (*Copyright: Howard Talbot*)

Ken Furphy welcomes new signing John O'Mara to the club in September 1972. O'Mara cost £30,000 from Brentford but failed to make the expected impact at Ewood Park. (*Copyright: Howard Talbot*)

midfielder, arrived from the Goldstone Ground on a free transfer. A few weeks later more firepower was added to the squad when John O'Mara was signed from Brentford. The 6ft 4in lanky centre-forward had attracted the attention of several First Division clubs and Furphy had to part with £30,000 to secure his signature.

There was no immediate revival and between mid-August and October 1972, the club remained entrenched at the wrong end of the table. However, a 2–2 draw at Swansea, on 21 October 1972,

Barry Endean forces his way into the Wrexham penalty area during the 1–1 draw at Ewood Park on 3 March 1973. (*Copyright: Howard Talbot*)

triggered the start of an unbeaten run of 19 League games. It was the most successful unbeaten run in the club's history and the team soared up the table as a result. There were, however, two blemishes during this sequence. Crewe Alexandra knocked the club out of the FA Cup at Ewood Park and Chesterfield inflicted a home defeat on the club on Boxing Day. However, it transpired that Jim Brown, the Chesterfield goalkeeper, had not been properly registered and the Football League ordered the game to be replayed.

The long unbeaten stretch came to an end at Port Vale, on 10 March 1973, and four days later the Rovers lost the replayed home game with Chesterfield. After victory over Swansea, the Rovers travelled south for two key games against promotion rivals Bournemouth and Charlton Athletic. A heavy defeat against Bournemouth also cost the Rovers the services of McNamee. Fortunately, the players rallied against Charlton and a 2–1 victory kept the promotion hopes alive. The next game brought a crowd of 33,309 to Burnden Park to watch the Rovers beat top-of-the-table Bolton by a single goal. Six points out of the next eight meant that the Rovers travelled to Notts County on Easter Saturday in the knowledge that a victory would take them into second place in the table, with just two games left to play.

With the exception of the injured Napier, the Rovers were at full strength for the trip to Meadow Lane. It was, therefore, all the more ironic that Don Hutchins, the man who replaced Napier, should miss the best scoring opportunity for the Rovers. Ultimately, a miraculous piece of goalkeeping by Roger Jones prevented the home side from scoring but, nonetheless, a goalless draw left the Rovers as outsiders for promotion. County duly gained the points they required and the Rovers ended the season in third place, just two points behind the Nottingham club. A few weeks later it was announced that in future the three leading clubs in divisions two, three and four would be promoted.

1973-74

Three of the first five League games of the new season were lost as the defence began to show an unexpected frailty. The summer had brought the release of McNamee and Furphy had attempted to use the astute footballing brain of Don Martin at the heart of the defence. On 6 October 1973, the manager gave a first-team debut to John Waddington, a former Liverpool apprentice, who had been playing for Darwen since his release from Anfield. Fortunately, Waddington and Fazackerley proved a successful combination at centre-back, and results gradually began to improve.

Six wins and three draws hauled the team up the table and talk, once more, turned to promotion. It was at this point that the club was struck a significant body blow when Ken Furphy accepted the manager's job at Sheffield United. While the chairman, William Bancroft, offered to match the terms that United had offered Furphy, he couldn't overcome the lure of First Division football. Nor could he overcome the fact that Ewood's limited resources had eventually frustrated Furphy's ambitions. The directors asked Richard Dinnis to take charge on a temporary basis and the team responded with a victory at Rochdale, in the first match after Furphy's departure.

John O'Mara in training. The expensive centre-forward proved a major disappointment and the club released him on a free transfer at the end of the season. (Copyright: Howard Talbot)

However, despite the best efforts of Dinnis, the team struggled for consistency and vital ground was lost in the League, while interest in the FA Cup ended in a 3–0 defeat at Everton. On 14 January 1974, it was announced that the Rovers had appointed Gordon Lee, the Port Vale manager, as the successor to Furphy. Dinnis, who had done an excellent job in difficult circumstances, remained at the club to continue working with the reserve team.

It quickly became apparent that Lee was far from enamoured with the team he had inherited. The promotion challenge began to fade as results continued to fluctuate and only one of the final 11 League games was won as the season drifted to a disappointing conclusion.

During the latter stages of the campaign, Furphy returned to Ewood Park to sign Tony Field and Terry Garbutt, while David Bradford moved to Bramall Lane at the end of the season. However, the club was able to show a handsome profit on the departure of all three players and might well have added to their finances if John O'Mara had accepted a return to Brentford after a £17,500 fee had been agreed.

Long before the end of the season, it had become clear that Lee wished to dismantle Furphy's team and rebuild his own. To this end the directors backed their new manager and took the brave decision to release Ben Arentoft, Kit Napier, John O'Mara and Dave Turner, players who had previously cost the club a total of £60,000.

(Left) Gordon Lee became manager of Blackburn Rovers in January 1974. (*Copyright: Howard Talbot*)

(Right) The decision to sell top goalscorer Tony Field to Sheffield United proved an unpopular one for the fans but the financial needs of the club dictated transfer policy. (*Copyright: Howard Talbot*)

1974–75

Although the club was still overdrawn at the bank to the tune of £130,000, the income that had been generated by Lee enabled him to embark on a rebuilding programme during the summer of 1974. His first signing was Ken Beamish, a big, powerful forward whom Lee rated as possibly the best striker in the Third Division. When Lee paid £25,000 to prise Beamish away from Brighton and Hove Albion, it was the largest fee that he had spent in his entire managerial career up to that point. Another major acquisition was that of Graham Hawkins from Preston North End. Hawkins, who cost £20,000, was a robust centre-half who elected to join the Rovers over Plymouth Argyle, because it meant he would not have to leave his Lytham home or the Preston garage that he owned.

Other summer transfers brought Pat Hilton, a young winger, from Brighton and Hove Albion on a free transfer while Graham Oates, a utility player, joined the Rovers from Bradford City in exchange for Don Hutchins and a small fee. The final arrival was Jimmy Mullen, Rotherham United's outside-left.

The team that Lee had assembled made a flying start to the new campaign with three wins from the opening four matches. With the season barely underway, Lee signed Andy Burgin, from Halifax Town, and immediately installed him at right-back with Mick Heaton swapping over to the left. Roger Jones remained an automatic choice between the posts while John Waddington edged ahead of Derek Fazackerley in the race to partner Hawkins at the centre of defence. In midfield Lee opted

Don Martin scores the second goal for Blackburn Rovers in the 5–2 win over Plymouth Argyle at Ewood Park on 15 February 1975. (*Copyright: Howard Talbot*)

for Stuart Metcalfe, Oates, Tony Parkes and Hilton while Beamish and Don Martin provided the cutting edge in attack.

The team maintained a challenging position from the very outset and the first real blip didn't occur until a 6–3 defeat at Hereford United in December 1974. That result led to the restoration of Fazackerley, in place of Waddington. The versatility of the players enabled Lee to use Oates in attack on occasions while Burgin could operate in midfield. The availability of players like Mick Wood to cover in defence was also a major bonus for Lee.

Injuries disrupted the club's progress at the turn of the year with Heaton being sidelined for a spell and Mullen suffering a broken leg in a 1–0 home defeat by Peterborough United. Three days after the Mullen injury, Plymouth Argyle not only beat the Rovers at Home Park, but also robbed them of the leadership of Division Three. On the bench at Plymouth was Mike Hickman, a utility player whom Lee had signed from Grimsby Town for £10,000, just 24 hours before the injury to Mullen.

After the defeat at Plymouth, Lee included Hickman at centre-forward for next match, which was away at Bury. Having gone behind, the Rovers drew level with a brave diving header from Hickman. A typically nimble piece of footwork by Martin enabled him to slot home the winner and keep the Rovers in second place in the table.

Seven days later the Rovers played hosts to Plymouth Argyle in a top of the table encounter. The West Country team were still ahead of the Rovers in the League and things appeared bleak when

Mike Hickman puts the Rovers into the lead against Plymouth Argyle with the third goal in the 5–2 victory. (*Copyright: Howard Talbot*)

they raced into a two-goal lead in an electrified atmosphere. The Rovers then spurned an opportunity to cut the deficit when Martin failed to score from a penalty. Fortunately, just before half-time, Martin and Oates presented Beamish with the opportunity to reduce the arrears with a neatly headed goal.

The second half brought a complete transformation, with the Rovers gaining the upper hand from the very outset. Metcalfe and Oates created a chance for Beamish to set up Martin for the equalising goal. As the Blackburn attack swarmed all over the Plymouth defence the visitors began to buckle under the pressure. Two minutes after Martin's goal, Hickman pounced on a slip by Green and poked the ball past the advancing Jim Furnell. Then, Beamish was sent through as a static defence appealed in vain for offside. Although Beamish hit his shot straight at Furnell the ball

Stuart Metcalfe scores from the penalty spot against Chesterfield. The 2–0 win ensured that the Rovers clinched promotion from Division Three. (*Copyright: Howard Talbot*)

Ken Beamish and
Gordon Lee
embrace after
promotion is
achieved with the
2–0 win over
Chesterfield.
(*Copyright: Howard
Talbot*)

rebounded to Hickman, who promptly put the ball in the back of the net. Within three minutes the
Rovers had added a fifth when Hickman's angled cross-shot beat Furnell and presented Martin with
the opportunity to tap it over the line. The Blackburn fans, in the 17,818 crowd, were totally ecstatic
as the referee blew for time and signalled the return of the Rovers to the top of the table.

The victory gave the Rovers a fresh impetus and the acquisition of Huddersfield's Bobby Hoy, in
exchange for Barry Endean, gave Lee further attacking options. Promotion was achieved with a 2–0
home win over Chesterfield and a week later the championship was virtually guaranteed when the
Rovers stormed to a 4–1 win at Port Vale. Two days later the title was officially won with a goalless
draw against Wrexham, at Ewood Park, in front of 21,290 jubilant fans.

1975-76

The summer of 1975 ought to have been a time of celebration, but instead the club was thrown into
turmoil. News that the club was £221,000 in the red, coupled with the departure of Gordon Lee to
Newcastle United, quickly dampened the celebratory mood.

Undeterred, William Bancroft managed to persuade Jim Smith to leave Colchester United and,
at 34, become the youngest manager in the club's history. With Richard Dinnis following Lee to St
James' Park, Smith had to recruit his own backroom staff and in due course appointed Norman
Bodell as his assistant and John Pickering as reserve and youth-team coach.

There was no transfer activity during the close season and when the campaign began the Rovers had just one overriding aim – survival. The Rovers enjoyed a good pre-season and qualified for the knock-out stages of the Anglo-Scottish Cup. This was followed by a somewhat flattering start that brought five points from the first three games. The first signs that the team might well encounter difficulties came with elimination from the Football League Cup at the hands of Preston North End. However, reality really began to bite when the Rovers went 11 League matches without a win. During this spell the club was also knocked out of the Anglo-Scottish Cup by Motherwell. It proved to be a baptism of fire for Smith as injuries kept key players out for weeks and, in some cases, months.

For various reasons, Lee's Championship squad began to break up. Injuries forced both Mick Heaton and Andy Burgin into premature retirement, while other players departed for pastures new. Don Martin, coming to the end of his career, returned to Northampton Town, while Mike Hickman left for Torquay United and Pat Hilton moved to Gillingham.

To plug the gaps the manager borrowed Geoff Hutt, a full-back, from Huddersfield Town and Gordon Hindson, a traditional type of winger, from Luton Town. His attempts to make a permanent signing to strengthen the attack were thwarted when Paul Cannell refused to move from Newcastle United after terms between the clubs had been agreed. Fortunately, the manager had better luck when he signed Bobby Svarc, a goalscorer whose capabilities he knew all too well, from Colchester United for £25,000.

William Bancroft had made it clear that the club didn't have the funds to make another major signing and, as a result, both Hutt and Hindson had to return to their clubs at the end of their loan periods. This led to further opportunities being given to Mick Wood, John Kenyon and Bobby Hoy at a time when their futures at the club seemed in doubt.

With the club embroiled in a relegation battle, it proved an inauspicious time to celebrate the club's centenary. The official centenary match took place on 8 November 1975 when Bolton Wanderers visited Ewood Park for a Second Division fixture. The match, which ended 1–1, was played out in front of 24,439 spectators, the largest League attendance at Ewood Park since March 1967.

After being knocked out of the FA Cup by Luton Town in the third round, the manager again turned to the loan system in an attempt to bring an 'older' head into the team. The man he signed was Dave Wagstaffe from Wolverhampton Wanderers. The veteran winger made a huge impression during his initial month at the club but, once again, the manager had to allow him to return to his former club because he hadn't got the funds to sign him.

As the transfer deadline approached, and with the Rovers involved in a grim relegation battle, both Roger Jones and Graham Oates were sold to Newcastle United. The influx of cash allowed

(Left) Bobby Svarc scores against Chelsea only to have his goal ruled out by the referee. Svarc had previously played for manager Jim Smith at Boston United and Colchester United before his £25,000 move to Ewood Park. (*Copyright: Howard Talbot*)

(Right) Neil Wilkinson was drafted into the team following long-term injuries to regular full-backs Mick Heaton and Andy Burgin. Wilkinson appeared in 21 League matches during the course of the season. (*Copyright: Howard Talbot*)

Roger Jones gathers the ball under pressure from the Sunderland attack while loan signing Geoff Hutt (No.3) provides support for his goalkeeper. (*Copyright: Howard Talbot*)

Smith to sign Wagstaffe and also acquire the services of Gordon Taylor, another experienced winger, from Birmingham City. The manager also arranged the loan of Steve Downes from Rotherham United, to cover the loss of Svarc, who had been ruled out since late February with cartilage problems.

A sequence of five wins from six matches, between mid-March and mid-April 1975, ensured Second Division survival. Furthermore, the final stages of the campaign had seen the emergence of a number of talented youngsters like Paul Bradshaw, Kevin Hird and John Bailey, which augured well for the future.

1976-77

The financial situation meant that Smith had to be selective in the recruitment of new players. Bobby Mitchell, a young midfield player, was signed on a free transfer from Sunderland, while another youngster, Andy Needham, came from Birmingham City without a fee. The major signing arrived within a week of the new campaign getting underway when Glenn Keeley, an England Under–23 defender, was signed from Newcastle United for £30,000.

At the start of the season William Bancroft had issued a stark warning that existence in the Second Division was no easy task for a club like the Rovers. Indeed, his words were quickly illustrated when, after an opening-day win over Bolton Wanderers, the Rovers went six games without a win and tumbled out of the Football League Cup at the hands of Stockport County, who were managed by Eddie Quigley. Fortunately, the team rallied and finished the campaign one point and three places better off than 12 months earlier. In truth, apart from those first few weeks, the club was never in any danger of relegation and a mid-table place seemed their destiny throughout the campaign. There were, of course, some rather bleak periods, but there were also sudden spurts of success to maintain the equilibrium and on three occasions the team enjoyed a hat-trick of League wins.

The chief weakness in the team was in the goalscoring department. In September, Smith had gambled on the return of John Byrom, now well into the twilight of his career, to provide the missing spark. Byrom, who had enjoyed 11 years at Bolton Wanderers, found that age was a foe that

(Left) Andy Needham was signed from Birmingham City on a free transfer but failed to make much impact at Ewood Park, with just seven starts and two substitute appearances for the club. (*Copyright: Howard Talbot*)

(Right) Dave Wagstaffe became the first player to receive a red card in domestic football when he was sent off at Orient on 2 October 1976. (*Copyright: Howard Talbot*)

couldn't be mastered. Nonetheless, his five goals earned a win at Wolverhampton and a draw at Blackpool and, perhaps most importantly, a share of the spoils against Burnley at Ewood Park.

With the club heavily in debt, the manager had again to turn to the loan system to fill short-term gaps. Peter Silvester came from Southend United to help out the attack in the autumn, while Blackpool's Terry Alcock was used to prop up the defence over the Christmas and New Year period.

Matters were not helped when the club became embroiled in a dispute with Newcastle United over the Keeley transfer that resulted in a transfer embargo being placed on the club. The dispute arose over an outstanding payment of £15,000 that the Rovers owed to Newcastle as part of the Keeley deal. However, the directors at Ewood had been incensed by the way in which the St James' Park club had handled the payment of the fee for Roger Jones. The deal for Jones had involved a number of payments based on appearances but after just five games, Jones was left out because of injury and Newcastle claimed it was severe enough to refuse any further payments to the Rovers. Faced with the embargo and opposition from the Football League, the Rovers had little choice but to make the outstanding payment for Keeley. Newcastle duly released Jones, on a free transfer, and the former Rovers goalkeeper went on to enjoy a long and successful playing career that lasted until May 1985.

The season also brought notoriety to the club when Dave Wagstaffe was sent off at Brisbane Road in October 1976. When he was dismissed from the field for dissent, he became the first player in the English game to be shown the infamous 'red card', as the red and yellow card system had been introduced at the start of the campaign.

1977–78

Although the Rovers finished fifth in the Second Division, the club's highest standing since 1966–67, there was a feeling of huge disappointment at the season's finale. The failure to clinch promotion, after being in the thick of the battle for so long, was the reason for the discontent.

The financial position meant that little could be done during the summer of 1977 to strengthen

Jack Lewis puts the Millwall defence under pressure in the 2–1 win at Ewood Park on 17 December 1977. (*Copyright: Howard Talbot*)

the team. John Curtis, a full-back from Blackpool, and Noel Brotherston, a young and untried Irish winger from Tottenham Hotspur, were both signed on free transfers. Grimsby Town's Jack Lewis, whom Smith saw as a replacement for the freed John Byrom, spent a week at the club during pre-season training but was forced to return to Grimsby when a deal couldn't be struck. Fortunately, after the opening day of the campaign, terms were agreed and Lewis arrived to lead the forward line in a 0–0 draw with Tottenham Hotspur at Ewood Park.

Until the middle of February the team appeared well set to mount a serious bid for the First Division. The first half of the campaign had produced some excellent football with Kevin Hird and John Bailey used as attacking full-backs. Of course, there were occasional blips – a 4–0 defeat at Colchester United in the Football League Cup being the most obvious. However, there was also a good deal to admire in the flair and style that Smith instilled into his team. A meeting with Southampton, appropriately on 5 November 1977, produced fireworks of a different variety at Ewood Park. The visitors' star-studded line-up was beaten 2–1 in a match that ended with Southampton being reduced to nine men after Peter Osgood and Steve Williams were both sent off.

The season reached its peak during a scintillating first-half display at Turf Moor on Boxing Day. Goals from Dave Wagstaffe, Keith Fear – who was on loan from Bristol City – and Brotherston gave the Rovers a commanding lead at the interval. However, early in the second half, Alan Stevenson produced a wonderful save to prevent Fear from adding to the lead from the penalty spot. It encouraged a spirited fight-back by the Burnley players and the Rovers were glad to hear the final whistle as they clung to a 3–2 lead. The following day the Rovers were held to a 1–1 draw by Sunderland at Ewood Park, and four days later the team was trounced 4–0 at White Hart Lane as the club's First Division credentials came under the closest of scrutinies.

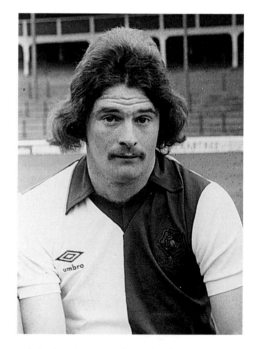

Dave Hargreaves was snapped up from non-League Accrington Stanley but his attempts to break into the senior game were plagued by injury. Hargreaves made senior appearances in February 1978. (*Copyright: Howard Talbot*)

Confidence received a further dent at the beginning of February when Blackpool, who were relegated at the end of the campaign, inflicted a 5–2 defeat on the Rovers just days after Smith's team had been eliminated from the FA Cup by Orient. In a bid to inject new life into the faltering campaign, Smith invested £35,000 in West Ham United's John Radford, the former Arsenal and England centre-forward. He made an immediate impact with a goal on his debut in a 4–2 win over Oldham Athletic, but, ultimately, his inclusion disrupted the intricate attacking football that Smith had developed. In a bid to capitalise upon Radford's aerial power, the team began to play too many long, hopeful balls towards their new centre-forward.

With 12 games left, the Rovers suffered a catastrophic blow when Smith opted to leave Ewood Park to become manager of Birmingham City. In truth, the Rovers had already lost their way in the promotion race, but Smith's departure proved to be the final nail in the coffin. Norman Bodell took

charge until Jim Iley, Barnsley's manager, took control on 15 April 1978. Bodell left for Birmingham as Iley tried to reassure supporters that he would not alter the attacking style of football they had become used to.

'I like the way Rovers play. They play my kind of football and I want to see players going forward,' was Iley's comment on taking charge. A talented midfield player in his day with Tottenham Hotspur, Nottingham Forest and Newcastle United, Iley also pointed out that he felt the team could improve defensively. Certainly that was a view that most supporters would have agreed with as far too many sloppy goals had been given away during the course of the campaign.

John Radford was signed from West Ham United to provide more firepower to the Blackburn attack as the club mounted a serious promotion challenge. (*Copyright: Howard Talbot*)

1978-79

The previous campaign had produced a profit of £110,648, which allowed the club to slash its debts by about a third. It was, therefore, all the more frustrating that the improvement in the financial position should coincide with the club's relegation back to the Third Division.

Iley appointed John Pickering as the new assistant manager and brought in Bobby Kennedy, the old Manchester City defender who had previously been manager at Bradford City, to look after the reserve team. Like Smith and Lee before him, the new manager had a reputation for being able to work with a shoestring budget and the acquisition of John Aston, Martin Fowler and Peter Morris was achieved with little financial expenditure. Aston, a former European Cup-winner with Manchester United, was in the twilight of his career when plucked from the relative obscurity of Mansfield Town. Fowler, an industrious midfielder, had spent his career traversing the divisions with Huddersfield Town, while Morris was an unknown youngster who had been released by Preston North End.

The club parted company with Gordon Taylor, Jack Lewis and Bobby Mitchell during the summer, and in August 1978 controversy surrounded the departure of Dave Wagstaffe to Blackpool. Rightly or wrongly, Iley bore the brunt of the criticism for the loss of the popular winger. In a bid to strengthen his limited attacking options the manager took Dave Gregory on loan from Stoke City with a view to a permanent deal.

The season opened on a note of controversy when Stuart Metcalfe, who had been relegated to the bench by Iley, entered the fray and scored the goal that rescued a point against Crystal Palace at Ewood Park. Away defeats at Preston North End and Notts County in the League were followed by

an ignominious defeat at Exeter City in the Football League Cup. Further misery was heaped on the manager when Gregory rejected the opportunity to join the Rovers and instead opted for Third Division football with Bury.

Criticism of the new regime followed thick and fast as the Rovers hovered in a perilous position in the League. Attempts to stem the tide of disenchantment brought Joe Craig, a Scottish international centre-forward, from Celtic for £40,000 while the veteran midfielder, Alan Birchenall, joined the Rovers from the American club Memphis Rogues. Both players made their debuts in the home defeat by Charlton Athletic and 48 hours later the club was under new management. Iley's tenure at Ewood Park had lasted for just 172 days.

The search for a new manager proved more difficult than usual and, as a result, John Pickering found himself in charge for an extended period. As the team continued to struggle at the foot of the table the directors promoted John Radford to the position of player-coach, in December 1978, in a bid to give Pickering more support.

By February 1979, the club was struggling against relegation and had been knocked out of the FA Cup by Liverpool, albeit after a spirited display at Anfield. Nonetheless, the directors had been impressed with the way in which Pickering had dealt with the situation in which he found himself and appointed him manager on a short-term basis with a contract that ran until the summer. Aware of his lack of experience, the club appointed Jimmy Armfield, the former Bolton Wanderers and Leeds United manager, as 'honorary chief executive'. Ironically, Armfield had been one of the men who had already turned down the opportunity to become the club's manager. The club then

appointed Brian Green, another ex-Leeds United backroom man, as coach, but his stay proved to be only fleeting and, within a week, he had moved on. There were also changes in the boardroom, as William Bancroft stepped down as chairman due to ill health to become vice-president, while Derek Keighley took the helm as the new chairman.

The sale of Kevin Hird to Leeds United for £375,000 enabled Pickering to strengthen his squad prior to the transfer deadline. Mick Rathbone, a full-back from Birmingham City, was signed for £40,000 and a similar amount secured Russell Coughlin, a midfielder from Manchester City. However, the most spectacular move was the one that brought Duncan McKenzie to Ewood Park for a club record fee of £80,000. McKenzie, who was signed from Chelsea, was one of the game's great entertainers and hugely popular on the terraces.

The new arrivals not only reawakened interest in the club but also brought an upturn in results. Of the final 13 games, seven were won and one was drawn but, unfortunately, there was too much leeway to make up. Between 11 November 1978 and 24 March 1979 the team had taken just five points from 16 matches, a sequence which had left them in a desperate position. The club was officially relegated on 25 April 1979 when Newcastle United enjoyed a 3–1 win at Ewood Park. At that stage there were still four games left to be played. Ironically, with no pressure on them, the Rovers won three of those games.

The final match brought a 2–1 win over Fulham at Ewood Park in front of 4,684 hardy souls. The supporters invaded the pitch at the end of the match and in a scene of high emotion, continually chanted their support for Pickering. However, the directors had opted for a different strategy and on 15 May 1979 it was announced that Pickering's contract would not be renewed.

Dave Wagstaffe returned to the Rovers in March 1979 but injury restricted him to just two appearances. (*Copyright: Anne Barry*)

1979–80

In June 1979, the club appointed its first player-manager when Howard Kendall took the helm at Ewood Park. The former Stoke City player-coach had gained a wealth of experience during a playing career that had begun at Preston North End and then taken him to Everton and

Howard Kendall became the club's new player-manager during the summer of 1979. (*Copyright: Howard Talbot*)

Birmingham City. However, he had no managerial experience, although he had helped Stoke to win promotion to the First Division during 1978–79.

Kendall arrived at Ewood Park to find morale low. Matters were not helped when he had to oversee the sale of John Bailey to Everton for £300,000. Kendall asked Richard Dinnis, whom Pickering had appointed, to continue as first-team coach, with Mick Heaton in charge of the reserves. However, on the playing front the manager had little room for manoeuvre. Two goalkeepers, Neil Ramsbottom and Mark Shipley, had both been released and to fill the void Kendall signed Jim Arnold from Stafford Rangers. Although he had just celebrated his 29th birthday, Arnold, a former England semi-professional international, had yet to appear in the Football League. Another new arrival, Stuart Parker, was a much-travelled centre-forward who joined the Rovers after a short stint in Holland with Sparta Rotterdam.

The first 10 League games produced just one win, while Nottingham Forest brought an abrupt end to interest in the Football League Cup. By the end of October the club occupied a relegation place in the Third Division. It was at this juncture that Kendall made changes to both the coaching and playing personnel. The club parted company with Richard Dinnis, although the manager was quick to point out that the parting was not connected with the disappointing run of results. Mick Heaton was promoted to first-team coach, while Tony Parkes was asked to combine playing with the first team with looking after the second team.

Kendall also made two further signings when Andy Crawford, a young striker, from Derby County arrived for £50,000, while Jim Branagan, a tough-tackling full-back, joined from Huddersfield Town. At the time of their transfer, both players were languishing in the reserve teams of their respective clubs.

Initially, the team slowly clawed its way from the bottom of the table while progress was made in the early rounds of the FA Cup. The season's watershed came with a 2–1 win at Grimsby Town on 12 January 1980, as this began a sequence of 15 games of which 14 were won and one was drawn. Thus, between mid-January and early April 1980 the team dropped just one point out of a possible 30 and leapfrogged into the promotion race. At the same time the club enjoyed a profitable run in the FA Cup that saw Coventry City, of the First Division, beaten at Ewood Park in the fourth round. The Rovers then went on to hold Aston Villa at home before bowing out at Villa Park by the narrowest of margins, 1–0, after a titanic battle.

Duncan McKenzie holds the ball as Brentford's Steve Perryman contemplates a challenge during the Rovers' 3–1 victory on 1 March 1980. (*Copyright: Howard Talbot*).

The team that Kendall built was founded on a rocklike defence. Arnold proved to be an outstanding goalkeeper, while Jim Branagan, Glenn Keeley, Derek Fazackerley and Mick Rathbone developed into a tight defensive unit. In midfield,

(Above) Simon Garner outpaces a Reading defender during the 3–1 win at Ewood Park on 19 April 1980. (*Copyright: Howard Talbot*)

(Left) Andy Crawford was signed from Derby County in October 1979 and ended the season as the top goalscorer with 23 League and Cup goals. (*Copyright: Howard Talbot*)

Kendall himself provided the inspiration, while Tony Parkes worked tirelessly to plug gaps and make forward runs. Noel Brotherston proved a constant threat from his berth on the right wing, while Duncan McKenzie was given a roving role that enabled him to exploit his talents to the full. Like Wagstaffe before him, McKenzie enjoyed a glorious 'Indian summer' to his career as he merrily destroyed Third Division defences. In attack the manager had initially partnered Joe Craig and Crawford, before opting to use Simon Garner and Crawford as his twin spearhead. Ironically, the manager had tried to raise funds earlier in the season by allowing Garner to join Halifax Town. Fortunately, the player declined the opportunity of a move to Yorkshire.

Two defeats in April, against Exeter City and, more importantly, against fellow promotion rivals Sheffield Wednesday, proved nothing more than a hiccup. The Rovers clinched promotion in the penultimate game of the season with a 2–1 victory over relegation threatened Bury. It was celebrated by a large contingent of Blackburn supporters who had made the short trip to Gigg Lane. A few days later Bury visited Ewood Park in the final game and clinched a 2–1 win but, sadly, this proved insufficient to save them from relegation. The Rovers finished the season in second place, just three points behind Grimsby Town, who lifted the Third Division championship.

1980–81

The summer of 1980 brought only minor changes to the Ewood Park squad as Kendall prepared to consolidate the club's position in the Second Division. A fee of £40,000 was spent on Mickey Speight, Sheffield United's former England 'B' international midfield player. Jimmy Hall, an inexperienced midfielder, was signed from Blackpool on a free transfer. At the other end of the scale the Rovers signed Roger De Vries, Hull City's experienced left-back, who had made some 318

Mick Speight was signed from Sheffield United to strengthen the midfield. (*Copyright: Anne Barry*)

League appearances for his former club. The summer also enabled both Mick Heaton and Tony Parkes to gain FA coaching qualifications at Lilleshall.

If consolidation was the aim, then the Rovers more than achieved their target. On the last day of the season only goal difference prevented a return to the First Division. However, within days of missing out on promotion the club lost the architect of this success when Howard Kendall accepted the manager's position at Goodison Park.

Ultimately, it was a lack of goals that prevented the Rovers from reaching the top flight. Only 42 goals were scored in 42 League games and, while it proved sufficient to keep the club in the promotion race, it was the Achilles' heel that Kendall couldn't overcome.

The club had been rocked by a transfer request from Andy Crawford early on and his traumas off the field, combined with injuries, meant that he played just a dozen games for the club. In November 1980, the manager had tried to remedy the problem with the acquisition of John Lowey from Sheffield Wednesday. However, the former Manchester United apprentice, who had previously appeared for the Rovers' Central League team, managed just two goals in 19 League games. Indeed, he looked happier as a provider of chances than as a goalscorer. Unfortunately, Duncan McKenzie struggled to find his best form and, with financial clouds gathering on the horizon, he was allowed to cross the Atlantic to join Tulsa Roughnecks. Viv Busby, the former Sunderland and Fulham striker, made the trip in the opposite direction to add some experience to the Blackburn attack. However, once again the move was not a success in terms of goals, with Busby netting just once in eight appearances.

Duncan McKenzie on the ball during the Rovers' 2–1 win at Cardiff City on the opening day of the season. (*Copyright: Anne Barry*)

With limited financial resources at his disposal, Kendall was hit by devastating injury blows to Tony Parkes and Noel Brotherston. Parkes suffered a broken leg that would end his career, while Brotherston's injury, which came just two days after the transfer deadline had elapsed, ruled him out for the rest of the campaign.

During the final stages of the season the lack of goals resulted in too many drawn games. Three successive goalless draws in April proved disastrous for the club's promotion hopes. On the final

Howard Kendall blasts a shot towards the Swansea City goal during the 0–0 draw at Ewood Park on 1 November 1980. (*Copyright: Howard Talbot*)

Kevin Stonehouse beats Swansea City goalkeeper David Stewart to the ball during a 0–0 draw at Ewood Park. (*Copyright: Howard Talbot*)

Tony Parkes suffered a badly broken leg against Wrexham on 21 February 1981. The midfield dynamo had scored 46 goals in 409 senior appearances for the club. He went on to become a prominent member of the management team at Ewood Park until October 2004. (*Copyright: Howard Talbot*)

day of the season the Rovers enjoyed their first victory over Bristol Rovers at the Eastville Stadium for well over 20 years. Unfortunately, it was not enough to clinch promotion as a victory for Swansea, at Preston, ensured that it was the Welsh club that accompanied Notts County and West Ham United into the top division.

Six days after the season ended it was announced that Kendall, who earlier in the season had rejected the chance to become manager of Crystal Palace, had accepted the manager's position at Everton. There was simply no way that the Rovers, with all their financial problems, could compete with the lure of Kendall's former club. The manager also took Mick Heaton with him to work as his assistant at Goodison Park.

1981–82

After two successful seasons it would be a difficult task for Kendall's successor to maintain the momentum that had built up at Ewood Park. The man who was given this unenviable task was Bobby Saxton, the manager of Plymouth Argyle. The new manager readily accepted that to many supporters a fifth-place finish would be deemed as unacceptable. Saxton quickly settled into his new environment by making sure he was surrounded by familiar faces. A number of his former backroom staff at Home Park followed him to Lancashire. Jim Furnell, the former Plymouth goalkeeper, was handed responsibility for the reserve team, while Tony Long replaced Jack Cunningham as physiotherapist. Eddie Quigley was ousted as chief scout and replaced by Harold Jarman, but Tony Parkes, who had retired from playing, was promoted to first-team coach.

Saxton also had to make changes on the field. Kendall returned to Ewood Park to sign Jim Arnold for £200,000 – a fee that enabled the Rovers to make a handsome profit on a player who had been signed for £25,000 just two years earlier. Saxton spent £60,000 on Southampton's Terry Gennoe to fill the gap left by Arnold. A similar sum was spent on Ian Miller, a speedy outside-right from Swindon Town. In November the manager paid another hefty fee to sign Norman Bell from Wolves.

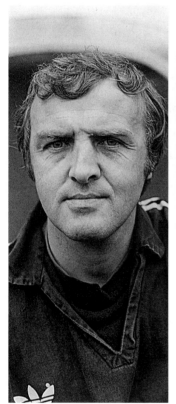

(Left:) Bob Saxton, the Plymouth Argryle manager, was the man appointed to succeed Howard Kendall at the helm at Ewood Park. (*Copyright: Howard Talbot*)

(Left) Norman Bell joined the Rovers from Wolverhampton Wanderers in November 1981. (*Copyright: Howard Talbot*)

(Right) Goalkeeper Mike Salmon made his only senior appearance for the club in the final home game of the season, a 1–1 draw with Chelsea. (*Copyright: Howard Talbot*)

With a new manager at the helm there was always going to be a period of readjustment but, against all expectations, Saxton managed to keep the club in the promotion hunt until the final two months of the season. After a 2–0 win over Grimsby Town, on 13 March 1982, the Rovers found themselves in third position in the Second Division. Unfortunately, the team was not quite good enough to claim a place in the top flight after an absence of 16 years.

Although Kendall the manager had been suitably replaced, the club had failed to replace Kendall the midfield dynamo. During the middle of the campaign, Saxton had been able to use the loan system to boost his midfield strength. However, once Kevin Arnott was re-called by Sunderland, after a four-month loan period, the midfield looked sterile and barren of creativity. Matters had also been further complicated when Mickey Speight became embroiled in a protracted pay dispute and appeared in just 13 League games.

For a second successive season April proved to be the month that tested the club's promotion credentials to the full and found them wanting. Only one point was taken and only one goal was scored during the five matches that were played during that month. The following month brought more goals but just four points out of 12.

Under a new manager a period of transition had always been a possibility: now it became a reality. However, once again, finances or, more accurately, the lack of them had cast a cloud over Ewood Park as the season came to its disappointing conclusion.

1982-83

In comparison with the previous three seasons, 1982–83 proved to be mundane in the extreme. The club became becalmed in mid-table and, as a result, the average home attendance dropped to 7,069 – the lowest average since the turn of the century. It was, therefore, not surprising that the financial constraints placed upon the manager restricted his options with regard to strengthening his squad.

During the summer of 1982 he had tried to solve his midfield problems by investing £40,000 in

Noel Brotherston spent the summer of 1982 in Spain with the Northern Ireland World Cup squad. (*Copyright: Howard Talbot*)

Plymouth Argyle's Colin Randell. A former Welsh Under-23 international, Randell had already clocked up 327 League appearances before arriving at Ewood Park. Although not the quickest of players, Randell had a reputation for being able to read the game and was noted for his passing ability. These were exactly the type of qualities that Arnott had brought to the team the previous season but, unfortunately, although Sunderland had made the player available, he was beyond the price range of the Rovers. The only other new face that Saxton added to his squad was Vince O'Keefe, who arrived from Torquay United to act as backup to Terry Gennoe.

The season began in disastrous fashion for the Rovers with four defeats in the opening five games. However, a steady improvement during November and December 1983 lifted the club to the mid-table spot that they occupied throughout the campaign. In view of the difficult financial position the manager did well to guide the team to a final position of 11th in the Second Division.

Interest in the FA Cup ended at the first hurdle when Liverpool enjoyed a fairly routine win at Ewood Park. There was only the briefest of flirtations with the Football League Cup as the Rovers fell to Brentford, over two legs, at the second-round stage.

The manager was further handicapped when a contract dispute robbed him of the services of Glenn Keeley for much of the season. Indeed, at one point Keeley was loaned to Everton, in November 1982, and made his debut in a Merseyside derby at Goodison Park. However, a professional foul resulted in his dismissal after 30 minutes and he returned to Ewood Park. Earlier in the season, Saxton had tried to fill the void by arranging the loan of David Barton from Newcastle United. He appeared in the opening half-dozen games of the season before being sent off at Grimsby. After a two-match suspension, Barton returned for a couple of games but badly twisted his knee against Chelsea, when his studs caught in the turf. Following the injury he returned to St James' Park and Saxton promoted David Mail, an untried youngster he had signed from Aston Villa, in January 1982, on a free transfer. Mail seized his opportunity and made the number five shirt his own until he was switched to right-back to allow for Keeley's return for the last half-dozen League games. The emergence of Mail was one of the few pluses that the manager could take out of the season.

Unfortunately, Randell failed to make much of an impact and Saxton again brought Arnott to the club on loan. However, this time he was borrowed from Sheffield United, the club he had joined in the summer from Sunderland. Sadly, he struggled to maintain the same level of performance as

(Left) Norman Bell rises above Bolton's Mike Doyle during the 1–1 draw at Ewood Park on 20 November 1982. (Copyright: Howard Talbot)

(Right) Glenn Keeley joined Everton on loan in October 1982 but, sadly, was sent off on his debut in the Merseyside derby. He returned to Ewood Park and continued to give excellent service to the Rovers. Always a popular character with the fans, Keeley appeared in 370 League games for the Rovers. (Copyright: Howard Talbot)

he had done during his previous spell at the club. Indeed, inconsistency blighted the performances of many of the players during what was a fairly mediocre season.

1983–84

Although the Rovers continually threatened to become involved in the promotion race, the truth was that it was more a flirtation than a serious challenge. Nonetheless, in view of the dire financial situation and the continuous list of injuries and illnesses to key personnel, a sixth-place finish was a remarkable achievement. Once again the manager had been forced to make do with very little in terms of transfer funds. In the summer he snapped up Chris Thompson, a centre-forward, from Bolton Wanderers, while November brought David Glenn, a young full-back, from Wigan Athletic.

The arrival of Thompson proved timely as Norman Bell received an injury on the opening day of the season that ended his playing career. On 1 October 1983 the manager received another blow when Mick Rathbone broke his leg, while Noel Brotherston's season was dogged by one injury after another. With David Mail ruled out by illness before the season began, the manager did extremely well to maintain the club's position in the top half of the Second Division. Indeed, when the Rovers visited Ipswich Town, in the Football League Cup, in October 1983, they did so with just over half a team fully fit. Even so the team put up a tremendous fight against First Division opponents and were unfortunate to lose by the odd goal in seven. When Ipswich visited Ewood for the second leg of the tie the Rovers were unable to turn the game around and lost again, this time by a 2–1 margin.

Although they remained unbeaten at Ewood Park in the League until the penultimate home match, the Rovers were unable to convert too many home draws – 11 in all – into wins. However, the real difference between the Rovers and the clubs who won promotion was spending power. Chelsea, Sheffield Wednesday and Newcastle United finished well clear of the chasing pack and the

Simon Garner fires in a shot against Preston North End at Ewood Park in the pre-season Lancashire Manx Cup Competition. (*Copyright: Howard Talbot*)

gulf between their average attendances and that of the Rovers was all too plain to see. Although the average attendance had marginally increased, the fact remained that the club was not competing on an even playing field in terms of revenue generated through the turnstiles.

With finance at a premium, the emergence of Simon Barker and Mark Patterson, two home-grown youngsters, was a welcome boost for Saxton as he began to build a team that could launch a serious promotion assault.

1984-85

With only the addition of Swindon Town's Jimmy Quinn to his squad, Bobby Saxton was able to forge a team that looked good enough to clinch promotion. During the first half of the season the team looked the equal of anyone in the division and went into the New Year at the top of the table.

The form of Simon Garner and Chris Thompson meant that Quinn had to be content with a place on the substitute's bench. However, in December he came off the bench to score two goals in the 3–1 victory over Sheffield United at Ewood Park and the following week he replaced the injured Garner and scored a brace in the 3–0 win at Wolves. It meant that for the first time since he arrived at the club, Saxton had genuine competition for the striking positions.

Another factor in the upturn in fortunes had been the improved form of Colin Randell in midfield. Having been virtually discarded the previous season, Randell forged a successful partnership with Simon Barker in the centre of the Rovers' midfield. With Miller and Brotherston posing a threat down the flanks, the Ewood faithful entered 1985 with genuine cause for optimism.

A 2–1 win over Leeds United at Ewood Park on Boxing Day cemented the club's position at the top of the Second Division. However, three days later a home defeat at the hands of Huddersfield Town suggested that there were vulnerabilities in the team that needed to be addressed. When the next three League games each ended 1–1, questions began to surface about the strength of the squad. These doubts were confirmed when promotion rivals Oxford United, under the management of Jim Smith, came to Ewood Park and left with a point. A week earlier, the club had, as expected, bowed out of the FA Cup at the hands of Manchester United in front of 22,692 fans at Ewood Park.

(Left) Northern Ireland international winger Noel Brotherston gets in a cross during the third-round FA Cup victory over Chelsea at Ewood Park. (*Copyright: Howard Talbot*)

(Right) John Lowey beats Manchester City's Neil McNab to the ball on a snow-covered Ewood Park on 21 January 1984. The Rovers beat City by a margin of 2–1. (*Copyright: Howard Talbot*)

Jimmy Quinn was signed from Swindon Town in the summer of 1984 but had to wait until December 1984 before he was given the opportunity to start a League game. During his time at the club he scored 17 League goals. (*Copyright: Howard Talbot*)

David Mail (No.5) and Jimmy Quinn put the Portsmouth players Scott McGarvey (No.12) and Billy Gilbert under pressure during the third-round FA Cup tie at Ewood Park on 26 January 1985. (*Copyright: Howard Talbot*)

Three successive defeats followed the disappointment of the Oxford draw and the promotion challenge began to look rather fragile. Suddenly, a team that had seemed so purposeful in attack looked jittery and uncertain. Defensive errors began to creep in as the pressure started to mount. A brief respite brought a 2–1 home win over Birmingham City to confirm the club's third-place position. However, the following week the team capitulated at Shrewsbury and slumped to a 3–0 defeat. That result sent the club down to fifth position in the table but still within two points of second-place Oxford United.

The need for a new, authoritative driving force in midfield went unanswered as the Rovers steadfastly refused to enter the transfer market before the approaching deadline. Ultimately, it was to prove to be a decision that many believe cost the club its best chance of promotion since 1966–67.

Nonetheless, with six games remaining, four of which were at home, the club was still in the thick of the promotion race. The first of these produced a convincing 3–0 win over Middlesbrough at Ewood Park. However, the next three were all lost, by the same 1–0 margin, so that even a 3–1 win at Sheffield United in the penultimate match did little more than delay the inevitable until the final day of the season. The Rovers duly won their final match, 3–0 at home to Wolves, but sadly it proved too little too late, as the club finished in fifth position, just one point behind third-place Manchester City.

Unlike previous near misses, the failure to win promotion this time brought fierce criticism from the terraces. The fact that the club had achieved a higher points total than in any other season in their history or the fact that the club had scored more goals than for a number of years cut little ice with the Blackburn faithful. There was a belief that the club had squandered an excellent opportunity to make the top flight. In particular, there was criticism about the decision not to enter the transfer market at the crucial stage of the season.

1985-86

After the heartache of the previous campaign, 1985–86 proved to be nothing short of a disaster. Just 12 months after narrowly missing out on a place in the top flight, the club was involved in a grim struggle against relegation. Those who had questioned the quality of the squad proved to be vindicated as the Rovers' wafer-thin resources were stretched to the limit.

The manager had opted not to strengthen the squad, preferring to stick with the players that he knew so well. It appeared to be a sound decision when the Rovers remained unbeaten during the opening six games of the campaign. By mid-October, although they had lost heavily in a two-legged League Cup tie against Wimbledon, the Rovers had climbed to second spot in the League table.

The team had a familiar look about it, with Terry Gennoe in goal and a back four of Jim Branagan, who sat out the early part of the season, Glenn Keeley, Derek Fazackerley and Mick Rathbone. Ian Miller and Noel Brotherston occupied the wide positions while Simon Barker, in the centre of midfield, was usually partnered by either Mark Patterson or John Lowey. In attack Jimmy Quinn had replaced Chris Thompson as Simon Garner's strike partner, with the former Bolton player now occupying the role of backup. David Hamilton, who had occupied the right-back spot early in the campaign, was generally used to cover gaps in midfield, while Mail was the understudy for the centre of defence. It was a tight-knit group that had served the club so well in the past. However, after a 1–0 win at Millwall, on

Alan Ainscow, the veteran midfielder, joined the Rovers from Wolves on a non-contract basis in December 1985. He went on to appear in 65 League games for the club. (*Copyright: Howard Talbot*)

12 October 1985, the team went eight matches without a win. It sent the club spiralling to 10th in the League, some eight points adrift of the third promotion spot but, more worryingly, the same number of points away from the third relegation place.

Victory over Leeds United at Ewood Park, on Boxing Day, lifted the gloom in Blackburn, but only 8,666 fans turned out to watch it. Once again, the club had found that support continued to ebb away as the team struggled to make much headway. Sadly, there was little to entice the public to Ewood, as the team didn't win another League game until 1 March 1986. By this time the club had been knocked out of the FA Cup by Everton and was stranded in the lower half of the table. After the victory over Portsmouth, at the beginning of March, the team went a further 10 games with success. Crucially, the last of these matches had seen fellow strugglers Huddersfield Town win 1–0 at Ewood Park, the fifth successive defeat that the team had suffered at home. It left the Rovers in a dire situation just two points above the relegation places.

John Lowey fires in a shot during the 0–0 draw with Preston North End in the pre-season Lancashire Manx Cup Competition. (*Copyright: Howard Talbot*)

163

Against all expectations the Rovers thrashed Sheffield United 6–1 in their penultimate home game of the season. However, a week later they visited London and suffered a 3–0 defeat at Charlton Athletic. The Rovers went into the final weekend of the season knowing that survival was no longer in their own hands. Fulham were already relegated, but Middlesbrough remained just a point behind the Rovers, while Carlisle United had the same number of points as the Rovers but, crucially, had a game in hand.

It was then that fate intervened and lent the Rovers a helping hand. Grimsby Town were due to visit Ewood Park on the final Saturday of the season, but a torrential downpour made the pitch unplayable and led to a postponement until the following Monday. Carlisle, in the meantime, lost to Charlton Athletic to put matters back in the Rovers' own hands. The final game was just 42 seconds old when Garner calmed nerves when he headed home a cross from Miller. Not only did he give the Rovers a lead, but he also registered his 100th League goal for the club. However, nerves jangled again when Kevin Moore headed an equaliser from a left-wing corner after just four minutes, with O'Keefe and his defenders looking at each other and wondering who to blame. Fortunately, the Rovers came back with a gem after 32 minutes. Barker got Garner away and, although his cross was not the best, Thompson showed a smart piece of control before setting up Hamilton, who was able to pick his spot from 12 yards out. A second-half penalty was converted by Barker to ensure that the club survived what Bob Saxton described as 'a frightening experience, the worst 90 minutes of my 25 years in football.'

1986-87

Mark Patterson shows his delight at scoring in the 2–2 draw at Millwall on 27 September 1986. (*Copyright: Anne Barry*)

The summer of 1986 finally brought changes to the playing personnel at Ewood Park. Chris Thompson, John Lowey and David Hamilton all left the club, while the manager brought in Chris Price and Scott Sellars. Price, an attacking right-back, had played over 400 games for Hereford United while Sellars, a left-sided midfield player, was signed from Leeds United.

Both players immediately brought a fresh impetus to the first team and the opening three League games were all won. Indeed, the third of these produced a scintillating display of attacking football as Simon Garner scored four goals in the 6–1 defeat of Sunderland at Ewood Park.

Unfortunately, the team merely flattered to deceive and after the Sunderland result an unexpected slump set in. Just two points were gained from the next 10 League games while Queen's Park Rangers ended the club's interest in the Football League Cup. Once again it was the home form that undermined any chance of progress. Between September and December 1986, just one point was gained from seven home games. As the team slipped down the table the supporters began to vent their anger on both the board and the manager while on the field and Jimmy Quinn became the main target of the frustration felt by the supporters.

As things went from bad to worse, demonstrations became a familiar sight at home matches. As pressure began to mount, Saxton took an uncharacteristic gamble. He allowed Quinn, who was already on the transfer list, to return to Swindon Town, and recruited Paul McKinnon from Sutton United to replace him. Although McKinnon had never played in the Football League, he was a prolific goalscorer in the semi-professional game. Furthermore, he had spent a considerable amount of time in Scandinavia and had gained experience in European competitions while playing for Malmö FF.

McKinnon made his debut against Sunderland, at Roker Park, just four days before Christmas. A 3–0 defeat ensured that there was little in the way of festive spirit when Huddersfield Town turned up at Ewood Park on Boxing Day. While their Yorkshire visitors were bottom of the table the Rovers were only one point better off and defeat was unthinkable. The game began with an early exchange of goals as Duncan Shearer, a future Blackburn player, put the visitors ahead before Simon Garner equalised. The game turned into a grim struggle for survival and appeared destined to end in a draw until disaster struck in the final two minutes. A Simon Barker own goal gave the visitors maximum points and confirmed that there was no merry Christmas at Ewood Park.

In the wake of the defeat, and the resultant unrest among the fans, the players issued a statement of support for their besieged manager. However, the pressure finally forced Bill Fox, the chairman, to end Saxton's reign. Fox, who had always been a keen supporter of his former manager, was quick

Vince O'Keefe catches the ball under pressure from Derby County's Bobby Davison as Chris Price watches on. The Rovers beat Derby 3–1 at Ewood Park on 17 April 1987. (*Copyright: Howard Talbot*)

to defend Saxton's record. He pointed out that the manager had not only taken the club to the brink of the First Division, but had also worked with the directors to help bring financial stability to the club. In this respect he had sold players to the value of £475,000 while spending £343,000.

The directors asked Tony Parkes to take charge on a temporary basis and one of his first acts was to allow Derek Fazackerley, who was no longer a regular in the first team, to move to Chester City as player-coach. Fazackerley left Ewood Park after making a record 596 League appearances for the club. Parkes was in charge until Don Mackay was appointed manager on 31 January 1987. Although the club slipped out of the FA Cup in the third round against Portsmouth, the team remained unbeaten in the League under Parkes. Two days before the arrival of the new manager the club had signed Sean Curry, a forward, from Liverpool, while a week earlier goalkeeper Bobby Mimms had joined on loan from Everton. Mackay, who had previous managerial experience at Dundee and Coventry City, had been on the backroom staff at Glasgow Rangers prior to his appointment at Blackburn.

While the League situation gradually improved, the club began to enjoy success in the Full Members' Cup. The early rounds had largely gone unnoticed, but an excellent 3–0 win over Chelsea, at Ewood Park, took the club into the semi-final. Once again the Rovers had a home tie, against Ipswich Town, and were just one win away from a Wembley Final. On the eve of the game Mackay spent £30,000 on an unknown youngster from Dundee. Colin Hendry could play centre-half or centre-forward, but was a total unknown outside of the city of Dundee. At the same time Mackay took Chris Sulley, a left-back, on

Derek Fazackerley left for Chester City in January 1987 after making a record number of appearances for the club. Fazackerley appeared in 596 League games plus 40 FA Cup ties and 38 Football League Cup games for the Rovers. (*Copyright: Howard Talbot*)

BLACKBURN ROVERS: AN ILLUSTRATED HISTORY

Don Mackay was appointed to succeed Bobby Saxton as the new manager of Blackburn Rovers. (*Copyright: Anne Barry*)

Simon Barker (left) holding his 'Man of the Match' award and Ian Miller (right) hold aloft the Full Members' Cup after beating Charlton Athletic 1–0 at Wembley. (*Copyright: Howard Talbot*)

loan from Dundee United to replace the unfortunate Mick Rathbone, who had broken a leg in the game against Chelsea. With Keeley ruled out of the Ipswich tie, both Hendry and Sulley made their debuts and helped the Rovers to a 3–0 win.

The Final of the Full Members' Cup was played at Wembley on Sunday 29 March 1987. Rovers' opponents were Charlton Athletic of the First Division and the Rovers travelled to London as the underdogs. Some 28,000 Blackburn fans also travelled to the capital as the town was suddenly struck with Cup fever. While the game itself was a disappointing affair, the Blackburn fans created a carnival atmosphere. Vince O'Keefe, who had largely been in the shadow of Terry Gennoe during his time at Blackburn, proved to be the hero with a string of outstanding saves. Then, with five minutes remaining, Ian Miller raced past a defender and sent in an inch-perfect cross that tempted Bob Bolder off his line. However, the Charlton 'keeper, at full stretch, failed to hold the cross and the ball dropped conveniently at the feet of Hendry, whose angled shot flew off the inside of the near post and into the net. It was the goal that won the trophy for the Rovers and made Hendry a cult figure among Blackburn supporters.

A civic reception awaited the team on their return to Blackburn and the success at Wembley lifted performances in the League. Ultimately, a 12th-place finish and victory in a Wembley Final

seemed a highly satisfactory conclusion to what had, at one point, threatened to be a disastrous campaign.

1987-88

The success of the previous campaign enabled Mackay to wheel and deal during the summer of 1987. He returned to Ibrox to sign Ally Dawson, a Scottish international defender, for £50,000. The experienced Nicky Reid was brought from Manchester City to play in midfield while John Millar, a young Scottish full-back-cum-midfield player, was snapped up from Chelsea. Another move brought Howard Gayle, a former Liverpool and Birmingham City forward, from Stoke City. However, speculation that Mackay was contemplating a move for Barcelona's Steve Archibald was dismissed as a flight of fancy.

There was nothing during August and September 1987 to suggest that the new additions would make any spectacular improvement. However, a 1–1 draw against Aston Villa on 30 September 1987 began a 23-match unbeaten run that took the club to the top of the Second Division. It was in the midst of this run that Mackay pulled off a coup that rocked the football world. In December 1987, he persuaded Barcelona to loan him Steve Archibald until the end of the season. Amid reports of a £6,000-per-week salary, Archibald refuted claims that he had come to Lancashire to earn easy money. 'I came to Blackburn Rovers because they made me feel wanted,' was Archibald's response, 'and I am here to play football – not for the money.'

Archibald made his debut on 19 December 1987 against Birmingham City, and immediately showed his silky touch with an adept piece of skill that set up a goal for Colin Hendry in the 2–0 win. As one might expect, the signing of Archibald began to attract disillusioned fans back to Ewood Park. While the former Tottenham Hotspur and Scottish international did not score many goals for Blackburn, he certainly created numerous chances for his colleagues. Two of his most important goals came on 20 February 1988, when his double strike helped to defeat top-of-the-table Aston Villa at Ewood Park. It was a victory that enabled the Rovers to leapfrog over Villa and head the Second Division. The win was also the team's seventh successive victory and, once again, talk of promotion reverberated round the town.

Nicky Reid was signed from Manchester City in July 1987 and featured in every game during the 1987–88 season. (*Copyright: Anne Barry*)

The long unbeaten run ended in a 2–1 defeat at Stoke City on 5 March 1988. However, there had also been an unexpected home defeat, at the hands of Portsmouth, in the FA Cup in the midst of this run. A week after the upset at Stoke, the Rovers enjoyed a comfortable victory over Bournemouth at Ewood Park. However, the following week the Rovers were fortunate to rescue a point against Leicester City at Ewood Park, having to come from behind to snatch an injury-time equaliser. It was a game that amplified the need for a more experienced head in the team.

Once again, the manager caused a major sensation when he landed Ossie Ardiles, Tottenham's Argentinian World Cup star, on loan. Although in the twilight of his career, he possessed the type of experience and ability that Mackay hoped would take the Rovers into the First Division. There were only eight games left when Ardiles arrived but, unfortunately, an injury on his debut meant he missed out on two vital matches over the Easter period.

Defeat at Oldham on Good Friday and a home draw with Shrewsbury Town the following day seriously dented the club's promotion hopes. Fortunately, a brace of goals from Archibald brought

Don Mackay shocked the football world when he took Steve Archibald from Barcelona on loan. (*Copyright: Howard Talbot*)

maximum points from a visit to Swindon Town and, with four games left, the Rovers were in fourth place, equal on points with third-place Middlesbrough and just one point behind second-in-the-table Bradford City.

Sadly, inconsistency affected the team at the crucial stage of the campaign and, as a result, only five points were taken from the last four matches, with home draws against Swindon Town and Reading proving extremely costly.

A fifth-place finish meant the Rovers had to enter the play-offs and face Chelsea, who had finished 19th in the First Division. Handicapped by the loss of Archibald and with Ardiles only fit enough for the bench, the Rovers slipped to a 2–0 defeat in the first leg. The return game at Stamford Bridge brought the reappearance of Archibald and Ardiles but the deficit proved too great to make up. A 4–1 defeat merely underlined the gulf that still existed between the Rovers and the First Division.

1988-89

Colin Hendry salutes his goal during the 3–0 defeat of Birmingham City at Ewood Park on 24 September 1988. Tony Finnigan is the other Blackburn player in the background. (*Copyright: Anne Barry*)

Failure to clinch promotion brought another bout of transfer activity during the summer of 1988. Steve Archibald and Ossie Ardiles duly departed at the end of their loan periods and Simon Barker was sold to Queen's Park Rangers for £400,000. Chris Price, who had only been at the club for a couple of seasons, was sold to Aston Villa for £150,000, while Mark Patterson, who had become a peripheral figure, joined Preston North End for £20,000. Mackay replaced Price with Mark Atkins, a teenage defender who was signed from Scunthorpe United for £45,000. A similar fee was spent on Tony Finnigan, a midfield player from Crystal Palace, while another midfielder, Ronnie Hildersley, arrived on a free transfer from Preston North End. The most significant investment was the £50,000 spent on Andy Kennedy, a tall, well-built centre-forward who also possessed plenty of pace.

The Rovers made an excellent start to the new campaign with five wins and a draw from their opening six games. While the Rovers continued to challenge at the top of table they were unfortunate to bow out of the Littlewoods Cup at the hands of Tottenham Hotspur. Indeed, the Cup competitions brought little cheer to the club, with Ipswich Town ending interest in the Simod Cup and Brentford pulling off a giant-killing act at Ewood Park in the FA Cup.

However, as February 1989 drew to a close, the Rovers were handily placed in third position in the table. The only strengthening that Mackay had carried out was the loan of David Byrne from Millwall. Unfortunately, before a

decision could be made with regard to Byrne's future, Plymouth Argyle had stepped in and given him a permanent contract at Home Park.

With Chelsea and Manchester City cementing their positions at the top of the Second Division, the Rovers slipped to fifth in the table. Once again, the Rovers were destined for the lottery of the play-offs. However, before that point was reached they displayed their First Division credentials with a 4–0 win over Manchester City at Ewood Park. The significance of the win and the fact that a hat-trick by Simon Garner made him the club's all-time leading goalscorer was overshadowed by the tragedy that had unfolded at Hillsborough. The loss of life at the semi-final between Liverpool and Nottingham Forest made talk of footballing matters appear shallow.

Three wins in the final five games confirmed the club's fifth-place finish in the Second Division and led to a play-off semi-final against Watford. Once again, the Rovers were at home in the first leg and were held to a goalless draw. Ultimately, Mackay had to rely on a piece of Simon Garner opportunism to snatch the goal that gave the Rovers a 1–0 win at Vicarage Road and a place in a two-legged Final against Crystal Palace.

Andy Kennedy scored some spectacular goals during an injury-plagued season at Ewood Park. (*Copyright: Anne Barry*)

A crowd of 16,421 watched the Rovers enjoy a 3–1 win over Palace in the first leg. The club's position might even have been stronger had Howard Gayle, who had already scored two goals, not missed a penalty. Nonetheless, a 3–1 lead appeared to put the Rovers in a strong position.

The second leg was played out in a white-hot atmosphere at Selhurst Park. A fiercely partisan crowd created an intimidating environment for the men from Ewood Park and, sadly, a number of them began to wilt under the pressure. Ian Wright whipped up the home fans with a 16th-minute

(Left) David Byrne was brought from Millwall on loan and made four appearances for the club before his loan was controversially ended when he agreed to join Plymouth Argyle permanently. (*Copyright: Anne Barry*)

(Right) Darren Collier made his debut for the Rovers on the final day of the season in the 2–0 defeat at Ipswich Town. Collier, a former Middlesbrough trainee, kept goal for the Rovers on 31 occasions. (Copyright: Ann Barry)

goal that reduced the arrears and sent panic through the Rovers' ranks. Although they held out until half-time, the Rovers were hit with a quick-fire goal just two minutes into the second period. It was a highly controversial goal as the referee, George Courtney, adjudged a clash between Mark Atkins and Eddie McGoldrick to be a deliberate foul. Maddern converted the penalty, which meant the Rovers had to score to prevent Palace gaining promotion at their expense. The game went into extra time and late on Perry Suckling made a superb save to deny Garner the opportunity to score. Then, four minutes from the end, McColdrick's cross was headed home by Wright. Yet again, another golden opportunity had slipped from their grasp and the Blackburn fans who made the long trek back north began to wonder if the club would ever lose its 'Nearly men' tag.

The first-team squad with two former Old Trafford favourites, Frank Stapleton (left) and Kevin Moran (right) at the front. (*Copyright: Anne Barry*)

1989-90

For a third successive season the Rovers reached the Second Division play-offs and for a third successive season they failed to achieve their objective. However, in truth the 1989–90 campaign was a lacklustre affair that failed to generate the same interest as the previous two seasons.

In the summer of 1989, Mackay had added Frank Stapleton, the former Arsenal and Manchester United centre-forward, to his squad. Although the Republic of Ireland international scored only three League goals during the season, his wealth of experience proved invaluable and he created numerous opportunities for others. Simon Garner bagged another 18 League goals, Scott Sellars hit 14 in the League and Andy Kennedy weighed in with 13. The only other summer acquisition was Neil Oliver, a full-back from Berwick Rangers, who found it impossible to dislodge Mark Atkins and Chris Sulley from the full-back berths.

In December 1989, the manager made another swoop that captured national headlines when he signed Kevin Moran from Sporting Gijon. The former Manchester United and Republic of Ireland defender was a welcome addition to a defence that had begun to become somewhat porous. Defensive problems had stemmed from a contract dispute between the Rovers and Colin Hendry

(Left) Don Mackay welcomes Alan Irvine (left) to Ewood Park after signing the winger on loan from Dundee United in October 1989. The following month Irvine signed for the club on a permanent basis. (*Copyright: Anne Barry*)

(Right) Manager Don Mackay (centre) placed his trust in two young centre-backs during the early part of the campaign. David May (left) and Keith Hill (right) had both graduated from the club's youth scheme to become first-team regulars. (*Copyright: Anne Barry*)

David Mail blasts home from the penalty spot against Ipswich Town, at Portman Road, on 28 April 1990. The Rovers went down to a 3–1 defeat. (*Copyright: Anne Barry*)

at the start of the season. Hendry had been included on just a handful of occasions before being sold to Manchester City. The manager had overlooked the claims of David Mail and opted for a youthful partnership of David May and Keith Hill at the centre of the defence. With Terry Gennoe missing through injury, Darren Collier was recalled to keep goal and the three youngsters began to endure a torrid time after initially making a favourable impression. The inclusion of Moran, in partnership with the re-called Mail, produced a welcome return to defensive solidity, especially when Gennoe recovered from injury.

While the Rovers maintained their challenge for a play-off spot, the season produced more disappointment with regard to Cup competitions. The Rovers were humbled by Exeter City over two legs in the Littlewoods Cup, while Leeds United ended interest in the Zenith Data Systems Cup. The FA Cup brought two closely fought third-round matches with Aston Villa, before the Rovers bowed out in the replay at Villa Park.

Having finished the season in fifth position, the Rovers faced Swindon Town in the play-off semi-final. Managed by Ossie Ardiles, Swindon visited Ewood Park in the first leg and left with a 2–1 win under their belts. The return match at Swindon brought further disappointment for Ewood's long-suffering fans, with the Rovers going down to another 2–1 defeat.

1990–91

After three seasons of chasing the dream of First Division football, the Rovers were faced with the nightmare scenario of relegation to the Third Division during 1990–91.

The summer had seen a new club record transfer fee reached when Lee Richardson, a highly rated midfielder, joined the Rovers from Watford. Valued at £250,000, the Rovers were able to finance the deal by allowing Andy Kennedy, who was valued at £190,000, to move to Vicarage Road

together with £60,000 in cash. The only other major transfer had brought Mick Duxbury, the former England international, to Ewood Park on a free transfer from Manchester United.

Unfortunately, Mackay was hit by a crippling injury list. Gennoe was injured on the opening day of the campaign and didn't reappear. Hernia problems restricted Scott Sellars to just nine League appearances, while a similar complaint kept Simon Garner out for all but 12 League matches. Indeed, no fewer than eight senior players were ruled out for periods of up to three months.

Disappointing results reflected the threadbare nature of the squad and Mackay was forced to move into the loan market to cover the gaps. Jim Beglin arrived from Leeds United to fill the left-back berth and when he returned to Elland Road he was replaced by Bernard Gallacher from Aston Villa. Mark Grew, an experienced goalkeeper, was signed from Port Vale on an extended loan after Darren Collier had again suffered a traumatic period between the posts. The attack was briefly boosted by Phil Starbuck, who came on loan from Nottingham Forest. Nor did the manager restrict his search for new talent to the British Isles. Lars Frisch, a Danish full-back, was given a trial in the Central League team, while Claus Reitmaier, a German goalkeeper, was loaned from the Austrian club Wiener SC. Reitmaier was given a trial in goal in the Zenith Data Systems Cup defeat against Everton at Ewood Park in December 1990. Although the Rovers lost 4–1, Reitmaier could hardly be faulted for any of the goals but, nonetheless, the manager declined to sign him on the grounds of cost and his lack of experience of English football.

Home defeats over the festive period had put the club in a perilous position – just four points ahead of bottom-placed Hull City. However, December finally brought a long-term replacement for Terry Gennoe, when Bobby Mimms was signed from Tottenham Hotspur for £250,000.

After early exits from the Rumbelows Cup, at the hands of Queen's Park Rangers, and the Zenith Data Systems Cup, the FA Cup ended abruptly in a third-round replay at Liverpool, after the Rovers had almost defeated their more illustrious opponents at Ewood Park.

On 17 January 1991, it was announced that Jack Walker had taken control of the club with the full support of the existing board. A lifelong supporter, Walker, who was based in Jersey, had started out in business in Blackburn in the humblest of circumstances. However, with his brother Fred, he had gone on to create Walker Steel, which was reported to have been sold for £330 million. Walker was also involved in a variety of business activities, including ownership of Jersey Airlines, which continued to add to his empire.

(Left) Phil Starbuck misses out with this shot against Portsmouth at Fratton Park on 22 September 1990. (*Copyright: Anne Barry*)

(Right) Phil Starbuck, seen here surrounded by Ipswich Town defenders, was one of six players who were brought in on loan during 1990–91. (*Copyright: Anne Barry*)

(Left) Lenny Johnrose battles with an Ipswich Town defender at Portman Road in September 1990. (*Copyright: Anne Barry*)

(Right) Jason Beckford, on loan from Manchester City, puts the Oldham Athletic defence under pressure at Ewood Park on 23 March 1991. (*Copyright: Anne Barry*)

Jack Walker took control of Blackburn Rovers in January 1991 and began his Ewood Park revolution. (*Copyright: Howard Talbot*)

(bottom left) Plymouth Argyle's Nicky Marker shields the ball at Ewood Park. He joined the Rovers in September 1992 as a utility player and became a valuable member of the squad.

(bottom centre) Frank Stapleton, the former Manchester United and Arsenal star spent two seasons at Ewood Park as manager Don Mackay utilised Republic of Ireland international's vast experience to the full.

(bottom right) Steve Livingstone scored nine goals in 1990-91 to ensure the club's survival in the Second Division.

Walker had clearly been behind the move for Bobby Mimms and on the day that he took control the Rovers spent a further £750,000 on Tony Dobson and Steve Livingstone from Coventry City. Livingstone, a physically imposing centre-forward, scored nine goals in 18 appearances, while Dobson formed an impressive partnership with Kevin Moran at the heart of the defence. Both men, together with Mimms, proved timely acquisitions and helped the Rovers to finish the season in the relative safety of 19th position in the League.

1991-92

Despite the financial backing of Jack Walker, the club could not overcome the question of credibility when trying to lure expensive new signings to Ewood Park. During the summer attempts to sign players of the calibre of Gary Lineker, Paul Stewart, Mike Newell and Teddy Sheringham all came to nothing. A new club record was established when Steve Agnew was signed from Barnsley for £750,000, while Stuart Munro, a Scottish international full-back, arrived from Rangers. However, only David Speedie, a £500,000 capture from Liverpool, was deemed a 'big name' signing.

One point from the first three League games, coupled with a surprise exit from the Rumbelows Cup, led to drastic action being taken. On 2 September 1991, Don Mackay's four-and-a-half year reign was brought to an end and Tony Parkes again took charge on a temporary basis.

Parkes was faced with the loss of Steve Agnew, who was sidelined for the majority of the campaign by injury. Nonetheless, he gradually pulled the club into a mid-table position with the introduction of younger players like Richard Brown, Craig Skinner and Lenny Johnrose. While Parkes improved the position in the League, Jack Walker had targeted the man who could attract the calibre of player required at Ewood Park. On 12 October 1992, on the morning of a home match with Plymouth Argyle, Walker revealed his new management team. Kenny Dalglish, the former Liverpool manager, had agreed to take the helm at Ewood Park and had appointed Ray Harford, a

Manager Don Mackay welcomes David Speedie to Ewood Park in August 1991. (*Copyright: Howard Talbot*)

Steve Agnew skips past a Bury defender during the Lancashire Manx Cup match at Gigg Lane. This pre-season game was one of just four appearances that Agnew made for the club before injury wrecked his Ewood Park career. (*Copyright: Anne Barry*)

respected coach and former manager of Luton Town, Fulham and Wimbledon, as his assistant. Dalglish had also insisted on Tony Parkes remaining at the club as first-team coach.

News of the new managerial appointments brought a crowd of 10,830 to watch the Rovers, still under the control of Parkes, romp to a 5–2 victory over Plymouth. The new management team gave the Rovers the credibility that had previously been missing and in the wake of their arrival a plethora of new players appeared. Alan Wright, Blackpool's diminutive left-back, arrived for £500,000, while the hugely popular Colin Hendry returned from Manchester City for £700,000. The pulling power of Dalglish prised Mike Newell from Everton for £1.1 million – a new record fee for the Rovers. In November 1991, Dalglish made the astute acquisition of Gordon Cowans, Aston

Roy Wegerle scores for the Rovers at Watford on 11 April 1992. (*Copyright: Anne Barry*)

Villa's veteran England international midfielder.

The team now had a completely new look about it. Bobby Mimms was the automatic choice in goal following Gennoe's move to the backroom staff. Richard Brown and Alan Wright proved a youthful but reliable full-back pairing, while Kevin Moran and Hendry were a formidable partnership in the centre of defence. The Rovers used Jason Wilcox and Scott Sellars on the flanks, while Cowans and Mark Atkins were given the central midfield positions. Speedie and Newell formed the strike force, while long-serving Simon Garner and Steve Livingstone were relegated to a back-up role.

Mike Newell's return from injury was vital in ensuring that the Rovers reached the play-offs to decide the final place in the newly formed Premier League. (*Copyright: Anne Barry*)

Although the first match under new management, away to Swindon Town, was lost, the Rovers quickly began to make an impression on the Second Division. On 7 December 1991 the club stood third in the League. However, it was at this point that tragedy struck with the death of Bill Fox, the club chairman. Like Walker, Fox was a lifelong supporter of the Rovers and had fought a difficult battle in the 1980s to keep the club afloat. He was a highly respected and popular figure in the game and was president of the Football League at the time of his death. It was the cruellest twist of fate that the man who had led the club through difficult times should be robbed of the opportunity to share the success that he had striven for so long to achieve.

As the club entered the New Year both points and new players were collected with equal vigour. Chris Price returned to the club from Aston Villa while Tim Sherwood, a talented midfielder, was signed from Norwich City. When Newell suffered a broken leg in February 1992, the manager spent £1 million to sign Roy Wegerle, Queen's Park Rangers' talented striker. On the eve of the transfer deadline, Matt Dickens arrived from Lincoln City to provide cover for Mimms, while Duncan Shearer, Swindon's leading goalscorer, was added to the attack.

Incredibly, despite such an array of talent, the team suffered a run of six successive defeats as the season reached its critical point. From being almost certain champions the team now clung to the final play-off spot. Fortunately, the return of Mike Newell sparked a revival that ensured sixth position and a place in the play-offs.

Derby County visited Ewood Park in the first leg of the semi-final. The opening phase of the game had a depressingly familiar look about it as the Rovers were two goals adrift after just 15 minutes. However, a typical long-range effort from Scott

Duncan Shearer was signed from Swindon Town just before the transfer deadline. However, Swindon's leading goalscorer found life difficult at Blackburn and only scored once in seven appearances before being sold to Aberdeen. (*Copyright: Anne Barry*)

Sellars reduced the arrears and, on the stroke of half-time, an unstoppable shot from Newell found the back of the Derby net. David Speedie, the club's talisman, scored twice in the second period to give the Rovers a 4–2 lead.

Memories of Crystal Palace resurfaced when Andy Comyn gave Derby a 1–0 lead after 23 minutes of the second leg. However, on this occasion the Blackburn defence, superbly marshalled by Kevin Moran, held firm. Indeed, in the second half, it was Moran himself who ventured forward to launch himself bravely at a corner and bundle the ball into the net past a host of Derby defenders. Although Ted McMinn pulled a goal back for Derby, the Rovers maintained their 5–4 lead and clinched a place in the play-off final.

Simon Garner drew the curtain down on his Ewood Park career when he moved to West Bromwich Albion in August 1992. Garner created a new goalscoring record with 168 League goals being recorded during his time at the club. (*Copyright: Howard Talbot*)

BLACKBURN ROVERS: AN ILLUSTRATED HISTORY

The final carried more significance than usual with the advent of the Premier League the following season. Officials of both the Rovers and Leicester City realised the financial implications of failure, which put extra pressure on both sets of players. The Rovers, in an all-yellow strip, were led out by Tony Parkes after Kenny Dalglish had insisted that the long-serving coach should be at the head of the team.

The first half proved a tight, nervous affair, with both teams adopting a 'safety first' attitude. Just before half-time the key moment in the match occurred when Speedie clashed with Steve Walsh in the Leicester penalty area. George Courtney, the man who had refereed the play-off final with Crystal Palace, ruled that Speedie had been fouled and awarded a penalty. The vehement protests of the Leicester players, so reminiscent of the protests of the Blackburn players at Selhurst Park in similar circumstances, were to no avail as Mike Newell calmly stroked the ball home against one of his former clubs.

The second half brought the expected response from Leicester and the Rovers had to defend for long periods. Fortunately, the defensive skills of David May, Kevin Moran, Colin Hendry and Alan Wright stood firm, with Bobby Mimms in good form between the posts. As the players wilted in the terrific heat, Mark Atkins continued to chase every ball in midfield and it was from one of his breaks from defence a move that led to a second penalty being awarded to the Rovers. However, on this occasion Newell's effort was saved to ensure a nervous final few minutes for Blackburn fans.

When the final whistle blew the Blackburn players swapped their yellow jerseys for the traditional blue and white halves, before mounting the Wembley steps to collect their play-off trophy. An ecstatic Blackburn contingent in the crowd of 68,147 celebrated the end of a quarter of a century outside the top flight of English football. The following day the team returned to Blackburn and paraded through packed streets before being given a civic reception at the Town Hall. Jack Walker's investment, Dalglish's shrewd man-management, Harford's coaching skills and the ability of Parkes to spark an early season rival had all contributed to the resurrection of the club.

1992-93

The full impact of Jack Walker's buying power was amply illustrated during the summer of 1992. A new British transfer record was created when Alan Shearer moved to Ewood Park in a deal that was said to be worth £3.3 million. That the Rovers could land a player like Shearer, in direct competition with Manchester United, demonstrated the magnetism that Dalglish had among young players. Stuart Ripley had already been signed for £1.2 million, while youngsters Lee Makel and Wayne Burnett arrived from Newcastle United and Leyton Orient respectively with a view to being developed in the Central League.

While new players arrived a number of the existing squad departed as Dalglish and Harford prepared for life in the Premier League. Duncan Shearer and Lee Richardson both moved to Aberdeen, while Paul Shepstone also travelled north of the border to link up with Motherwell. Chris Sully joined Port Vale on a free transfer while Simon Garner, the club's record goalscorer and cult hero, linked up with Ossie Ardiles at West Bromwich Albion in a £30,000 deal. The departure of Scott Sellars to Leeds United for £800,000 came as something of a surprise and supporters were shocked to learn that David Speedie was to join Southampton as part of the Shearer deal.

After an absence of a quarter of a century the Rovers adapted surprisingly well to life in the top flight. Dalglish proved an excellent man-manager while

The goalkeeping fraternity at Ewood Park at the start of the 1992–93 season. From left to right, back row: Bobby Mimms, Terry Gennoe (goalkeeping coach), Matt Dickens. Front row: Darren Collier, Frank Talia, Alec Ridgeway. (*Copyright: Anne Barry*)

179

Harford demonstrated his credentials as one of the finest coaches in the country. On 3 October 1992, Norwich City travelled to Ewood Park as the early pacesetters in the newly founded Premier League. However, a stirring performance by the Rovers, with two goals apiece from Shearer and Wegerle, together with goals from Sherwood, Cowans and Ripley, resulted in a 7–1 victory that sent Blackburn Rovers to the top of the table.

Although unable to retain the top position, the Rovers remained in the top eight throughout the season and for the most part were in the top six. Indeed, in finishing sixth in the final table the Rovers achieved their highest League position for 78 years. However, the Cup competitions brought the disappointments of the season. In the Coca-Cola Cup the Rovers lost over two legs to Sheffield Wednesday in the semi-final, while Sheffield United ended the club's interest in the FA Cup at the sixth round. The United defeat was particularly unfortunate as the Rovers went down 5–3 on penalties after two drawn games.

Throughout the season the manager continued to add to the impressive array of talent at his disposal. Nicky Marker, Plymouth Argyle's utility defender and midfield man, arrived early in the campaign in exchange for Keith Hill and Craig Skinner. Simon Ireland, a right-sided midfield player, was signed after he had performed well against the Rovers for Huddersfield Town in the Coca-Cola Cup. In January 1993, two Scandinavian defenders, Henning Berg and Patrik Andersson, were signed from Lillestrom and Malmö FF respectively. Steve Livingstone was allowed to move to Chelsea as part of the deal that brought Graeme Le Saux, a left-back, to Ewood Park for £650,000. Another deal worth £1.5 million brought Kevin Gallacher to Ewood Park from Coventry City while Roy Wegerle moved in the opposite direction.

(Above) Roy Wegerle, the South African-born American international, scored two goals in the 7–1 win over Norwich City at Ewood Park on 3 October 1992. The win took the Rovers to the top of the Premier League. (Copyright: Anne Barry)

(Left) Ray Harford's coaching expertise was a major factor in the club's successful transition to top-flight football in 1992–93. (Copyright: Anne Barry)

(Right) Patrik Andersson failed to settle in English football and made only 15 senior appearances before joining Borussia Mönchengladbach. (Copyright: Anne Barry)

The success that was achieved was all the more remarkable given that the club had lost the services of Alan Shearer in January to a cruciate ligament injury. Shearer had suffered the injury in the 3–1 win over Leeds United on Boxing Day but had battled back to feature in the Coca-Cola Cup match with Cambridge United on 6 January 1993. At the time it was thought that Shearer had suffered cartilage problems but when he collapsed in the Cambridge match the full extent of his injury became known. He was faced with surgery and a lengthy recovery period to overcome what was a career-threatening injury.

In February 1993 the Darwen End was demolished as ambitious plans for an all-seater stadium got under way. Unfortunately, the revamp was not without its problems and the Football Association threatened to have the home match with Sheffield United in the FA Cup played at another venue unless the Rovers found a way to give their visitors more tickets for the match. It led to the Sheffield contingent being given the Blackburn End enclosure as the club struggled to accommodate supporters with their reduced capacity.

By the end of the season the club was slowly being transformed from a small-town club into one that could compete with the best in the land and have the facilities to match.

1993-94

Apart from the signing of Andy Morrison, a young, robust defender from Plymouth Argyle, the summer of 1993 was a quiet affair in terms of transfer activity. The main focus of attention was the race to get Alan Shearer fit as soon as possible. Dalglish refused to rush his young protégé back too quickly and the season began with Shearer on the substitutes' bench. However, on 29 August 1993 at Newcastle United he left the bench and scored his first League goal of the season to rescue a point for the Rovers. Nonetheless, he didn't make his first start for the club until the visit of AFC Bournemouth in the Coca-Cola Cup on 21 September 1993. Once again, he demonstrated his fitness with the only goal of the match and from that point he resumed his centre-forward role.

Nicky Marker proved a useful squad player, with his ability to play in the centre of defence or in midfield. Marker made 28 appearances during the course of the season, of which seven came from the bench. (*Copyright: Anne Barry*)

By the time Shearer returned to League action the Rovers were in eighth position, some five points adrift of leaders Manchester United. Dalglish had also further strengthened his squad with the purchase of Paul Warhurst from Sheffield Wednesday. The utility man cost the Rovers £2.7 million but tragically suffered a broken leg on only his fifth appearance for the club. Dalglish snapped up Ian Pearce, Chelsea's promising young defender, for a modest fee, while David Batty, the Leeds United and England international midfielder, was signed for £2.75 million. The Rovers beat Liverpool for the signature of Tim Flowers who arrived from Southampton for £2 million – a record fee for a goalkeeper at that time.

Gradually a new team began to emerge. Flowers replaced Mimms in goal while Henning Berg and Graeme Le Saux developed into an outstanding pair of full-backs. In the centre of defence Dalglish could use the combined talents of Kevin Moran, Colin Hendry, David May and Nicky Marker. The arrival of Batty enabled Tim Sherwood to enjoy greater freedom to join the attack, while Stuart Ripley and Jason Wilcox posed a constant threat with their pace down the flanks. In attack the Rovers were able to call upon Shearer, Mike Newell and Kevin Gallacher – an embarrassment of riches. However, there was one significant departure when Patrik Andersson failed to settle in English football and was sold to Borussia Mönchengladbach.

By Christmas the Rovers had climbed to third position in the Premier League but remained 14

Stuart Ripley appeared in 49 League and Cup games during the season. (*Copyright: Anne Barry*)

Paul Warhurst signed from Sheffield Wednesday for £2.7 million. (*Copyright: unknown*)

points behind the leaders Manchester United. Interest in the Coca-Cola Cup had ended at Tottenham, while the FA Cup campaign came to an abrupt and unexpected halt in the fourth round. Having drawn away at Charlton Athletic, the Rovers suffered a shock 1–0 reversal in the replay at Ewood Park. Nonetheless, the Rovers continued to be a model of consistency in the League and slowly began to close the gap between themselves and Manchester United. At the same time the club now boasted two impressive new stands at the Darwen End and Blackburn End, while the Nuttall Street Stand was demolished in January 1994 as work began on the final phase of ground redevelopment.

When Manchester United visited Ewood Park, on 2 April 1993, the gap between the two clubs, which at one stage had been 16 points, had been reduced to just three. The title race had become a straight battle between Ewood Park and Old Trafford. Because of the redevelopment the crowd was restricted to 20,866. However, the fiercely partisan atmosphere created the perfect environment for the Rovers to try to get the better of their Championship rivals. The game came alight in the second half when Shearer's header beat Peter Schmeichel to give the Rovers the lead. As the visitors tried to retrieve the situation they were caught out by a long pass from Ripley that sent Shearer racing towards the United goal. The Rovers number nine got in front of Gary Pallister and wasted no time in rifling a powerful left-foot shot past Schmeichel to seal a 2–0 win for the Rovers.

Sadly, the Rovers were unable to maintain their challenge over the final stages of the season with only one win from their last five League games. Nonetheless, a second-place finish meant that the Rovers had qualified for European football for the first time in the club's history. On a personal level, Alan Shearer, who had scored 31 League goals, was voted Footballer of the Year by the Football Writers' Association.

1994-95

The Rovers players applaud their supporters at the end of the 1994 FA Charity Shield match against Manchester United. (*Copyright: Anne Barry*)

Kevin Moran retired from the game at the end of the 1994 World Cup Finals in the United States, while David May departed from Ewood Park to Manchester United following a contract dispute. However, the club set a new British transfer record when Chris Sutton, Norwich City's England Under-21 striker, was signed for £5 million. The manager also strengthened his midfield options by signing Robbie Slater, an Australian international, from the French club Lens.

Injuries blighted pre-season preparations to such an extent that both Kenny Dalglish and Tony Parkes had to play for the Rovers in a testimonial match at Aberdeen. Two days later, when the club faced Celtic at Hampden Park, Tony Gale, a vastly experienced centre-half who had been released by West Ham United, made his debut for the Rovers. In the wake of the departures of Moran and May, Dalglish moved swiftly to offer Gale a short-term contract at Ewood Park.

The Rovers also appeared at Wembley in the FA Charity Shield against Manchester United. It was the first time since 1928 that the Rovers had participated in this match and it was entirely fitting that Dalglish invited Jack Walker to lead out the Blackburn players. Unfortunately, an under-strength team was unable to hold the Premier League champions, who won the game 2–0.

The loss of David Batty, Kevin Gallacher and Nicky Marker to long-term injuries meant the team had a slightly unfamiliar look at the start of the season. Tim Flowers remained supreme in goal while the back four were now made up of Henning Berg, Tony Gale, Colin Hendry and Graeme Le Saux. Tim Sherwood was still the most prominent member of the midfield, with Mark Atkins replacing the injured Batty. Stuart Ripley and Jason Wilcox continued on the flanks with Robbie Slater and Paul Warhurst also being utilised in midfield. The strike force of Alan Shearer and Chris Sutton was backed up by the ever reliable Mike Newell.

By Christmas the title race had again developed into a battle between the Rovers and Manchester United.

The Carling Award for 'Player of the Month' was awarded to the 'SAS' strike force of Alan Shearer (right) and Chris Sutton (left) in November 1994. (*Copyright: Anne Barry*)

(Left) Ian Pearce replaced the veteran Tony Gale during the second half of the Championship-winning campaign. (*Copyright: unknown*)

(Right) Alan Shearer celebrates after scoring at Liverpool on the final day of the season. (*Copyright: Anne Barry*)

However, on this occasion it was the Rovers who held the advantage. While the League form was remarkably consistent, the club fared badly in Cup competitions. Swedish club Trelleborgs FF eliminated the Rovers from the UEFA Cup, while Liverpool inflicted a home defeat on the team in the Coca-Cola Cup. The FA Cup also brought a home defeat, at the hands of Newcastle United, after the Rovers had drawn at St James' Park in the third-round tie.

The Rovers entered 1995 at the top of the Premiership, having lost just two League games. By this time the more youthful Pearce had replaced Gale in the centre of the defence. However, the club suffered a major blow on 8 March 1995 when Jason Wilcox suffered a cruciate ligament injury in the 3–1 win over Arsenal at Ewood Park. This necessitated Graeme Le Saux being moved into midfield but, as Alan Wright had recently been sold to Aston Villa, the gap at left-back was covered by entering the transfer market. Jeff Kenna was signed from Southampton and appeared in the final nine League games. Dalglish also signed Richard Witschge, a Dutch international winger, on loan from Ajax. However, the Dutchman remained a peripheral figure during the closing stages of the season and only appeared on one occasion.

Both David Batty and Kevin Gallacher returned to action in the penultimate home game of the season. However, the 2–1 win over Crystal Palace was marred when Gallacher, who scored the winning goal, suffered another broken leg. The injury came at a time when the Rovers had begun to show signs of nerves as the finishing line came in sight. An eight-point lead over Manchester United had been cut to just two when Newcastle United visited Ewood Park on 8 May 1995.

Newcastle United still required points for UEFA Cup qualification and the home fans, in a crowd of 30,545, endured an uncomfortable night as the visitors pounded away at the Blackburn goal. Tim Flowers was in truly inspired form and produced several breathtaking saves to ensure that the Rovers clung on to the 29th-minute lead that Alan Shearer had given them. At the final whistle the Blackburn fans greeted the victory with a mixture of delight and relief. The fans streamed out of the ground in party mood and the VE Day celebrations were hijacked as the fans celebrated Victory at Ewood night.

A victory for Manchester United over Southampton two days later meant that the title would be decided on the final day of the season. While United travelled to London to face West Ham United, Dalglish would have to take his Blackburn team to his beloved Anfield to gain the win that would assure the Rovers of the Championship.

The afternoon of Sunday 14 May 1995 provided one of the most dramatic conclusions to a

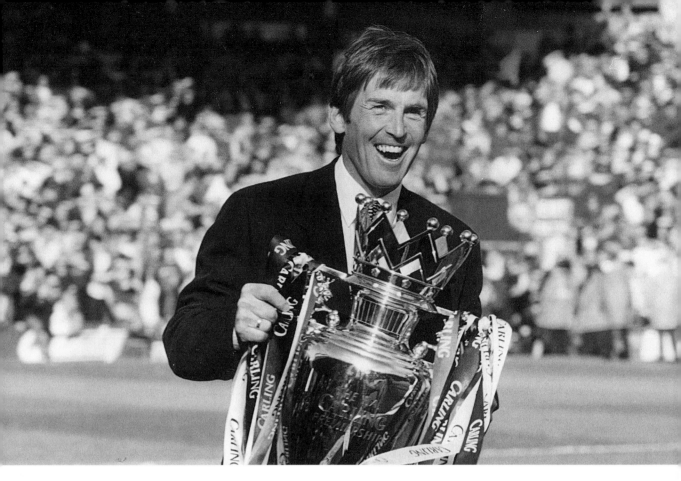

Championship race in the history of the game. When Alan Shearer put the Rovers ahead, after 20 minutes, the title seemed destined for Ewood Park. The Blackburn fans were still celebrating when news arrived that West Ham had taken the lead against Manchester United. On 64 minutes the Championship race took another twist when John Barnes equalised for Liverpool and news of a United goal further dampened the spirits of the Blackburn contingent. Nerves had begun to play

A delighted Kenny Dalglish with the Premiership trophy after the Rovers were crowned champions at Anfield. (*Copyright: Anne Barry*)

tricks on the Rovers players and 10 minutes from the end Chris Sutton's tentative effort was cleared by John Scales as it moved tantalisingly close to the goal-line.

As the game moved into injury time, and with United still pressing a besieged West Ham goal, Liverpool were awarded a free-kick just outside the penalty area. Rovers fans stood in shocked silence as they watched Jamie Redknapp launch an unstoppable shot into the top corner of the net. However, before the full realisation of what had happened had fully registered with Blackburn fans news filtered through from London that Manchester United had been held to a draw. The Rovers had clinched the Championship by just one point.

Scenes of wild celebration followed as the Liverpool fans stayed behind to join in the celebrations. Jack Walker, eyes

Alan Shearer and Colin Hendry, two of Blackburn's favourite adopted sons, lift the Premiership trophy at the official presentation that took place at Ewood Park on Monday 15 May 1994. (*Copyright: Anne Barry*)

The men who guided Blackburn Rovers to the Premiership title. From left to right: Ray Harford, Tony Parkes and Kenny Dalglish, with his daughter on his shoulders and holding the Manager of the Year trophy. (*Copyright: Anne Barry*)

filled with tears of joy, paraded the trophy in front of the Blackburn crowd to rapturous applause.

Two days later the trophy was officially presented to the club in front of a packed Ewood Park. The crowd paid homage to the players, manager and coaching staff who had delivered the club's first League Championship since 1914. However, the greatest cheer was that given to Jack Walker, the man who had delivered a dream.

Kenny Dalglish, only the third man in the history of the game to win the League Championship with two different clubs, was named as Manager of the Year, while Alan Shearer had earlier collected the PFA Player of the Year award. Shearer, who ended the season as the country's leading goalscorer, had also been runner-up in the Football Writers' Association Footballer of the Year award, while Colin Hendry had come third. Tim Sherwood had been nominated for the PFA award, while Chris Sutton was among the nominations for the Young Player of the Year award. Such was the respect that the players at Ewood Park had earned from their fellow professionals that the PFA Premiership team of the season included Flowers, Le Saux, Hendry, Sherwood, Shearer and Sutton. A flood of international honours had been bestowed upon the team with Flowers, Berg, Le Saux, Hendry, Shearer and Kenna all representing their various countries, while Sherwood, Sutton and Wilcox had been awarded England 'B' caps with Pearce and Shay Given winning Under-21 caps for their countries.

1995–96

The major talking point of the summer of 1995 was the shock decision of Kenny Dalglish to step down from the manager's position. His wish to escape the rigours of modern-day management led to him being offered the nebulous title of Director of Football, while Ray Harford stepped up to become manager. For Harford the task was immense, as he was asked to follow the man who had taken the club to its most successful season since 1913–14.

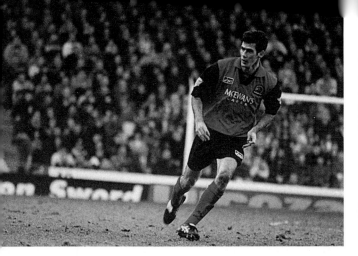

Although the team had looked somewhat jaded during the final weeks of the previous campaign, the manager opted against a major infusion of new blood. Mattie Holmes arrived from West Ham United, while Robbie Slater left for Upton Park. Tony Gale returned to the capital to join Crystal Palace, while a young centre-back, Adam Reed, was signed from Darlington.

The season began in a disappointing manner with defeat in the FA Charity Shield at the hands of Everton, followed by four defeats in the opening six League games. The Rovers also lost their first match in the Champions' League – 1–0 to Spartak Moscow at Ewood Park.

Harford had strengthened his backroom staff with the appointment of Newcastle United's Derek Fazackerley, the former Ewood favourite, as first-team coach. Following Harford's elevation to manager the club had promoted Tony Parkes to become his assistant.

In the wake of such a poor start, the manager began to make new signings. In October 1995, two new midfield players arrived in Billy McKinlay, from Dundee United, and Nottingham Forest's Lars Bohinen. The deal to sign Bohinen had been particularly controversial as the Norwegian international had exercised a clause in his contract that allowed him to leave Nottingham for a bargain fee. Thus, when Forest fans visited Ewood Park on 18 November 1995, for what was the official opening of the newly redeveloped Ewood Park, they hurled a stream of abuse at their former player. However, Bohinen had the last laugh as he scored two goals in the 7–0 demolition of Forest.

Unfortunately, McKinlay and Bohinen were ineligible for the Champions' League campaign and the inclusion of some of the club's younger players on the substitutes' bench for these games highlighted the threadbare nature of the squad. The Rovers suffered severe criticism for their performance in Europe and yet, if the team had beaten Leiga Warsaw at home, the club would have qualified for the quarter-finals. However, the fracas that involved David Batty and Graeme Le Saux, who came to blows with each other in Moscow, was the image that made the greatest impression on the media. Ironically, the Rovers ended their European adventure on a high note with a 4–1 home win over Rosenborg that included a Mike Newell hat-trick.

In the wake of the Champions' League disappointment, Harford again turned to the transfer market. Chris Coleman was signed from Crystal Palace in December 1995 to bolster the defence, and Graham Fenton, an England Under-21 international, arrived from Aston Villa to provide more options in attack. Another new face arrived in December when Niklas Gudmundsson was signed on extended loan from Halmsted before his move was later made permanent.

While home form remained impressive in the League, the Rovers struggled to make any impression in away matches. Indeed, the club's first away win wasn't achieved until a 1–0 win at Queen's Park Rangers on 14 January 1996.

Following the clash between Le Saux and Batty, relations between the club and the former Leeds United player became somewhat frosty. Batty remained in the team until mid-January 1996 and the following month the Rovers allowed him to join Newcastle United for £3.75 million, a new club record for an outgoing transfer.

Despite his many critics, Harford steered the team to a seventh-place finish in the League and only missed out on UEFA Cup qualification on the final day of the season. The club had allowed Alan Shearer to miss the last few matches of the season to have minor surgery that would ensure

(Left) Mike Newell scored a hat-trick in the 4–1 victory over Rosenborg in the European Champions' League at Ewood Park on 6 December 1995. (*Copyright: Anne Barry*)

(Right) Lars Bohinen is felled by QPR's Ray Wilkins during the match at Loftus Road in January 1995. The 1–0 win gave the Rovers their first away win of the season in the Premiership. (*Copyright: Anne Barry*)

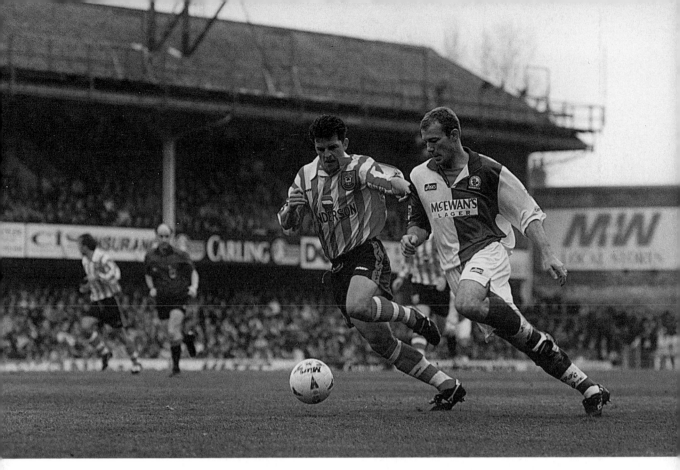

his fitness for England at Euro '96. In so doing, the club sacrificed their own chances of European qualification. Furthermore, Harford had been robbed of the services of Gallacher, Le Saux, Pearce, Wilcox, Warhurst, Ripley and Bohinen for long periods while a combination of injury and loss of form had restricted Sutton to just 13 League appearances. Ultimately, Harford could take some satisfaction in what he had achieved in such trying circumstances.

1996-97

The departure of Alan Shearer cast a shadow of despair over Ewood Park that proved almost impossible to lift. It undermined the stability at the club, ultimately cost Ray Harford his job, and almost destroyed everything that had been achieved since the arrival of Jack Walker. Rarely can one decision have had such devastating repercussions on a football club.

There had been continual speculation with regard to Shearer's future after Euro '96. However, just when it appeared that the persuasive tongue of Jack Walker had talked Shearer into remaining at Ewood Park, Kevin Keegan intervened. Unfortunately, the lure of Tyneside was too great for the Geordie to resist and on 29 July 1996 it was announced that Alan Shearer would join Newcastle United for a world-record fee of £15 million.

The sense of loss among the Ewood faithful was immeasurable. The manager's plans were in tatters as he had constructed his transfer activity around Shearer. Georgious Donis, a Greek international winger, had been signed from Panathanikos to supply ammunition for Shearer. Harford had also hoped to sign Christophe Dugarry, to link the French striker with England's premier centre-forward. However, when Shearer left and the Dugarry deal failed to materialise the manager's plans disintegrated. The summer of 1996 also brought the departure of Mike Newell and when Chris Sutton was injured in a pre-season game the Rovers entered the new campaign in crisis.

Graham Fenton and Kevin Gallacher led the line on the opening day of the season, but the campaign got off to a lacklustre start. Tottenham Hotspur enjoyed a 2–0 win at Ewood Park and

the Blackburn supporters, in a crowd of 26,960, quickly realised the impact that the loss of Shearer would have on the team. By the end of August the Rovers had just one point from three games and consecutive home defeats, against Leeds United and newly promoted Derby County, left the club anchored at the foot of the table.

While the loss of Shearer was still fresh in the memory the club announced that Kenny Dalglish and Blackburn Rovers had parted company. While his role as Director of Football had never been fully explained to the supporters, the fact remained that two of the key men of the Championship season had now left the club. With discontent among the supporters on the increase, Ray Harford had become an increasingly isolated figure at the club. The manager revealed that he had offered to resign on two occasions during 1995–96 and had again offered to tender his resignation in light of the disappointing start that the team had made. It was a gesture that spoke volumes about Harford's integrity and pride at what had been achieved since he and Dalglish first arrived at Ewood Park.

Both Jack Walker and the directors refused to accept Harford's offer of self-sacrifice. However, elimination from the Coca-Cola Cup at the hands of Stockport County at Ewood Park proved to be the final straw. On Friday 25 October 1996, Ray Harford resigned as manager of Blackburn Rovers just 16 months after taking over from Kenny Dalglish. The directors reluctantly accepted his decision and asked Tony Parkes to take control until a successor was appointed.

Slowly the situation under Parkes improved as he opted for the slightly more cautious approach of 4–3–3, which dispensed with the services of Donis in favour of a more combative midfielder. Parkes infused more confidence into the team and better results gradually lifted the Rovers off the bottom of the table.

Roy Hodgson, the first choice to succeed Harford, rejected the opportunity to move to Ewood Park in favour of remaining at Internazionale in Italy. However, in December 1996 it was announced that Sven-Göran Eriksson would assume control at Ewood Park on 1 July 1997, when his contract with Sampdoria was at an end. In the meantime, Parkes would continue his excellent work as caretaker manager.

December also brought a farcical situation in which Middlesbrough, suffering from an epidemic of illness and injuries, refused a Premiership edict to fulfil their match at Ewood Park on 21 December 1996. The club was docked three points and fined £50,000. Ultimately, the loss of three points cost them their place in the Premiership at the end of the season.

Tim Sherwood takes the ball past Arsenal's Lee Dixon during the 1–1 draw at Highbury on 19 April 1997. (*Copyright: Anne Barry*)

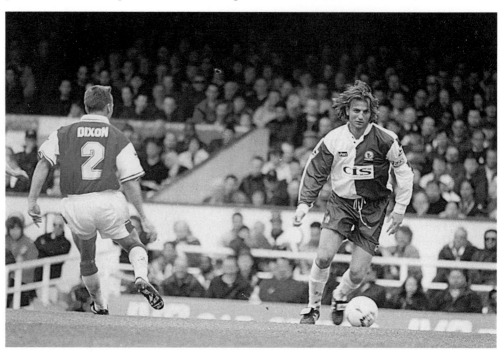

The New Year brought rumours from Italy that suggested that Eriksson might well have had a change of heart with regard to the Ewood job. In February 1997, it was announced that Eriksson would not be coming to Blackburn for personal reasons, amid rumours, which proved to be correct, that Lazio wished to employ him. Fortunately, Roy Hodgson had also had a change of heart and when offered the job again he readily agreed to take charge at Ewood Park in July 1997. The appointment of such a well-respected and successful figure as manager merely reiterated the ambitions that Walker still had for the club.

Parkes continued to guide the club to safety, with the only new signing being that of Per Pedersen, a Danish international forward, who came from Odense for £2.5 million. A 4–1 win over Sheffield Wednesday on 22 April 1997 virtually guaranteed survival and a 0–0 draw in the delayed game against Middlesbrough secured the club's place in the Premiership.

Prior to the final match of the season at Ewood Park, Jack Walker made a special presentation to Tony Parkes in appreciation of the wonderful job he had done for the club in the most difficult of circumstances. He was also rewarded with a Carling No.1 award during the summer – an award given to individuals who have made an outstanding contribution to the national game. No one at Ewood Park would deny that Parkes had made the greatest contribution of all during 1996–97.

Damien Duff made his League debut against Leicester City at Ewood Park on 11 May 1997. (*Copyright: unknown*)

1997-98

The summer of 1997 brought a flurry of activity as Roy Hodgson revamped the Ewood playing staff. Anders Andersson, a Swedish midfield international, who had been Hodgson's last signing when manager of Malmö FF, readily agreed to follow his former mentor to Ewood Park. Martin Dahlin, the renowned Swedish striker, arrived from AS Roma, while Swiss international centre-back, Stephane Henchoz, was signed from SV Hamburg. Patrick Valery, a former French Under-21 international full-back, arrived from Bastia while John Filan, an Australian goalkeeper, joined the Rovers from Coventry City.

Unfortunately, Henning Berg and Graeme Le Saux, each valued at £5 million, moved respectively to Manchester United and Chelsea before the season began. Shay Given, an outstanding goalkeeping prospect, left Blackburn to join Newcastle United in search of first-team football. Hodgson also unloaded Nicky Marker, Graham Fenton, Mattie Holmes, Niklas Gudmundsson and Paul Warhurst during the early stages of his reign.

Per Pedersen, seen in action in a pre-season friendly at Wolverhampton Wanderers, failed to make any impression on Roy Hodgson and made just 13 appearances for the club. (*Copyright: Anne Barry*)

Hodgson was happy to work with the existing backroom staff, but added Arnaldo Longaretti as fitness coach. This appointment reflected the continental approach that the manager brought to training. All day sessions became the norm at the Brockhall training complex as Hodgson transposed the techniques with which he was so familiar on his new charges.

The Rovers made an encouraging start to the new campaign with two wins during the first week of the

Martin Dahlin was signed from AS Roma but was plagued by back problems during his stay at Ewood Park. Dahlin, who had been one of Europe's top strikers, scored just six goals for the Rovers in 30 appearances. (*Copyright: Anne Barry*)

(Left) Northern Ireland international goalkeeper Alan Fettis was signed from Nottingham Forest to cover for the injury to John Filan. (*Copyright: Anne Barry*)

(Right) Tore Pedersen, an experienced Norwegian international, failed to make the expected impact at Ewood Park and made just six starts and a further two substitute appearances during the 1997–98 season. (*Copyright: Anne Barry*)

campaign. The second of these games was a 4–0 demolition of Aston Villa at Villa Park. A home draw with Liverpool followed, in which Dahlin scored his first League goal for the club.

Two days after the Liverpool game the Rovers overwhelmed Sheffield Wednesday 7–2 at Ewood Park. Sadly, Filan suffered a badly broken arm and had to be replaced by Tim Flowers, who had just returned to fitness. Filan's injury ruled him out for virtually the rest of the season and, as a result, Hodgson snapped up Nottingham Forest's Northern Ireland international 'keeper, Alan Fettis. He also spent a further £500,000 to sign Tore Pedersen, a Norwegian international centre-back, who had enjoyed a rather nomadic career that had taken in clubs as diverse as Oldham Athletic and Safrecce Hiroshima in Japan. In October the manager offloaded Per Pedersen on a season-long loan to Borussia Mönchengladbach.

The players quickly responded to Hodgson's new methods and by Christmas were second in the

table behind Manchester United. The only slight blip had been elimination from the Coca-Cola Cup, at Chelsea, and even then the tie had gone to penalties. Some of the football produced during this period was simply sublime and the Rovers went into the New Year full of optimism.

Unfortunately, the second half of the season proved to be unexpectedly disappointing. After the 5–0 victory over Aston Villa, on 17 January 1998, the team only won two of their next 12 games. Dreams of the Championship quickly evaporated as the club desperately clung to a UEFA Cup place. A penalty shoot-out deprived them of further progress in the FA Cup, with West Ham United proving triumphant in the shoot-out at Ewood Park. Fortunately, two wins in the final three games proved sufficient to finish sixth in the Premier League and win a spot in the UEFA Cup. However, their European place had been in doubt right up to the very last moments of the final day of the season – when a late goal from Chris Sutton produced a 1–0 win over Newcastle United.

Ultimately, the manager had found himself without sufficient options when things began to go wrong. There was not enough quality in the squad and a number of the new signings had failed to impress. Dahlin endured an injury-hit campaign, while Andersson made no impression and started just one League game. Filan, until his injury, and Henchoz had been the pick of the new men but, ultimately, a string of injuries, particularly to midfield players, drained the limited resources at the club. While there was general satisfaction with the impact that the manager had made, it was clear that the squad would need further strengthening if progress was to be maintained.

Swiss international Stephane Henchoz was one of Roy Hodgson's more successful signings and became an automatic choice at centre-back. (*Copyright: Anne Barry*)

Kevin Davies became the club's record signing when he moved from Southampton for £7 million. (*Copyright: Anne Barry*)

1998-99

Having qualified for Europe, the manager again received the full financial support of Jack Walker. In signing Kevin Davies from Southampton, Hodgson created a new transfer record for the club when he parted company with £7.25 million for the young striker. However, the manager reaped some of the fee back by allowing Stuart Ripley and James Beattie to move to Southampton. Other new signings brought Darren Peacock, a vastly experienced centre-back, from Newcastle United under the Bosman ruling. James Corbett, an exciting young prospect from Gillingham, was also snapped up on a lengthy contract. The manager also allowed Patrick Valery, who had experienced an indifferent first season in English football, to return to France to join Bastia. Ironically, just a few weeks earlier Valery had helped persuade Sebastian Pérez to leave the Corsican club and join him at Ewood Park in a £3 million transfer.

Colin Hendry, who was about to start his testimonial year, rocked the club with a transfer request on the eve of the new season. Unable to persuade him to stay, the manager hurriedly arranged a deal with Rangers which brought in £4 million.

Sebastian Pérez was signed from Bastia, but the Frenchman never really settled in Lancashire and made just eight appearances for the club before returning to France. (*Copyright: Anne Barry*)

Jack Walker introduces Brian Kidd to Blackburn supporters before the game against Charlton Athletic on 5 December 1998. (*Copyright: Anne Barry*)

A goalless draw with Derby County opened the new campaign at Ewood Park and a few days later Christian Dailly, Derby's Scottish international centre-back, joined the Rovers for £5 million. His acquisition was timely as the manager had been hit by an epidemic of injuries from the very start of pre-season training.

Only one win from the opening seven League games ensured the Rovers began the campaign in the relegation zone. Furthermore, European interest ended at the first hurdle when Olympique Lyonnais enjoyed a 3–2 aggregate win in the UEFA Cup. In fairness to the manager, the injury situation was such that Damien Johnson and Martin Taylor, two of the club's youngsters, were given unexpected debuts in the second leg in France.

At the end of October the manager moved swiftly to strengthen his depleted squad with a trio of transfers. Oumar Konde, a 19-year-old Swiss Under-21 international midfielder, was signed from FC Basel, while Dario Marcolin, an experienced Italian midfielder, came on an extended loan from Lazio. Marcolin cost the Rovers £100,000 to fund the loan and the Italian club agreed an option for the Rovers to purchase him for £700,000 at the end of the season. A former Italian Under-21 international, Marcolin had a wealth of experience in Serie A and appeared a good acquisition for the club. The final signing, during a 48-hour period, was Nathan Blake, a Welsh international centre-forward who made the short journey from Bolton Wanderers. Blake was signed after Dion Dublin, the manager's first choice, rejected the chance to join the Rovers.

Unfortunately, Konde was injured before he could play for Hodgson and the inclusion of Marcolin and Blake had little impact initially. However, after a home defeat by bottom club Southampton, on 21 November 1998, a result that put the Rovers on the bottom of the Premier League, Jack Walker immediately met with Hodgson after the match and ended his reign at the club. Rumours of dressing room, unrest had been rife as Hodgson's attempts to bring a continental set-up to Ewood Park never quite won favour. While the highly literate and well-read manager had been touted as a possible England manager, he seemed a little too cosmopolitan for many of the Ewood faithful. However, it was the performance of Kevin Davies that seriously undermined the manager's credibility with the supporters. At the time of Hodgson's departure Davies had not scored a goal and was virtually a permanent substitute.

Tony Parkes took temporary charge for one League game, a 2–0 defeat at Liverpool, before Brian Kidd took charge on 5 December 1998. The former Manchester United assistant manager quickly won favour with the fans with an animated display from the touchline as the Rovers beat Charlton Athletic 1–0. Ironically, the goal was scored by Kevin Davies, who came off the bench to register his first goal for the club.

Kidd immediately brought Brian McClair from Old Trafford to assist him while Derek Fazackerley was axed from his coaching post. Backed by the finances of Jack Walker, Kidd immediately brought in a host of new players. Keith Gillespie, a Northern Ireland international winger, was signed from Newcastle United for £2.3 million. Ashley Ward, a well travelled centre-forward, arrived from Barnsley for £4.25 million, while

Damien Johnson in action against Newcastle United on 12 December 1998. (*Copyright: Anne Barry*)

another £4 million brought Matt Jansen, another striker, from Crystal Palace. The midfield was strengthened by the addition of Jason McAteer from Liverpool for another £4 million. A more curious deal, considering the situation of the club, brought Burton O'Brien and David McNamee from St Johnstone for £2.6 million. However, the two youngsters were immediately loaned back to the Scottish club for the rest of the season.

Kidd seemed to have eased relegation worries as the team gradually pulled away from the bottom of the table. When the Rovers gained a 1–1 draw at Chelsea, on 17 February 1998, the club seemed on course to survive. The Rovers were 10 points ahead of bottom-placed Nottingham Forest, six points ahead of next to bottom Southampton and had a three-point cushion over Charlton Athletic, who occupied the third relegation place. Indeed, the manager had felt sufficiently comfortable to be able to allow Tim Sherwood to move to Tottenham Hotspur.

However, after the draw at Stamford Bridge the Rovers then lost their next three games and found themselves back in the mire. In a desperate bid to strengthen the midfield the manager spent another £3,375,000 on Derby County's Lee Carsley. However, chances to gain vital points, in away matches against relegation rivals Southampton and Charlton Athletic, were not taken and when

Ashley Ward fires in a shot against Tottenham Hotspur at Ewood Park on 30 January 1999. (*Copyright: Anne Barry*)

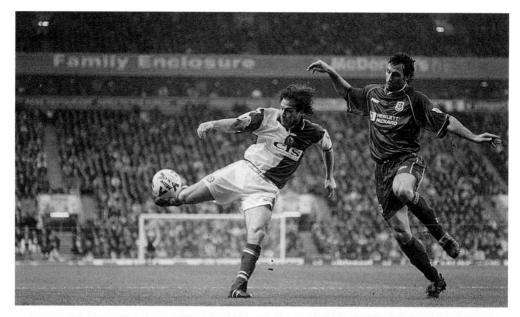

Chris Sutton made his final League appearance for the club at Newcastle United on 16 May 1999. During the summer he was sold to Chelsea for £10 million. (*Copyright: Anne Barry*)

already relegated Nottingham Forest won at Ewood Park, the Rovers were all but doomed. Kidd's patience with his players finally snapped as he dubbed them 'rubber dinghy men', indicating that they were only interested in their own survival rather than the club's.

Four days after the débâcle against Nottingham Forest, Kidd's former employer visited Ewood Park to deliver the *coup de grâce*. While some pride was regained in a 0–0 draw with Manchester United, it wasn't enough to prevent the club from being officially condemned to First Division football. While Kidd suffered the humiliation of relegation his former club went on to win the League, FA Cup and European Champions' League.

1999-2000

There was to be no fairytale return to the Premiership for the Rovers after their first season in Division One. Indeed, at one stage the club seemed more likely to slip through to an even lower level. It proved a traumatic season for followers of the club, with no fewer than three different managers taking control at various stages of the season before a final place of 11th position was achieved.

Relegation brought some expected departures from Ewood Park. Stéphane Henchoz was quickly snapped up by Liverpool for £3.5 million, while a £10 million deal took Chris Sutton to Chelsea. Tim Flowers was another to remain in the Premiership when he joined Leicester City on the eve of the new season. Both Dario Marcolin and Oumar Konde ended their disappointing spells at the club, the former returning to Lazio while the latter joined the German club SC Freiberg.

Although the club had dropped out of the Premiership, the manager was given funds to rebuild his shattered team. The summer brought Alan Kelly, a Republic of Ireland international goalkeeper, from Sheffield United, while Craig Short was signed from Everton to fill the vacancy left by Henchoz. Ironically, Short had previously turned down a move to Ewood Park during the early days of the Kenny Dalglish era at the club. Kidd also signed Simon Grayson, an experienced full-back, from Leicester City.

Once the season began the manager continued to wheel and deal as early results proved somewhat disappointing. Kevin Davies was allowed to return to Southampton, while Egil Ostenstad, a Norwegian international forward, moved in the opposite direction. Kevin Gallacher left to join Newcastle United for £700,000, while £1.75 million brought Per Frandsen from Bolton Wanderers. Another new arrival was Steve Harkness, a former Liverpool full-back, who arrived at the Rovers from Benfica.

Unfortunately, despite the quality of the squad, Kidd was unable to obtain any degree of consistency in terms of performances and results. When Queen's Park Rangers visited Ewood Park on 30 October 1999 and left with maximum points, the Rovers found themselves just two points

Northern Ireland international Keith Gillespie experienced a difficult season with just 11 starts in the League together with a further 11 substitute appearances. (*Copyright: Anne Barry*)

Jason McAteer and Matt Jansen (No.15) in action against Charlton Athletic at Ewood Park on 24 April 2000. (*Copyright: Anne Barry*)

above the relegation zone. Once again, Jack Walker was called upon to take drastic action and four days after the débâcle against Queen's Park Rangers, he sacked both Kidd and McClair.

Tony Parkes stepped into the breach once more and took control of playing affairs on a temporary basis, aided by Terry Darracott, the reserve-team coach. His relaxed style of management brought its usual improvement in results. Despite a loss to Leeds United, in the Worthington Cup, the Rovers continued to improve in the League and, as Christmas approached, the team had climbed to a comfortable mid-table position. The progress that the club made under Parkes persuaded him to accept Jack Walker's offer and take the manager's job until the end of the season.

One of the first duties that Parkes had to perform was to oversee the sale of Jason Wilcox, to Leeds United, for £3.7 million. However, despite the loss of Wilcox the Rovers entered the New Year in excellent form. A 1–0 win over Liverpool, at Anfield, in the fourth round of the FA Cup underlined the improvement that Parkes had brought to the team. While Newcastle United ended interest in the competition in the next round, promotion, via the play-offs, was still a distinct possibility.

As always, Parkes was happy to work with the players at his disposal and his only move into the transfer market was to sign Alan Miller, an experienced 'keeper, from West Bromwich Albion to provide cover for Alan Kelly and John Filan.

Unfortunately, the ground lost during the early part of the campaign proved too much of a handicap in terms of a realistic promotion bid. As a result, a disappointing sequence that brought one point from 12, early in the New Year, seriously undermined any bid for place in the play-offs.

In March the club appointed their third manager of the campaign when Graeme Souness accepted an offer to take control at Ewood Park. The new manager appointed Phil Boersma as his coach and Alan Murray as his chief scout, while Tony Parkes reverted to the role of assistant manager. Three successive wins, over Birmingham City, Nottingham Forest and Sheffield United, revived hopes, however slim, that the play-offs could still be reached. However, a 2–1 defeat at Wolverhampton Wanderers was followed by three drawn games and two defeats. The Rovers finished the campaign in 11th position in the First Division, some 14 points behind a play-off spot.

2000-01

The death of Jack Walker on 17 August 2000 at the age of 71 devastated an entire town. Thousands converged on Ewood Park to sign books of condolence and leave personal tributes fixed to the railings that surrounded the Jack Walker Stand. The area became a sea of flowers as a town paid homage to one of its favourite sons.

For Graeme Souness and his players, promotion was not only a matter of necessity; it was now a personal crusade in memory of the club's benefactor. The visit of Norwich City, in the aftermath of Walker's death, proved to be an emotional affair for all concerned. Prior to the match thousands gathered in hushed silence among the floral tributes that now surrounded the Jack Walker Stand. A moving tribute was then screened prior to the match and was greeted by a standing ovation on all sides of the ground. The Blackburn players each laid flowers in the centre circle while the Norwich City team paid their respects and laid a bouquet in respect for Walker. On a day when football seemed so trivial the players gave Walker the tribute he would have appreciated most – a 3–2 victory.

Due to Walker's failing health, Souness had not met him during the summer but had, nonetheless, begun to rebuild the team with the funds available to him. John Curtis, an England Under-21 full-back, arrived from Manchester United for £1.5 million, while Stig-Inge Bjørnebye, a Norwegian international full-back, was signed from Liverpool for £300,000. A fee of £2.25 million was required to capture Craig Hignett, Barnsley's midfielder, who spent the early weeks of the campaign on the sidelines with injury.

Once the season had begun the manager brought Henning Berg back to the club, initially on loan, before a permanent deal was finalised in December 2000. Souness also took the opportunity to have a look at Kabia Diawara, the former Arsenal forward, who was brought to Ewood on loan from Paris Saint Germain, before discarding him.

Fulham and Watford both made excellent starts to the season and when the latter enjoyed a controversial win at Ewood Park, it caused a minor slump in Rovers' fortunes. By mid-October the club had slipped to 11th in the table, some 14 points behind second-placed Watford and a massive 18 points behind Fulham.

Egil Ostenstad scored one of the goals in the 4–0 home win over Portsmouth in the first leg of the second-round Worthington Cup tie at Ewood Park on 19 September 2000. (*Copyright: Anne Barry*)

It was at this point that Souness pulled off a masterstroke and snapped up Mark Hughes from Everton. Although almost 37 years of age, the Welsh international manager brought a wealth of experience to the club and proved a steadying influence on the team. Hughes also brought his battling qualities and ability to score spectacular goals, as demonstrated by his two-goal debut against Grimsby Town on 21 October 2000.

November 2000 proved a busy month for the club as Souness continued to add to his squad with the acquisition of Brad Friedel and Marcus Bent, while preparations were also underway to celebrate the club's 125th anniversary. Friedel, who signed on a free transfer from Liverpool after

Mark Hughes scores the opening goal in a 2–1 win over Stockport County at Ewood Park on 27 November 2000. (*Copyright: Anne Barry*)

(Left) Matt Jansen and Sheffield Wednesday's Des Walker collide during the Rovers' 2–0 win on 13 January 2001. (*Copyright: Anne Barry*)

(Right) Marcus Bent under challenge against Derby County in the fourth-round FA Cup meeting at Ewood Park in January 2001. (*Copyright: Anne Barry*)

work permit problems were ironed out, had previously worked with Souness in Turkey when both were at Galatasaray. The manager made no secret of his admiration for the experienced American international, and after he made his first-team bow, in a friendly at Yeovil, he became the first-choice custodian. Bent, who was signed from Sheffield United for an initial fee of £1.35 million, was a speedy type of front-runner who also had a good goalscoring record. The weekend of 18 November 2000 brought a victory over Wolverhampton Wanderers, when the Rovers wore a specially commissioned strip for the occasion, and a host of special events took place to celebrate the club's anniversary. However, perhaps the most poignant moment was the parade before the Wolves game of former stars from the previous six decades.

As Christmas approached the Rovers added Alan Mahon, the former Tranmere Rovers midfielder, to their squad after signing him on loan for the remainder of the season from Sporting Lisbon. Mahon was on the bench when the Rovers visited Turf Moor, on 17 December 2000, when goals from Jason McAteer and Marcus Bent ensured that Blackburn supporters enjoyed a very merry Christmas.

The victory over Burnley proved to be the launching point for a run of results that took the club into second place in the League and the sixth round of the FA Cup. Away victories against promotion rivals Watford, Birmingham City and Bolton Wanderers established the club's Premiership credentials and a 5–0 win over Burnley, appropriately on 1 April 2001, lifted the club into second place in the table for the first time since the opening week of the season. By this time

David Dunn gets in his shot before Burnley's Kevin Ball can make a tackle during the 5–0 demolition of Burnley on 1 April 2001. When the clubs had met earlier in the season Ball had been sent off because of a challenge on Dunn. (*Copyright: Anne Barry*)

the manager had added further to the wealth of talent at his disposal with Eyal Berkovic, an Israeli international midfielder, being brought on extended loan from Celtic.

Defeat at the hands of Arsenal, in the FA Cup, counted for little among the fans as the quest for promotion had always been the main priority. During the final weeks of the season it became a two-horse race between the Rovers and Bolton Wanderers for the right to join Fulham in one of the two automatic promotion places. Ultimately, a 1–0 win at Preston North End, on Wednesday 2 May 2001, ensured promotion and was the signal for mass celebrations at Deepdale. Skipper Gary Flitcroft removed his shirt to reveal a T-shirt that carried the simple message 'Jack This is 4 You'. It was a poignant moment and a sentiment that every Blackburn fan felt.

At the height of the celebrations, Graeme Souness stood in front of the media and paid homage to the man who had made it all possible. 'I'm sure Jack will be looking down on us and he'll probably be on his second bottle of expensive Bordeaux by now. He'll be drinking all to himself knowing him,' said Souness. 'But, as I've said many times,' he added more seriously, 'this football club is all about Jack Walker – the stadium we have, the training ground we have, the academy we have, and the wages the club pays. And it's only because of one man that all this was possible. That is something we are all very grateful for and we must never forget that. There will never, ever be another Jack Walker, and this is for him.'

2001-02

The first season back in the Premiership brought mixed emotions for the supporters. The high point of the season was undoubtedly winning the Worthington Cup at the Millennium Stadium in Cardiff. The supporters also saw the club create a new transfer record when £7.5 million was spent to sign Andy Cole from Manchester United in December 2001. However, on the other side of the coin the club struggled to maintain its Premiership status and survival was only assured during the final weeks of the season. Excellent progress in the FA Cup was halted in the fifth round when a controversial refereeing decision resulted in a 1–0 defeat at Middlesbrough. Nonetheless, the Blackburn faithful had cause for celebration when the campaign ended with the Rovers in 10th place in the Premiership, a major trophy won and a place in the following season's UEFA Cup assured.

The manager was given substantial financial support by the club to ensure the Rovers remained in the Premiership. The summer had seen Alan Mahon make his switch from Sporting Lisbon permanent at a cost of £1.5 million. Souness opted not to sign Eyal Berkovic and instead spent £1.3 million on Tugay, a Turkish international playmaker who arrived from Rangers. Gordon Greer, a strapping young central defender, was signed from Clyde for £200,000, with a view to being developed for the future. However, the transfer that made the headlines during the summer was the £6.75 million signing of Corrado Grabbi from Ternana, an Italian Serie B club. Grabbi, popularly known as Ciccio, was a major gamble as he was virtually unknown outside his native Italy. Within weeks of the new season getting underway, Souness had replaced John Curtis, at right-back, with the Australian international Lucas Neill, who was signed from Millwall. Another defender arrived in October 2001 when Nils-Eric Johansson, a Swedish Under–21 international centre-back, was signed from German club Nürnberg.

Then, in December 2000, the manager created a new transfer record with the signing of Andy Cole. Immediately prior to the Worthington Cup Final, Souness brought Hakan Unsal, a Turkish international left-back, from Galatasaray, while Spanish striker Jorge González Dias, more popularly known as 'Yordi', came on loan from Real Zaragoza. Indeed, 'Yordi' made his debut as a late substitute at Cardiff.

The huge outlay on new players meant that several familiar faces were allowed to leave Ewood Park. Thus Nathan Blake moved to Wolverhampton Wanderers for £1.5 million, Jason McAteer joined Sunderland for £1 million and £3.5 million took Marcus Bent to Ipswich Town. A fee of

Andy Cole (left) came from Manchester United for a club record £7.5 million.

Breaking into the first team was Damien Duff (right).

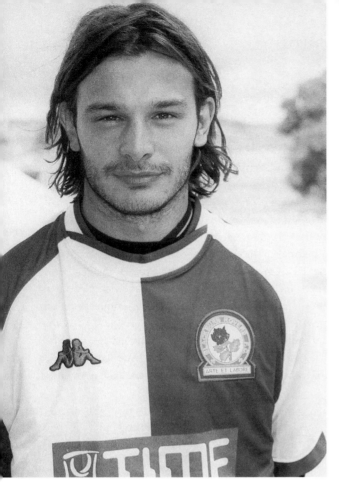

£6.75 million signing Corrado Grabbi (left) arrived from Ternana and Lucas Neill was signed from Millwall.

£600,000 was paid by Wigan Athletic for John Filan, while free transfers took Jeff Kenna to Birmingham City and Marlon Broomes to Sheffield Wednesday.

Among all this transfer activity the manager continued to stress the importance of the club's younger players, Damien Duff and David Dunn. Both became key members of the team as the season progressed. Indeed, in the latter stages Duff produced some electric displays on the left-flank that secured vital goals in the quest for survival.

Unfortunately, not all of the manager's new signings proved successful. As the club became embroiled in a relegation battle the manager agreed to allow Grabbi to return to Italy, on loan, to Serie B club Messina, until the end of the season. The Italian had struggled to make any impression at the club and at the time of his departure was out of the first team. Mahon also lost his place before Christmas, while Greer never threatened to win a place in the first-team squad. Johansson, too was not an automatic choice and was used as cover for Berg and Short, undoubtedly the best two centre-backs at the club.

The Worthington Cup Final, on 24 February 2001, came as a welcome relief from the rigours of fighting for Premiership points. As the Rovers occupied one of the relegation places at the time, it was their opponents Tottenham Hotspur who went into the game as favourites. The Rovers' cause was not helped by the fact that Tugay, Short and Flitcroft were all unavailable. The key to the Rovers' success was the inclusion of Mark Hughes in a central midfield role. The Welsh manager quickly stamped his authority on the match from the very beginning and simply overwhelmed Darren Anderton in the Tottenham midfield. With seemingly boundless energy, the Welsh veteran anchored the midfield, which allowed David Dunn to show off his tricks and darting dribbles at the Tottenham defence. On the left flank, Damien Duff galloped up and down, both creating and covering in equal measure.

In the 24th minute, a Keith Gillespie shot deflected off Ben Thatcher into the path of Matt Jansen. The Blackburn striker's shot was low and hard and went straight through the legs of Neil Sullivan in the Tottenham goal. The London club responded on 33 minutes when Christian Ziege put them on level terms. It was the signal for Tottenham to pour forward and keep the Rovers

Managing the Welsh national side and making a difference in Rovers' midfield was Mark Hughes, a bargain from Everton.

defence at full stretch. Fortunately, Brad Friedel was in truly inspired form and his 'Man of the Match' performance helped keep Tottenham at bay. In the second half, a long pass from Berg was miscontrolled by Ledley King and Jansen quickly worked the ball across to Andy Cole. The former England forward wasted no time in applying a deft finish that beat Sullivan in goal to put the Rovers ahead.

The final whistle was greeted by wild celebrations from the Blackburn fans in the crowd of 72,500. In capturing the Worthington Cup the club had ensured a place in the following season's UEFA Cup. However, with relegation still a real possibility, the manager insisted that any civic celebrations were put on hold until the club's Premiership place was secured.

The win at Cardiff was followed by important home victories over Aston Villa and Ipswich Town that took the Rovers out of the relegation zone. The victory at Cardiff inspired the team and just one of the final seven League games was lost as the club climbed to a creditable 10th place in the Premiership.

Turkish international Tugay arrived from Rangers for £1.3 million.

2002-03

Having spent much of the season comfortably ensconced in mid-table, a late run of eight wins from 12 matches brought the club European qualification with a sixth-place finish. While the team couldn't match the silverware of 12 months earlier, they did reach the Worthington Cup semi-final, only to bow out over two legs to Manchester United. Nonetheless, Graeme Souness continued to build on the strong foundations that he had laid since his arrival at the club.

Once again, the manager could have no complaints with regard to the financial backing that he received from the boardroom. Andy Todd, a no-nonsense centre-back, was brought from Charlton Athletic during the close season. He was followed by Sebastian Pelzer, a young German full-back from FC Kaiserslautern and Dwight Yorke from Manchester United. If the former was something of a gamble, Souness believed that reuniting Yorke and Cole would guarantee goals for the club.

During the summer of 2002 a number of the players had been preoccupied with the World Cup. Hakan Unsal and Tugay were part of the Turkish squad that won third place in the competition, while Brad Friedel had kept goal for the American team that surprised many with the progress it made. Alan Kelly and Damien Duff were both members of the Republic of Ireland squad that was involved in the tournament. One man who had hoped to be involved in the England squad was Matt Jansen, but unfortunately he missed out at the last minute and spent part of the summer on holiday in Italy. It was here that he was involved in a tragic motor accident that resulted in serious head injuries.

The new season began with Jansen on the sidelines and Ciccio Grabbi back at Ewood Park. Souness opted to make another change to his squad before the transfer window closed. Hakan Unsal was allowed to return to Galatasaray to fund the signing of David Thompson, a combative right-sided midfielder, from Coventry City. The introduction of the transfer window, together with

Dwight Yorke (left) and David Thompson (right) were two more arrivals, brought in by Graeme Souness.

Much was expected from Hakan Sukur, a free transfer signing.

a crop of injuries, provided an opportunity for some of the club's younger players to appear in the senior team. Thus, the likes of Neil Danns, Jonathan Douglas, Paul Gallagher and Marc Richards all received first-team call-ups. However, the primary beneficiary was Jay McEveley, who made his first-team debut against Walsall in the Worthington Cup on 6 November 2002. When Pelzer was injured, just 30 minutes into his debut, McEveley entered as a substitute left-back and gave an excellent display. He then went on to start 14 first-team games and enjoyed a particularly successful game at Old Trafford, in the first leg of the Worthington Cup semi-final, when he kept David Beckham quiet for much of the match.

In December 2002, the manager was able to sign Hakan Sukur, the 'Bull of the Bosphorus', as he was out of contract. Sukur joined the club until the end of the season with a view to a more permanent arrangement if both parties were happy. With over 80 Turkish caps to his credit and with Inter Milan, Parma, Torino and Galatasaray among his employers, Sukur appeared to be an excellent investment. Cole and Yorke had been unable to repeat their successful partnership, while Grabbi remained an enigma who was largely confined to the reserve team. With Jansen still suffering from the after-effects of his head injury, the need for a proven goalscorer had become a priority. However, on the day before Sukur was due to make his debut against Manchester United on 22 December 2002, he suffered a broken leg in a training ground accident.

In January 2003, Jansen made a triumphant return to first-team football with a two-goal salvo against Aston Villa in the FA Cup. Sadly, he was unable to maintain this level of performance and quickly faded from the first-team scene. Of equal concern was the fact that both Damien Duff and David Dunn had become increasingly prone to muscle injuries, while Henning Berg had missed a large chunk of the season due to injury. As the January transfer window neared its close the manager signed Vratislav Gresko on loan until the end of the season. An experienced Slovakian international, Gresko arrived from Parma to make the left-back position his own until injury, at Leeds on 26 April 2003, brought his season to a premature end.

Whilst the team maintained a comfortable position in the Premiership, there were mixed fortunes in the Cup competitions. The Rovers progressed to the second round of the UEFA Cup by beating CSKA Sofia on the away goals rule. However, a two-legged encounter with Celtic proved disappointing, particularly as the Rovers had been unfortunate to lose 1–0 at Celtic Park in the first leg. A below par performance at Ewood Park allowed Celtic to win the tie by a 3–0 aggregate. A penalty shoot-out ended interest in the FA Cup at Sunderland, while Manchester United prevented a second appearance at the Millennium Stadium with a 3–1 aggregate win in the semi-final of the Worthington Cup.

Without the distraction of Cup football the Rovers enjoyed an excellent end-of-season run that enabled the club to finish in sixth position in the Premiership and ensure European football for a second successive season.

2003–04

After the success of the previous couple of seasons, 2003–04 came as a major shock to Blackburn supporters. Far from building on the sixth-place finish of the previous season, the club became involved in a desperate relegation battle.

The summer had brought a radical overhaul of the playing staff at the club that resulted in two of its brightest stars, David Dunn and Damien Duff, both leaving. The town had been rife with

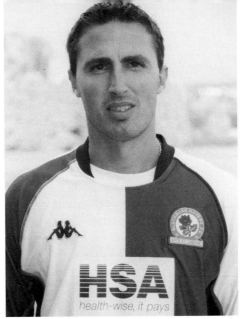
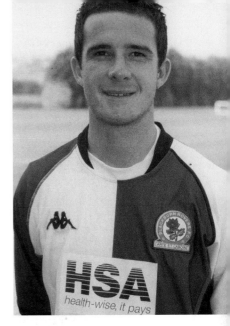

Markus Babbel
(left), Dino Baggio
(centre) and Barry
Ferguson (right)
were more
additions to the
Blackburn squad.

rumours that Dunn and Souness did not see eye to eye on the role of the former. Thus when the player turned down a new contract the manager allowed him to move to Birmingham City for £5.5 million. The departure of Duff was an altogether different matter, as the player opted to join the Chelsea revolution that Roman Abramovitch had begun at Stamford Bridge. A fee of £17.5 million was a huge sum to the Rovers at a time of financial restraint. According to John Williams, the managing director, the fees received for Dunn and Duff would secure the medium-term financial future of the club and allow the Rovers to stay competitive at Premiership level.

The manager also unloaded Keith Gillespie, Craig Hignett and John Curtis to Leicester City, while Henning Berg was released to join Rangers. Hakan Sukur was not retained and Gordon Greer was allowed to join Kilmarnock on a free transfer. Throughout the season the manager also allowed a number of the fringe players to go out on loan and thus Andy Todd, Alan Mahon, Jonathan Douglas and Neil Danns all spent time away from Ewood Park.

While the manager didn't spend as much money as in the previous summer, there were still some substantial signings made during the close season. Brett Emerton, an Australian international midfielder, joined the Rovers from Feyenoord for £2.2 million, while £1.4 million was spent to sign Lorenzo Amoruso, an experienced centre-back, from Rangers. Steven Reid, a Republic of Ireland international winger, was signed from Millwall for a fee of £1.8 million that was to rise to £2.5 million depending upon appearances. However, the manager was quick to point out that Reid was not a replacement for Duff as the two were different types of players. The manager also ensured that Vratislav Gresko, who had impressed during this loan period, remained at the club in exchange for £1.2 million. Souness also paid a fee of £100,000 to sign David Yelldell, a young German goalkeeper from Stuttgart Kickers.

However, in August 2003, football matters seemed of little importance when the death of Ray Harford was announced. Harford had been the man who had coached the Championship team of 1994–95 and had made a huge contribution the development of so many of the players that Dalglish had signed.

The manager continued to add to his squad throughout August with the addition of three experienced internationals. German defender Markus Babbel was signed on a season-long loan from Liverpool, while Italian midfielder Dino Baggio came on loan from Lazio for the season. However, a fee of £6.5 million was required to bring Scottish midfielder Barry Ferguson from Rangers.

Perhaps one of the most surreal sights in the history of the club occurred on 3 September 2003 at Christie Park, Morecambe, when Dino Baggio, with over 60 Italian caps to his name and a former star of Juventus, Inter Milan, Parma and Lazio, made his debut for the club against Leeds United reserves. The spartan surroundings and a crowd of 767 must have seemed a far cry from the glamour of Serie A.

Unfortunately, too many of the new arrivals failed to make the expected impact for one reason or another. Amoruso and Reid were both plagued by injury and reduced to minor roles, while Baggio failed to make any impression. Ultimately the Rovers cut their losses and allowed Baggio and Grabbi to join Italian club Ancona in January 2004. Barry Ferguson, after a difficult start to his Ewood career, was just coming into form when he suffered a broken knee-cap in the match at Newcastle United on 28 December 2003, which ruled him out for the rest of the season.

The January transfer window allowed the manager to strengthen his struggling squad without spending too much money. Aston Villa's reserve goalkeeper, Peter Enckelman, who had already been on loan at Ewood Park, joined on a permanent basis to provide experienced cover for Brad Friedel. Michael Gray, a former England full-back, joined the club on a free transfer from Sunderland, while Jonathan Stead, Huddersfield Town's promising young striker, joined the Rovers for £1,250,000.

After the opening-day win against newly promoted Wolverhampton Wanderers, the Rovers had struggled to gain points at Ewood Park and won only four home games all season. It was this appalling home form that anchored them in the relegation zone. Nor was there any consolation to be gained from the three Cup competitions. Liverpool enjoyed a 4–3 win at Ewood Park in the third round of the Worthington Cup, while Turkish club Genclerbirligi ended interest in the UEFA Cup in the first round. The FA Cup brought the biggest disappointment of all. Just a few weeks after romping to a 4–0 win at St Andrews in the League, the Rovers returned to Birmingham in the third round of the FA Cup and slumped to a 4–0 defeat.

Home defeats by relegation rivals Portsmouth and Leeds United plunged the club into crisis as the team travelled to London to meet Fulham on Easter Monday. An amazing game ebbed and flowed in both directions until Jon Stead scored the final goal in a 4–3 win. It was Stead's fourth goal since joining the club and after the Fulham victory the Rovers went on to win their next three games and ensure their place in the Premiership.

2004–05

Rarely can the club have endured such a difficult season as 2004–05. It included managerial changes, hectic transfer activity, the embarrassing departure of a loyal clubman, a bitter dispute with another club over a transfer, the walkout of the captain, a wave of national hysteria about the tactics employed, the lowest number of goals scored in the history of the club and a substantial drop in attendances. Against this backdrop, the Rovers enjoyed a successful battle against relegation and reached an FA Cup semi-final at Cardiff.

After gaining two points from the first four matches, the loss of Graeme Souness and his backroom team to Newcastle United was greeted with some relief by many of the Ewood faithful. The supporters had witnessed the loss of a number of excellent players due to differences of opinion with the manager, while the team had only just escaped relegation the previous season. Andy Cole, who left for Fulham in the summer of 2004, was the latest player to leave in the wake of a disagreement. Indeed, if Andy Todd had not been injured during the summer he too might well have left at the same time as Cole. Supporters had also voiced their concerns at a number of signings that hadn't proved successful.

During the summer the manager had promoted Alan Murray to assistant manager, while Tony Parkes stepped down to reserve-team manager. Souness also brought in three new players during the summer, with Paul Dickov, a striker from Leicester City, being signed for £150,000. Dominic Matteo, a defender from Leeds United, and Javier de Pedro, a left-sided midfielder from Real Sociedad, were both signed on free transfers. Just before he left the club, Souness spent £1.5 million on Morten Gamst Pedersen, a young Norwegian international winger, and brought striker Jay Bothroyd from the Italian Serie A club Perugia on a season-long loan. He also allowed Dwight Yorke to move to Birmingham City.

The arrival of Mark Hughes and a new coaching team was warmly greeted by the supporters. Mark Bowen was appointed assistant manager, while Eddie Niedzwiecki arrived from Arsenal as first-team coach. Kevin Hitchcock, the former Chelsea goalkeeper, was brought from Watford as goalkeeping coach. A few weeks after Hughes had taken control it was announced that Tony Parkes would be replaced as reserve-team manager. The manager felt that Parkes was more suited to dealing with senior players but, with the arrival of his own backroom team, there was now no position for him. However, the manner in which Parkes was informed brought deserved criticism for the club. Parkes, who had spent 34 years at the club, learnt of his dismissal via the media as he was travelling to the training ground. Although John Williams, the chief executive, offered profound apologies it proved to be a massive 'own-goal' on the part of the club, with public

Andy Todd (left), Ryan Nelson (centre) and Paul Dickov (right)

sympathy firmly behind Parkes. Ultimately matters were settled amicably, and the club awarded Parkes a well-deserved testimonial.

Although Hughes introduced a more scientific approach to training, he expressed his concern about the initial fitness of the players. Bottom of the table in November, Hughes was faced with a difficult task to ensure safety. The signing of Youri Djorkaeff, the former French international who was a free agent, on a short-term contract, proved unsuccessful due to injury. However, in January 2005, Hughes was able to sign three new players for his squad. Aaron Mokoena, the South African captain, was brought from Racing Club Genk in Belgium while Ryan Nelsen, the captain of New Zealand, was signed from the American club DC United. The third signing, Robbie Savage, from Birmingham City for £3.5 million, was surrounded by controversy. Birmingham initially refused to allow him to leave and there were a number of unsavoury accusations before the player linked up with the Rovers. Indeed, the hostility was such that it was agreed that the player would not play for the Rovers at Birmingham that season.

As Savage arrived, the Rovers lost their captain when Barry Ferguson became unsettled and expressed a desire to return to Scotland to rejoin Rangers. Ultimately, the Rovers had little option but to agree to the move, but the timing of his departure meant that Hughes had no opportunity to use the funds for further signings.

After the disappointment of the Carling Cup, a second-round defeat at home to AFC Bournemouth, albeit on penalties, the FA Cup brought some relief from the grim relegation battle. Two games were required to beat Cardiff City while Jemal Johnson, one of a number of emerging youngsters, registered his first senior goal in the 3–0 win over Colchester. However, undoubtedly the highlight of the FA Cup campaign was the fifth-round meeting with Burnley. The vitriolic nature of the local derby received national coverage and was covered live on television. However, the first encounter, at Turf Moor, proved a dour affair that held little interest for the neutrals. The

Norwegian international Morten Gamst Pedersen (left) was one of Souness's last signings, and controversy surrounded Robbie Savage's transfer from Birmingham (right).

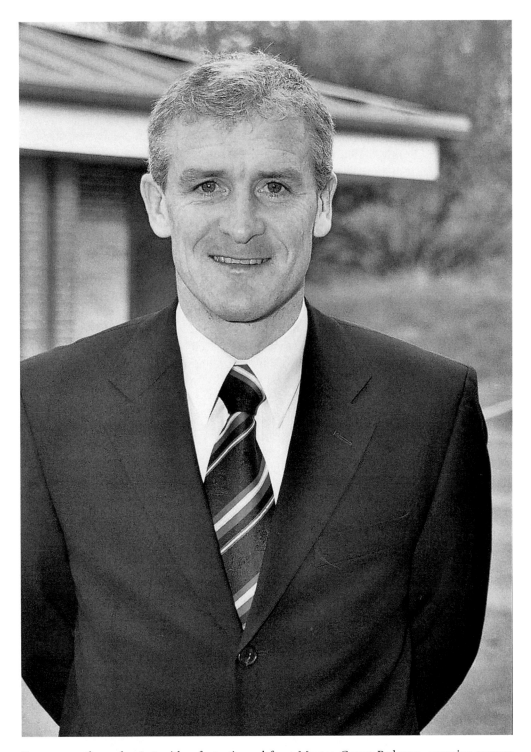

Mark Hughes returned as manager with Rovers deep in relegation trouble.

Rovers won the replay 2–1 with a fantastic goal from Morten Gamst Pedersen, ensuring passage into the next round. Pedersen emerged from the wilderness of reserve-team football in January 2005 and scored a number of vital goals in both the League and FA Cup.

Hughes adopted a more defensive approach as vital points were gained in the second half of the season. Brad Friedel remained in goal while the back four was usually made up of Lucas Neill, Andy Todd, Ryan Nelsen and Dominic Matteo. With Vratislav Gresko sidelined by injury and Michael Gray loaned to Leeds United, Nils-Eric Johansson was a capable understudy for the left-back spot. Aaron Mokoena was used as the defender in a five-man midfield. Brett Emerton, David Thompson,

Steven Reid, Garry Flitcroft, Tugay, Robbie Savage and Morten Gamst Pedersen were all utilised at different times in midfield, while Paul Dickov strove manfully in the role of lone striker. With Jonathan Stead suffering an indifferent season, the manager had to utilise the battling qualities of Dickov even when the Scottish international was not fully fit. Matt Jansen, who had been a peripheral figure since his accident, ended his season early after medical advice suggested a prolonged break from the game might aid his recovery.

While the Rovers clawed their way up the table they became victims of a media campaign that portrayed them as the Premiership's bullies. The hysteria reached fever pitch when the Rovers met Arsenal in the FA Cup semi-final at the Millennium Stadium, Cardiff. Overlooking the histrionics of certain Arsenal players, not to mention the robust tackling of Patrick Vieira, the media criticised the tactics used by Hughes and in particular they launched a vitriolic campaign against Andy Todd. An accidental collision with Robin Van Persie was immediately highlighted as being a premeditated attack by Todd. However, a subsequent hearing by the Football Association accepted Todd's explanation that it was nothing more than an accident.

A 3–0 defeat in the FA Cup semi-final ended the season for the injured Dickov, while Savage was also restricted to a peripheral role due to injury. However, the main aim, Premiership survival, was achieved with a 15th-place finish in the Premiership. Hughes described the task of keeping the Rovers afloat in the Premiership as his greatest achievement in football. Considering the glut of medals and honours he had won in the game it merely underlined the situation the club had found itself in at the start of the season. Hughes immediately dismissed talk of further relegation battles and insisted that the club build on the solid base that was now in place and move the Rovers forward.

2005-06

The summer of 2005 brought further changes to the club that were intended to establish the Rovers in a stronger position, both on and off the field.

In the boardroom the trustees of the late Jack Walker, the club's major shareholder, announced a slimmed-down, more executive-orientated board. John Williams relinquished his position as chief executive to become the club's new chairman, while Tom Finn, the club secretary, became the new managing director. Martin Goodman became the new finance director and David Brown, one of Jack Walker's most trusted business colleagues, became vice-chairman. Rob Coar, the previous chairman, and Richard Matthewman, the former vice-chairman, became executive directors. All of the other former directors became vice-presidents of the club, with Keith Lee being named as club president.

Another major change resulted in the senior squad moving into the state-of-the-art facilities at the Academy, while the club's younger players moved into the former senior training complex. The manager felt that the facilities at the Academy, which included a rehabilitation swimming pool and a full-size indoor pitch, were more in keeping with the scientific approach to training and preparation that he and his backroom team had introduced at senior level.

On the playing side the manager captured Shefki Kuqi, a big, strong Finnish international centre-forward, who was out of contract at Ipswich Town. However, a significant amount of money was required to sign Craig Bellamy from Newcastle United. Out of favour at St James' Park, Bellamy, a Welsh international forward who had played under Hughes for the national team, had been on loan at Celtic and was sought after by a number of top clubs. Fortunately, Hughes was able to persuade his fellow Welshman to join the Rovers when the pair met at the wedding of Clayton Blackmore, the former Manchester United and Welsh international defender.

As the transfer deadline came to a close, the manager added three loan players to his squad. Watford's young goalkeeper Richard Lee arrived to provide back-up for Brad Friedel and Peter

Enckelman. In defence the manager signed the Georgian international Zurab Khizanishvili from Rangers, while the midfield was strengthened with the addition of David Bentley, an England Under-21 international, who arrived from Arsenal after having spent the previous campaign on loan with Norwich City. Both Bentley and Khizanishvili later signed on a permanent basis.

Although the manager had talked pre-season of a push for European football, the early results suggested otherwise. Indeed, when Newcastle United inflicted a 3–0 home defeat on the Rovers, in mid-September, the club found itself in 18th position in the Premiership with just five points from the opening six games.

Following the Newcastle defeat, the team enjoyed a comfortable 3–1 victory over Huddersfield Town in the Coca-Cola Cup, with Bellamy, who had been in and out of the team with injury, notching two goals. Hughes then took his team to Old Trafford and surprisingly abandoned his tactic of using Aaron Mokoena as a defensive midfielder and opted for a more orthodox 4–4–2 system. The Rovers recorded an unexpected 2–1 win, thanks to a brace of goals from Morten Gamst Pedersen, and the result proved a turning point in the season.

The team gradually began to climb the table as a settled formation was found. Friedel remained the undisputed number-one custodian, while Neil continued to impress with his displays at right-back. The Manchester United game had provided an unexpected opportunity for Michael Gray, at left-back, and the former England international grasped it with both hands and remained in the team for the rest of the season. The central-defensive positions were occupied by Ryan Nelsen and either Khizanishvili or Andy Todd. In midfield Tugay rolled back the years and provided a number of virtuoso performances. Robbie Savage was his usual energetic self, while Steven Reid developed into a forging midfielder who could operate in the centre or the right-hand side of midfield. In attack the manager was hampered by a series of niggling injuries that restricted Bellamy's appearances during the first half of the campaign. However, Kuqi proved an energetic worker whose physical assets provided the manager with an alternative style to any of his other front men.

Shefki Kuqi (left) was brought to Ewood Park from Ipswich as an out-of-contract player.

Craig Bellamy (right), a favourite of manager Mark Hughes when in charge of the Welsh national side, was persuaded to join Rovers at a wedding they both attended. Bellamy was to leave after only one season and join Liverpool.

Fans' favourite,
Republic of Ireland
international
Steven Reid, who
extended his
contract during the
close season.

By the turn of the year the Rovers found themselves in ninth position in the Premiership and in the semi-finals of the Coca-Cola Cup – the second major Cup semi-final that Hughes had reached during his short tenure in management at Ewood Park.

The transfer window brought another acquisition to the squad with Florent Sinama Pongolle arriving on loan from Liverpool. The young French front-man was signed to inject a little more pace into the attack but, unfortunately, a combination of illness and injury restricted his impact. January also brought the senior debut of Sergio Peter, a young German winger who had graduated through the club's Academy system. However, while Peter progressed to the first-team squad, other products of the Academy were loaned out to gain vital experience. Jonathan Douglas spent the season with Leeds United and even featured for the Elland Road club against the Rovers in an early round of the Coca-Cola Cup. Paul Gallagher proved a success with Stoke City and ended the campaign as their leading goalscorer with 11 goals from 37 League appearances. Jay McEveley's stay at Ipswich Town was interrupted by injury, while lower Division clubs employed Matt Derbyshire, Jemal Johnson, Gary Harkins and Andy Taylor at various stages of the campaign.

The Coca-Cola Cup semi-final produced two extremely close games against Manchester United, with a 1–1 draw at Ewood Park being followed by a narrow 2–1 defeat at Old Trafford. Sadly, interest in the FA Cup ended rather abruptly at the fourth-round stage with the Rovers going down to a 4–2 defeat at West Ham United, despite the fact that Bentley had given the Rovers a first-minute lead.

The Rovers responded to defeat at Upton Park with a thrilling 4–3 win over Manchester United at Ewood Park in the Premiership. In spite of disappointing defeats at West Bromwich Albion and Everton, Mark Hughes was able to galvanise his squad into making a serious assault on a top-six finish. Indeed, for a spell the team challenged for fourth place and the final European Champions' League spot.

Unfortunately, April produced a slight stumble with two draws and two defeats that threatened to undermine the hard work that had gone on before. With three games remaining the squad produced the resilience that Hughes had instilled into them. Charlton were beaten at the Valley and then the Rovers clinched sixth place and a UEFA Cup spot with a 1–0 win over Chelsea, just three days after the London club had been crowned champions. The Rovers completed a hat-trick of victories to end the season with a 2–0 win over Manchester City.

Thus, at the end of his first full season in charge, Mark Hughes had not only achieved UEFA Cup qualification but had done so by adopting a style of football that had won plaudits from many of the club's former critics. The directors rewarded the manager and his backroom team with new, extended contracts as the club once again looked to the future with a genuine sense of optimism.